Sport Mega-Events, Security and COVID-19

This book examines contemporary issues of security at sports mega-events (SMEs). It focuses on the 2020 UEFA European Football Championship (Euro 2020) – subsequently postponed to 2021 – the third biggest SME in the global sporting calendar and a unique multi-city, multi-country event that took place in the eye of the COVID-19 storm.

Drawing on stakeholder interviews, policy documents, media sources and existing research, the book explores the constructions, meanings and perceptions of security in the efforts to secure this football mega-event. It argues that Euro 2020 is a powerful case through which to better understand wider security governance and security-related processes in present-day societies, which are increasingly preoccupied with notions of 'security', 'safety' and 'risk'. It assesses the precautionary logic and transnational knowledge transfer processes that guide security constructions surrounding SMEs in an uncertain and threat-conscious world and captures the dramatic moments in which COVID-19 transitioned into a security threat with severe impacts on the world of football and well beyond. *Sport Mega-Events, Security and COVID-19* advance existing debates in the sociology of football and sport, offering a critical understanding of security and safety in the modern world, and giving an insight into the changing 'new normalities' of security between 9/11 and the COVID-19 pandemic through the lens of global sport.

This is a fascinating reading for anybody with a professional or academic interest in sport management, event management, football, security studies, policing, risk and crisis management, the sociology of sport, the sociology of surveillance or political science.

Jan Andre Lee Ludvigsen is a Senior Lecturer in International Relations and Politics with Sociology at Liverpool John Moores University, UK. His research interests are the sociology and politics of sport. Jan's research on sport mega-events, security, risk and fandom has been published in journals including the *International Review for the Sociology of Sport*, *Journal of Consumer Culture*, *Leisure Studies* and *Journal of Sport and Social Issues*. Jan serves several editorial positions and has acted as Guest Editor for three special issues.

Critical Research in Football

Series Editors:
Pete Millward, Liverpool John Moores University, UK
Jamie Cleland, University of Southern Australia
Dan Parnell, University of Liverpool, UK
Stacey Pope, Durham University, UK
Paul Widdop, Manchester Metropolitan University, UK

The *Critical Research in Football* book series was launched in 2017 to showcase the inter- and multi-disciplinary breadth of debate relating to 'football'. The series defines 'football' as broader than association football, with research on rugby, Gaelic and gridiron codes also featured. Including monographs, edited collections, short books and textbooks, books in the series are written and/or edited by leading experts in the field whilst consciously also affording space to emerging voices in the area, and are designed to appeal to students, postgraduate students and scholars who are interested in the range of disciplines in which critical research in football connects. The series is published in association with the *Football Collective*, @FB_Collective.

Available in this series:

Football and Discrimination
Antisemitism and Beyond
Edited by Pavel Brunssen and Stefanie Schüler-Springorum

Football, Politics and Identity
James Carr, Daniel Parnell, Paul Widdop, Martin J. Power and Stephen R. Millar

Football, Family, Gender and Identity
The Football Self
Hanya Pielichaty

Sport Mega-Events, Security and COVID-19
Securing the Football World
Jan Andre Lee Ludvigsen

https://www.routledge.com/Critical-Research-in-Football/book-series/CFSFC

Sport Mega-Events, Security and COVID-19

Securing the Football World

Jan Andre Lee Ludvigsen

LONDON AND NEW YORK

First published 2022
by Routledge
4 Park Square, Milton Park, Abingdon, Oxon OX14 4RN

and by Routledge
605 Third Avenue, New York, NY 10158

Routledge is an imprint of the Taylor & Francis Group, an informa business

© 2022 Jan Andre Lee Ludvigsen

The right of Jan Andre Lee Ludvigsen to be identified as author of this work has been asserted in accordance with sections 77 and 78 of the Copyright, Designs and Patents Act 1988.

All rights reserved. No part of this book may be reprinted or reproduced or utilised in any form or by any electronic, mechanical, or other means, now known or hereafter invented, including photocopying and recording, or in any information storage or retrieval system, without permission in writing from the publishers.

Trademark notice: Product or corporate names may be trademarks or registered trademarks, and are used only for identification and explanation without intent to infringe.

British Library Cataloguing-in-Publication Data
A catalogue record for this book is available from the British Library

Library of Congress Cataloging-in-Publication Data
A catalog record has been requested for this book

ISBN: 978-1-032-19273-4 (hbk)
ISBN: 978-1-032-19275-8 (pbk)
ISBN: 978-1-003-25844-5 (ebk)

DOI: 10.4324/9781003258445

Typeset in Goudy
by KnowledgeWorks Global Ltd.

Contents

List of Tables		vi
Acknowledgements		vii
	Setting the Scene	1
1	The Dynamic Nexus between Sport, Mega-Events and Security: A Socio-Historical Sketch	16
2	The Meanings and (Re)productions of Security	36
3	Between Retrospective and Futuristic Processes of Security: Extending the 'Troika of Security'	57
4	Policing, Policy and Fan Networks	75
5	Pandemic Threats, COVID-19 and Euro 2020's Postponement: Ready, Set, Postponed	94
6	Redesigning, Re-Imagining and Delivering Euro 2020 in a Pandemic	123
7	Conclusions: Uncertainty, Legacy and New Threats	151
	Index	161

List of Tables

5.1 Selected competitions/events postponed in February and
March 2020   103

6.1 Euro 2020 host cities' stadium capacities and capacity limit
upon Euro 2020's commencement   127

Acknowledgements

This book should be considered the end product of many years work and there are so many people who deserve a special acknowledgement for their great help and support throughout the processes of researching for and writing-up this book. Fearful that I have forgotten some, I would like to begin this acknowledgements page by highlighting the very limitations of this page which in no way provides an all-inclusive list!

First, a huge thanks to every interview participant who gave up their time and expertise to help me complete this project. Within academia, I would like to thank Jamie Cleland, Mark Doidge and Matthew Millings who were the examiners on my Zoom PhD viva in December 2020. Our discussions really helped reshaping this project and developing it further into a book in constructive fashion. This, I'm extremely grateful for. Jamie also deserves a special mention as the Editor of the *Critical Research in Football* book series and for being a true source of support, inspiration and guidance. Special thanks are also due to Seamus Byrne, Joe Moran, David Tyrer, Chris Allen, Sara Parker, Elizabeth Peatfield, John Hayton, Alex Miles, Calvin Lau, Matthew Hill, Renan Petersen-Wagner, Dan Parnell, Dan Silverstone, Paul Widdop, David Webber and Mark Turner for friendship, collegiality and support. Thanks also to the Football Collective for providing a supportive environment that has benefitted me greatly. A special mention goes to my colleagues Dan Feather, André Keil and Jack Sugden, for interesting – dare I say intellectually stimulating discussions (at least occasionally!) as we watched many of Euro 2020's memorable matches together over the summer of 2021. A big thanks to Simon and Rebecca at Routledge for help and for providing direction. Thanks to Jodie Hodgson for her continual support whilst I wrote and thought about this book. A massive, massive thanks to my mentor Peter Millward for all the invaluable advice, support, supervision and friendship over the last decade. Pete has been a constant source of inspiration and guidance and has been (…and still is) absolutely instrumental in shaping my approach to academia and research, for which I am forever grateful.

Last but not least, I wish to dedicate this book to my dearest mum, dad, brother and grandparents. They have always supported me and been there for me. To be sure, this book will not repay anything of what you have given to me, nor the sacrifices you have made for me. Still, this book is for you.

Any inaccuracies or errors in this book are entirely my own.

Setting the Scene

Euro 2020 and its pan-European turn

By examining international security issues and policy mobilities at sport mega-events (SMEs) and arguing that SMEs represent expressions and end products of wider security trends and changes, this book puts down a significant marker in the sociology of sport and the critical study of security. Particularly so, in-between the epochal post-9/11 and coronavirus disease 2019 (COVID-19) timescapes. Sociologically, this book's empirically informed and theoretically elaborated on key argument remains significant because it demonstrates how wider, global security developments and their reflexive social changes influence mega-events, their spaces and stakeholders in a time where insecurity, security threats and management feature centrally on policy agendas and in the social and political scientific debates (Beck, 1992; Tsoukala, 2009; Zedner, 2009).

Although modern societies, since the late nineteenth century, have been structured around and preoccupied with the staging of mega-events and SMEs in particular, these socio-cultural landmarks have undergone a series of profound changes in recent times (Roche, 2017). Mega-events are 'large-scale cultural (including commercial and sporting) events which have a dramatic character, mass popular appeal and international significance' (Roche, 2000: 1). Whilst dramatic and popular, SMEs and the social universes encapsulating them are also packed with controversies, emerging trends and a multitude of sociologically important questions, leading Maurice Roche (2017: 282) to convincingly predict that '[t]he future facing mega-events as the twenty-first century unfolds evidently involves risks and challenges' that are associated to the major changes to our societies.

Within the powerful mega-event universe, the Union of European Football Associations (UEFA) European Championships in men's football – or the 'Euros', as the tournament is known as – are commonly considered to be the third largest SME globally (Klauser, 2013), after the Olympics Games and the *Fédération Internationale de Football Association* (FIFA) World Cup. And fundamentally, the Euros' 2020-edition would symbolize a remarkable break away from the usual way of hosting SMEs in one or two host countries (Lee Ludvigsen, 2019).

DOI: 10.4324/9781003258445-1

2 Setting the Scene

The rights to host Euro 2020 were initially granted to 13 host countries spread across the European continent, although this number was later reduced to 12 and then 11 countries. Whilst innovative and certainly untested, this pathbreaking hosting style also arrived with a large number of new and unanswered questions for football supporters, event organizers and social researchers alike. This book will address, engage with and seek to answer many of these questions – but primarily those related to the concept of 'security'.

SME preparations take several years. They are usually gigantic, costly and controversial affairs when taking into account stadium and infrastructure constructions or upgrades that commonly come with most mega-events' hosting rights (Boykoff, 2020; Millward, 2017; Roche, 2000). In recent years, one can therefore observe that cities, especially geographically located in the 'Global North', have become increasingly aware of mega-events' costs and reluctant towards bidding for SME hosting rights (Graeff and Knijnik, 2021). In that respect, a Euro 2020 scheduled to be staged in stadiums that predominantly were in-use *before* the tournament may have seemed a positive and welcome trend, albeit the format was criticized by some voices for the logistical challenges and financial costs imposed on travelling fans in a hectic summer holiday period (Lee Ludvigsen, 2019). 'The only person who could have come up with this plan', one interviewee told me, 'was someone who had their flights and hotels paid for by someone else' (Stakeholder 3). As other stakeholders commented, Euro 2020's format presented new, logistical difficulties and was a format which they did not expect to be employed again for the European Championships, which would be quickly departed from (Lee Ludvigsen, 2021a). Ahead of Euro 2020's final, between England and Italy, UEFA President Aleksander Čeferin also acknowledged in an interview with BBC (2021) that he would not support the format moving forward, commenting that it had been 'too challenging' and that it was 'not fair to fans' who had to travel across different jurisdictions, currency zones, EU and non-EU countries to follow their teams.

Notwithstanding, the speculations around a potential departure from the orthodox mega-event housing style emerged whilst Euro 2012 was still underway in host countries Poland and Ukraine (Lee Ludvigsen, 2021a). Whilst even the chief instigator of the new format, the then UEFA president Michel Platini, admitted that it was 'a bit of a zany idea', it was believed that the format would be one way to commemorate the competition's 60th anniversary (The Independent, 2021). However, it was not until September 2014 that UEFA confirmed Euro 2020's 13 host cities. Then, in 2017, 13 host cities were reduced to 12, when Brussels lost the city's assigned fixtures because the city's new stadium was unlikely to be completed in time for 2020 (Eurosport, 2017). Twelve host cities later became 11 when Dublin lost their hosting rights in April 2021 in the very final build-up to Euro 2020 (see Chapter 6). Therefore, the remaining 11 host cities of Euro 2020 included Amsterdam (the Netherlands), Baku (Azerbaijan), Bucharest (Romania), Budapest (Hungary), Copenhagen (Denmark), Glasgow (Scotland), London (England), Munich (Germany), Rome (Italy), Seville (Spain, which replaced Bilbao in April 2021) and Saint Petersburg (Russia). The tournament's fixtures would move between the mentioned cities during the tournament's group and knock-out stages and conclude in London, with Wembley – often considered to be the spiritual 'home of football' (Webber, 2022: 53) – being assigned both the semi-finals and the tournament's final. Euro 2020 and the associated celebrations concluded on the night of 11 July 2021 as Italy was crowned as the European football champion.

In many ways, Euro 2020 will always stand out as a very special and unforgettable SME. However, not merely for sporting-related reasons. A key rationale which this book is firmly anchored in is that the competition and its build-up, as a whole, remain sociologically illuminating, relevant and important. The event's final day was largely overshadowed by security issues and dramatic scenes of disorder as a number of ticketless fans stormed through the gates of Wembley before kick-off. Further, Euro 2020's build-up and staging reinforce the idea that European football have proven to be economically, politically, culturally and socially significant in modern societies (King, 2016[2003]). Perhaps fittingly, Euro 2020 was therefore branded and promoted pre-event as a 'Euro for Europe' (The FA, n.d.) whereas the tournament's official anthem, released in May 2021 – featuring Martin Garrix, Bono and the Edge – was titled 'We are the People'. Crucially, however, the tournament's geographies and European networked structures described above became its major weakness (Parnell et al., 2020) when the catastrophic COVID-19 pandemic – spreading worldwide in 2020 – impacted SMEs, sport and all human life worldwide and subsequently delayed the European-wide festival for a year. When Euro 2020 eventually commenced on 11 June 2021, it was the first SME to be staged during the COVID-19 pandemic.

Sport mega-events, security and COVID-19

Whilst there are multiple facets of Euro 2020 and contemporary SMEs that call for critical discussion and empirical examination from researchers situated in diverse fields, this book focuses primarily on two broad aspects. However, these aspects are intrinsically inter-connected and include *security* and the COVID-19 *pandemic* which caused the 12-month postponement of Euro 2020. Here, some context is necessary first. Following two landmark tragedies, the 1972 Olympics in Munich and the attacks on 11 September 2001 (9/11), the relationship between SMEs and security has grown immensely in its significance, scale and sociological importance (Boyle and Haggerty, 2009; Cleland, 2019; Giulianotti and Klauser, 2010). More broadly too, some scholars would argue that the present-day world is one defined by its preoccupation with 'safety' (Bauman, 2005), 'security' (Zedner, 2009) or 'risk' (Beck, 1992). Ultimately, this has meant that security's position on the frontiers of public policy, political agendas and sociological debates has been increasingly centralized in the twenty-first century.

As the next chapter unpacks, the security and policing operations associated with contemporary SMEs are now commonly described as warfare in peacetime.

4 Setting the Scene

Some operations even represent the largest security operations in the modern world (Armstrong et al., 2017). SME security efforts typically involve the militarization of public and urban spaces (Boykoff, 2020). They come at enormous financial and social costs and often remain in the cities long after the circus leaves the town as what Giulianotti and Klauser (2010) call 'security legacies' (see Chapter 1), as security is open to powerful forms of 'political exploitation' (Zedner, 2009: 18). Hence, as central to this book, sporting spaces have become *de facto* 'testing grounds' for new methods and innovations of social control, public/private security partnerships or surveillance technologies that can extend beyond an event's relatively short duration (Clavel, 2013; Tsoukala, 2009). This is often justified under the banner of 'security'. And undeniably, SMEs *are* threatened by a manifold of security threats and issues. These include 'terrorism', 'hooliganism', 'crime' (Boyle and Haggerty, 2012; Cleland, 2019; Giulianotti and Klauser, 2010) and, as evidenced by the events in 2020 and 2021: *pandemics*.

In 2007, Cheng et al. (2007: 683) described SARS-CoV viruses as 'timebombs' and warned of the 'possibility of the re-emergence of SARS and other novel viruses from animals or laboratories' which meant that 'the need for preparedness should not be ignored'. Thirteen years later, in the early months of 2020, the world witnessed the emergence of a new, unprecedented health and safety crisis. The COVID-19 pandemic is arguably the largest crisis of modern time. COVID-19 is an infectious disease caused by the *virus* officially named 'severe acute respiratory syndrome coronavirus 2' (SARS-CoV-2) believed to have zoonotic origins (Rothan and Byrareddy, 2020). Importantly, the main source of spread is human-to-human transmission between people in close proximity to each other, mainly through respiratory droplets, while some symptoms include fever, cough, tiredness and shortness of breath (WHO, 2020).

The initial reports of the novel coronavirus emerged on 31 December 2019 after it was detected in Wuhan, China. Whilst first treated as an epidemic, the infectious disease which was confirmed by the World Health Organization (WHO) as a pandemic in March 2020 (WHO, 2020) has – at the time of writing – caused more than 4 million deaths across the world. Worldwide, there have been reported more than 188 million COVID-19 cases.[1] Just days after COVID-19 was declared a pandemic, WHO's General-Director, Tedros Adhanom, also announced that Europe had become the pandemic's new epicentre 'with more reported cases and deaths than the rest of the world combined, apart from China' (*BBC*, 2020). In scale, it was argued that COVID-19 represented the most serious public health threat from a respiratory virus since the 1918 H1N1 influenza pandemic (Lodise and Rybak, 2020).

In their responses to the pandemic – and while a vaccine was under development (and, indeed, after vaccines had been *developed*) – nation states and their governments and policymakers introduced a series of strict health and safety measures (Bigo et al., 2021), including lockdowns, social distancing measures, quarantines and the restrictions on mass gatherings. As there are linkages 'between the mobilities of people and illnesses' and since 'places are immensely vulnerable to the movements of illnesses' (Urry and Larsen, 2011: 219), many countries also imposed strict restrictions on domestic and transnational travelling. The responses to the pandemic, in many ways, became synonymous with extraordinary measures and in several cases turned countries into 'states of exception' (Agamben, 2005) where public health and safety had to be balanced against risk prevention and where legal orders were temporarily suspended in the name of national security. Notwithstanding, it is also evident that the pandemic and its responses have had immense impact on sport both on elite and grassroots levels (Parnell et al., 2020). Already, there is a growing literature body examining the social impacts of the pandemic in sport (see Lee Ludvigsen, 2021b; Parnell et al., 2020; Rowe, 2020).

Because the infectious disease spread worldwide merely six months before Euro 2020 was originally due to kick-off at Rome's *Stadio Olimpico*, UEFA, who administrates the competition, had to make a decision on whether the mega-event could proceed as planned or not. Following a series of intense days in March 2020, packed with much speculation, UEFA confirmed on 17 March that Euro 2020 had been postponed for 12 months, until June 2021, over health concerns and to avoid pressure on national public services (UEFA, 2020). Consequently, this was the first time the Euros – which has been organized quadrennially since 1960 – was postponed. However, Euro 2020 was not the only mega-event or football tournament that could not proceed as planned in 2020. The Tokyo 2020 Summer Olympics were also postponed for a year, along with *Copa America* and numerous other domestic leagues around the world (Lee Ludvigsen, 2021b).

As this book captures, the pandemic, in distinctive ways, reconfigured the conceptual and practical meanings of security and safety at contemporary SMEs. The pandemic meant that an infectious disease proceeded from being *one* of the several threats that SME planners must account for, to becoming the main threat – where human proximity and contact in themselves could have devastating effects and impact transmission rates (Bigo et al., 2021) globally. The pandemic, however, did not only mean that Euro 2020's timeline was prolonged. It also significantly impacted the organization of security and safety which had to be revisited and integrated more distinctively with the politics of public health. As argued, Euro 2020 had to be substantially redesigned and re-imagined before it could commence on its new dates. In the pandemic epoch, SMEs did not solely have to be 'secure' and 'safe', but 'covid-safe' and 'covid-secure'. Yet, this also raised important political and public health related questions about what 'covid-security' could mean at a mega-event taking place across the 'whole' European continent. For example, England's group fixture against Scotland was linked to nearly 2,000 Scottish COVID-19 cases, and when 60,000 fans were allowed inside Wembley for Euro 2020's semi-finals and final, the German Chancellor Angela Merkel expressed her 'grave concern' towards the UK Prime Minister Boris Johnson over too many fans being allowed inside Wembley amidst the pandemic (Sky News, 2021).

The unpredictable and indeed exceptional events described above are, importantly, captured in this book. Essentially, they also impacted the original research

6 Setting the Scene

project which this book draws largely from. The research upon its initial design, as should be rightfully acknowledged, originally included plans of a participant observation with fan interviews in Euro 2020 host city London, during the tournament in June/July 2020. My plan here was to interview supporters about *their* perceptions of security and safety inside the vibrant fan zones where I would immerse myself. For this, I had booked accommodation and transport to the British capital. Yet, in the lead-up to the postponement announcement, I quickly realized that this would become impossible due to the likely postponement and wider restrictions on social research activities throughout the pandemic. I mention all this because much like Euro 2020 in itself, a rearrangement, re-imagination and redesign of my original plans were urgently required.

With the postponement directly induced by the pandemic, it became natural that this book also would have to cover and critically explore COVID-19 and its large-scale effects on Euro 2020 and football more generally. COVID-19 became the significant turning point on Euro 2020's almost decade-long preparation timeline. Thus, not accounting for this – and thereby failing to be responsive – would have been close to impossible from a sociological perspective. The pandemic and its impacts warrant sociological investigation and imagination. As Rowe (2020) reminds us, when it comes to asking crucial questions concerning the pandemic crisis, there are few – if any – academic disciplines that can remain completely detached. This book, therefore, covers the pre-event – and 'pre-COVID' planning and organization of Euro 2020, and the dramatic period in which COVID-19 struck and subsequently reconfigured the meanings of 'security' and 'safety' at present-day SMEs. It also tells the story of the delivery of Euro 2020 – in *2021* – which was staged amidst a global pandemic.

This book and its approach

To accomplish my empirically informed examination of Euro 2020's securitization and (COVID-related) security governance, the primary research aims that I set out to assess in the remainder of this book are the following:

- To explore which processes, activities, logics and policies that guided the construction of security before Euro 2020.
- Critically explore the meanings of 'security' in the context of mega-events.
- Question how COVID-19 impacted mega-event security and safety, and the delivery of Euro 2020.

Hence, although Euro 2020 figures as the case study that allows me to engage with all the above questions, the book itself can still speak to broader debates in the social worlds of football, sport and security. Whilst case study research should be approached with some caution in relation to the extraction of generalizable propositions or claims (Løkke and Sørensen, 2014), case study findings can still apply to wider research arenas (Millward, 2011). Perhaps particularly so because there are levels of resemblance between mega-event security templates across times/spaces (see Chapter 2). Moreover, in line with this book's approach and overarching topic, case study approaches have clear strengths in exploratory research concerned with contemporary phenomena and allows for the employment of multiple sources of data (Yin, 1994).

In my investigation, I draw upon a range of qualitative methods and data sources[2] and upon proceeding, it is important that each data source and method are regarded important in their own right. The empirical parts of this book draw from in-depth, qualitative semi-structured interviews with nine stakeholders of Euro 2020 with a role to play or general expertise in Euro 2020's security or the wider mega-event security nexus. These stakeholders included six individuals associated with European-wide or national fan networks, one Supporter Liaison Officer (SLO) in a Euro 2020 host city, one journalist covering Euro 2020 and one crowd safety professional.[3] The purposive selection of these stakeholders is mainly explained by two reasons. First, in order to ensure a continual expansion of mega-event scholarship, the stakeholders of the mega-event 'security field' (Giulianotti and Klauser, 2010) must and should not be conflated with authorities, law enforcements nor security agencies. Important stakeholders may encompass, *inter alia*, journalists, spectators, locals and nongovernmental organizations (ibid.). Second, fan networks like Football Supporters Europe (FSE) and SD Europe hold observer status on Council of Europe's Standing Committee of the Convention on Spectator Violence (T-RV) (Numerato, 2018). The formal recognition of these fan networks by UEFA and the Council of Europe (Cleland et al., 2018) and their involvement in Euro 2020's preparations (Council of Europe, 2019) demonstrate that fan networks are a part of the security-related discussions and consultation processes in the European football world. Notwithstanding, fan networks and their representatives' perspectives are often missing in the pre-existing mega-event/security literature, which provides an important rationale for my approach. Ultimately, limited research has concentrated on how security impacts 'one of sport's *key stakeholders*: the fans' (Cleland and Cashmore, 2018: 456, emphasis added).

Further, this book draws upon a framed discourse analysis (Goffman, 1974) of 780 pages of handbooks, manuals and policy documents related to Euro 2020 and European-wide football security. For example, this included UEFA's (n.d.) *Euro 2020 Tournament Requirements* in which the tournament's security requirements were laid out, and UEFA's (2005) *Good practices for safe and secure major sporting events: experiences and lessons from UEFA EURO 2004*. These should be deemed central policy documents that are publicly available, and it is the *discourses* within these documents that are subject to analysis. Finally, this book draws upon a collection of hundreds of digital media sources and official statements from sport governing bodies. Importantly, many of these media sources featured interview quotes and statements from key actors in Euro 2020's governance and organization. In fact, these individuals may be notoriously hard to access for academic research interviews (Rookwood, 2020). Moreover, when the COVID-19 pandemic

8 Setting the Scene

struck in early 2020, this did somewhat restrict the available arsenal of social research methods as terms like 'social distancing', 'quarantines' and 'self-isolation' became an integral part of global citizens' vernaculars. In that respect, my move towards media sources was also highly necessary in itself, pragmatic and compliant with the pandemic realities. All this is supplemented by further secondary sources in form of previous research on the mega-event and security relationship and mega-event policing.

Taken together, this rich material goes to inform the book's main arguments. First, it is argued that Euro 2020 proves an exemplary and powerful site for the understanding of wider security governance and security-related processes in the twenty-first century. This speaks to the transnational knowledge transfer processes of security-related knowledge and policies (Klauser, 2011a; Tsoukala, 2009) and to the adaption of precautionary processes that have been utilized by security officials and planners more broadly after 9/11 (Mythen and Walklate, 2008). Second, this book gives new insights into the several meanings of 'security' in a mega-event's 'security spectacle' (Boyle and Haggerty, 2009). Especially concerning how the meanings of 'security' intersect with football's commercial desires and policies, and then how the security meanings were impacted by the emerging threat of COVID-19 which created tensions and entangled national security, public health and the economy (Bigo et al., 2021). Subsequently, the idea of sporting spaces as a 'testing ground' for new security techniques, technologies and practices acquired a new set of meanings. This gives us a glimpse of the final key argument, which is that COVID-19, for now, has initiated a new era of SME security, in a similar yet also completely different fashion to other key moments such as the Munich massacre and 9/11 which, respectively, have redefined SME security (Chapter 1).

Therefore, the book ties into and advances debates in the social study of sport, football mega-events and security with its original insights from Euro 2020's securitization. Though, this book's contributions should be placed in some context. For decades, as Millward (2011: 17) writes, the sociology of sport and particularly the social study of football and fan activities and cultures have traditionally been 'responsive to the social issues which have emerged within it'. This speaks to a number of wider trends or processes, most notably 'commercialization' and 'globalization'. In a way, the same may be contended regarding the study on SMEs which largely has focused on these events as neoliberal projects of modern consumer societies (Boykoff, 2020).

This book is about another emerging issue and a significant process at play inside and outside of the worlds of sport and football. That is *security*. In recent years, one may see a growing academic engagement with mega-event securitizations (Boykoff, 2020; Boyle and Haggerty, 2009, 2012; Cleland and Cashmore, 2018; Clavel, 2013; Giulianotti and Klauser, 2010, 2012; Roche, 2017). However, scholars have convincingly argued for a more comparative study and underlined the importance of assembling transnational mega-event case studies in order to produce 'sustained, comparative studies of security issues, and processes at different events within varying contexts' (Giulianotti and Klauser, 2010: 58). On one level, this book responds to this, ties into and extends existing social scientific debates relevant to the securitization of and social control at SMEs, as well as the impact of COVID-19. Crucially, in doing so, it simultaneously situates, illuminates and empirically nuances the multiple roles of football fans and fan cultures within the complex nexus of football and security (Cleland et al., 2018; Numerato, 2018).

It is decades since Roche (2000: 5) observed that 'mega-events have attracted relatively little research attention'. Whilst much has been said and written about mega-events since then, many of the issues related to security remain subject to further empirical research and theorization. Importantly, mega-events 'seem to be becoming more important to us than they have ever been' whilst concurrently 'more criticised than ever before' (Roche, 2017: 1). The continued sociopolitical importance and the general media visibility of SMEs formulate an important backdrop for this book, which examines security complexes at modern-day SMEs and the related impacts of COVID-19, both of which require critical examination by social researchers.

And so, this book adds to the library of existing SME case studies, such as Euro 2008 (Klauser, 2011a, 2011b, 2012) and London's Olympic Games in 2012 (Armstrong et al., 2017; Fussey et al., 2011). The book does so by providing original insight into Euro 2020's securitization and breaking down the processes through which security was constructed in a completely novel and untested event context. These processes are conceptualized in what I have previously called the 'troika of security', which captures the coalescence of retrospective and futuristic assessments in the construction of security (Lee Ludvigsen, 2020). The 'troika of security' – whereby a 'troika' implies a set of threes – involves intersecting processes of (1) lesson-drawing, (2) the employment of institutional memory and (3) the precautionary securing efforts that attempt to manage a future characterized by uncertainty (ibid.). As I revisit and expand on the 'troika' in Chapter 3, this can serve as a framework for understanding how security is pursued and constructed in mega-event contexts. Yet, the updated 'troika of security' also calls into question some of the social trends and paradoxes evident within the conceptual framework.

By employing a mega-event as an appropriate point of entry, this book will analyze broader security trends and demonstrate exactly *how* and *why* sport can be analyzed to make sociological sense of governance mechanisms through which security is constructed, pursued or framed in the post-9/11 and 'post-pandemic' timescapes and societies. Particularly so, in relation to transient, urban, crowded and securitized contexts like SMEs. The book also contributes with an understanding of the meanings of the contested concept of security (Zedner, 2009) in a football-related context. Indeed, it is well established and accepted that SMEs are heavily securitized happenings. Yet, less is known about what exactly 'security' means or refers to when applied to a sporting or mega-event setting. Here, this book offers a theoretically and empirically informed analysis of the fluid, contextual and changing meanings of 'security' – and its practical implications and ramifications. The book empirically documents how mega-event spaces – accommodated by interconnected security-related and commercial policies and practices are 'tamed, sanitized [and] guaranteed to come free of dangerous ingredients' (Bauman, 2000: 99) like protests, anti-social behaviours, ambush marketing and political statements that can represent 'bad news' (Klauser, 2010: 334) in the eyes of the organizers and impede the much-desired festive event spaces. Yet, this again underscores the social meanings and roles of security (Jarvis and Lister, 2012). Whilst, in practice, it helps the event owners' desired sustainment of a mega-event's commercial appeal and attractiveness. The book therefore speaks to and contributes to wider debates on the relationships between processes of social control and the neoliberal political economy of professional sport (Giulianotti, 2011).

Finally, as aforementioned, this book captures the shocking outbreak of COVID-19, which played a completely central role in Euro 2020's extended securitization timeline and delivery. However, even before COVID-19, the impact of pandemics or epidemics on SME security represented a largely under-researched area (see Chapter 5). With a critical analysis of the unfolding events in 2020 and 2021 – as Euro 2020 was disrupted, postponed, rescheduled and eventually staged on its new dates – this book shows how the mentioned constructions and meanings of 'security' were reconfigured in line with COVID-19's devastating impact on societies. Finally, there are certain practical and policy-related ramifications of this book's original insights that may be valuable. Especially those findings related to the policing of football fans (Chapter 4) can provide practitioners lessons on how present-day football mega-events should be operated, policed and approached and how football fans should preserve a say in security-related matters in the modern football world.

Book contents: A summary

This introductory stage setter is followed by seven main chapters that are now broken down. Chapter 1 discusses the emergence of the dynamic nexus between SMEs and security. More specifically, it draws upon the relevant social scientific frameworks and literature and explores the socio-historical underpinnings of this problematic relationship, while revisiting some of the key conceptual tools and contemporary issues related to SME securitization and wider security governance in the post-9/11 society. In the case of Euro 2020, Chapter 2 will advocate for a critical approach to the reading of security and discuss the meanings of 'security'. It captures how the ideal conditions for 'security' – as pushed for – are evident in the official event-related document forms and discourses several years before the mega-event even took place. This chapter will explore for whom security ultimately was constructed, and whom or what that were secured against as potential security threats or issues. Overall, it documents how pre-emptive security-related policies and recirculated templates intersect with the event owner's and organizers' desires to ensure commercial attractiveness before, during and in-between the events.

Chapter 3 explains how security, before Euro 2020, was constructed. To do so, the chapter revisits and expands on the mentioned concept, the 'troika of security' (see Lee Ludvigsen, 2020), in which the recirculation of security practices and knowledge (Klauser, 2011a) and the reliance on institutional memory sit beside the exercise of future-oriented precaution (Boyle and Haggerty, 2012). Hence, it extends existing positions in the mega-event security literature into the novel case of Euro 2020. Yet, this chapter locates football fans more centrally within this conceptual framework than earlier, as subjects simultaneously to be protected *and* secured from, and as security stakeholders.

Building on this, Chapter 4 examines the policing of football and the roles of fans in consultation processes related to policing and security. Across European football cultures, the policing of European football is a contested topic (Numerato, 2018; Tsoukala, 2009). In fact, '[s]ecurity and repressive measures are one of the most commonly contested aspects of contemporary football culture' (Numerato, 2018: 14). Euro 2020 posed a unique football policing challenge and encompassed a high number of both security and fan cultures. This chapter will give an insight into the perceived national variations of policing across Europe and the impacts of the media discourses. In the contexts of pre-event consultation processes, the organization of Fans' Embassies and fan cultures, the chapter also highlights how fan networks like FSE and SD Europe operate as important agents of knowledge transfer *before*, *during*, and *in-between* football mega-events like the European Championships in football.

Chapter 5 examines the emerging threat of COVID-19 as Euro 2020's future became uncertain and the event eventually was postponed on 17 March 2020. The chapter revisits the relationship between security and public health before it examines how COVID-19 was framed as a safety and security threat and for whom it posed a threat to. This chapter is succeeded by Chapter 6, which explores the final preparations for – and, importantly, the eventual delivery of Euro 2020 in the organization of a 'covid-secure' Euro 2020 in June and July 2021. Euro 2020, it is argued, was both redesigned and re-imagined, so that it could be staged during the pandemic in front of spectators. Yet, the context of the pandemic enabled a series of new practices with profound implications for the mega-event/security relationship. The final preparations and the competition's commencement marked a new epoch within the nexus of sport and security, it is contended. Whilst SMEs historically have constituted moments for the testing of new security-related practices or partnerships (Clavel, 2013), such proposition acquired an extended set of meanings in light of COVID-19's climate of 'pilot' and 'test events'. As this chapter captures as it transpired, the new epoch is characterized by the increased embeddedness of public health into mega-event securitizations and SMEs, and SMEs like Euro 2020 playing an (in)direct role in the wider 'post-pandemic' societies' safe re-openings and futures.

12 Setting the Scene

Finally, the book's main conclusions are provided and discussed in Chapter 7. Importantly, it is also argued that the social study of mega-event security is continually developing. To elaborate on such point, pathways for future inter-disciplinary research are launched. These may help scholars in keeping up with this evolving academic field in the twenty-first century. The chapter marks the closure of this book with an epilogue that reflects on forthcoming mega-events in an uncertain, insecure and ever-changing (football) world.

Notes

1 Numbers from: https://www.worldometers.info/coronavirus/ (accessed 14 July 2021).
2 For a longer discussion *vis-à-vis* the interview methodology and data analysis, see Lee Ludvigsen (2020, 2021a, 2021b).
3 All the interviewees, interviewed between January 2019 and February 2020, signed consent forms. If they are cited, they have been given pseudonyms to respect their anonymity.

Bibliography

Agamben, G (2005) *State of Exception*. Chicago. University of Chicago Press.

Armstrong, G, Giulianotti, R & Hobbs, D (2017) *Policing the 2012 London Olympics: Legacy and Social Exclusion*. London. Routledge.

Bauman, Z (2000) *Liquid Modernity*. Cambridge. Polity.

Bauman, Z (2005) *Liquid Life*. Cambridge. Polity.

BBC (2020) Coronavirus: Europe Now Epicentre of the Pandemic, Says WHO. BBC. Available from: https://www.bbc.co.uk/news/world-europe-51876784 (Accessed 2 April 2020).

BBC (2021) Euro 2020 Unfair on Fans because of Travel Inequalities, Says UEFA President Aleksander Ceferin. BBC. Available from: https://www.bbc.co.uk/sport/football/57778285 (Accessed 10 July 2021).

Beck, U (1992) *Risk Society: Towards a New Modernity*. London. Sage.

Bigo, D, Guild, E & Kuskonmaz, EM (2021) Obedience in Times of COVID-19 Pandemics: A Renewed Governmentality of Unease? *Global Discourse* 11(1–2), 1–2.

Boykoff, J (2020) *NOlympians: Inside the Fight against Capitalist Mega-Sports in Los Angeles, Tokyo and Beyond*. Nova Scotia. Fernwood.

Boyle, P & Haggerty, KD (2009) Spectacular Security: Mega-Events and the Security Complex. *International Political Sociology* 3(3), 57–74.

Boyle, P & Haggerty, KD (2012) Planning for the Worst: Risk, Uncertainty and the Olympic Games. *British Journal of Sociology* 63(2), 241–259.

Cheng, VC, Lau, SK, Woo, PC & Yuen, KY (2007) Severe Acute Respiratory Syndrome Coronavirus as an Agent of Emerging and Reemerging Infection. *Clinical Microbiology Reviews* 20(4), 660–694.

Clavel, A (2013) Armed Forces and Sports Mega Events: An Accepted Involvement in a Globalized World. *Sport in Society* 16(2), 205–222.

Cleland, J (2019) Sports Fandom in the Risk Society: Analyzing Perceptions an Experiences of Risk, Security and Terrorism at Elite Sports Events. *Sociology of Sport Journal* 36(2), 144–151.

Cleland, J & Cashmore, E (2018) Nothing Will Be the Same Again after the Stade de France Attack: Reflections of Association Football Fans on Terrorism, Security and Surveillance. *Journal of Sport and Social Issues* 42(6), 454–469.

Cleland, J, Doidge, M, Millward, P & Widdop, P (2018) *Collective Action and Football Fandom: A Relational Sociological Approach*. New York. Palgrave.

Council of Europe (2019) The third consultative visit took place in Bilbao, Spain – Preparations for UEFA EURO 2020. Available from: https://www.coe.int/en/web/sport/-/preparations-for-uefa-euro-20-2 (Accessed 26 May 2020).

Eurosport (2017) Brussels loses right to host Euro 2020 matches as Wembley gains four games. *Eurosport*. Available from: https://www.eurosport.co.uk/football/euro-2020/2021/brussels-loses-right-to-host-euro-2020-matches-wembley-gains-four-games_sto6435836/story.shtml (Accessed 14 July 2021).

Fussey, P, Coaffee, J, Armstrong, G & Hobbs, D (2011) *Securing and Sustaining the Olympic City: Reconfiguring London for 2012 and Beyond*. Aldershot. Ashgate.

Giulianotti, R (2011) Sport Mega Events, Urban Football Carnivals and Securitised Commodification: The Case of the English Premier League. *Urban Studies* 48(15), 3293–3310.

Giulianotti, R & Klauser, F (2010) Security Governance and Sport Mega-Events: Toward an Interdisciplinary Research Agenda. *Journal of Sport and Social Issues* 34(1), 48–60.

Goffman, E (1974) *Frame Analysis: An Essay on the Organization of Experience*. Plymouth. Penguin.

Graeff, B & Knijnik, J (2021) If Things Go South: The Renewed Policy of Sport Mega Events Allocation and Its Implications for Future Research. *International Review for the Sociology of Sport* 56(8), 1234–1260.

Jarvis, L & Lister, M (2012) Vernacular Securities and Their Study: A Qualitative Analysis and Research Agenda. *International Relations* 27(2), 158–179.

King, A (2016 [2003]) *The European Ritual: Football in New Europe*. Oxon. Routledge.

Klauser, F (2010) Splintering Spheres of Security: Peter Sloterdijk and the Contemporary Fortress City. *Environment and Planning D: Society and Space* 28, 326–340.

Klauser, F (2011a) The Exemplification of "Fan Zones": Mediating Mechanisms in the Reproduction of Best Practices for Security and Branding at Euro 2008. *Urban Studies* 48(15), 3202–3219.

Klauser, F (2011b) Commonalities and Specificities in Mega-Event Securitisation: The Example of Euro 2008 in Austria and Switzerland. In C.J. Bennett & K.D. Haggerty (eds) *Security Games, Surveillance and Control at Mega-Events*. London. Routledge, 120–136.

Klauser, F (2012) Interpretative Flexibility of the Event-City: Security, Branding and Urban Entrepreneurialism at the European Football Championships 2008. *International Journal of Urban and Regional Research* 36(5), 1039–1052.

Klauser, F (2013) Spatialities of Security and Surveillance: Managing Spaces, Separations and Circulations at Sport Mega Events. *Geoforum* 49, 224–234.

Lee Ludvigsen, JA (2019) "Continent-Wide" Sports Spectacles: The "Multiple Host Format" of Euro 2020 and United 2026 and Its Implications. *Journal of Convention & Event Tourism* 20(2), 163–181.

Lee Ludvigsen, JA (2020) The 'Troika of Security': Merging Retrospective and Futuristic 'Risk' and 'Security' Assessments before Euro 2020. *Leisure Studies* 39(6), 844–858.

Lee Ludvigsen, JA (2021a) Mega-Events, Expansion and Prospects: Perceptions of Euro 2020 and Its 12-Country Hosting Format. *Journal of Consumer Culture* 0(0), 1–19.

Lee Ludvigsen, JA (2021b) When 'The Show' Cannot Go on: An Investigation into Sports Mega-Events and Responses during the Pandemic Crisis. *International Review for the Sociology of Sport* 0(0), 1–18.

14 Setting the Scene

Lodise, TP & Rybak, MJ (2020) COVID-19: Important Therapy Considerations and Approaches in This Hour of Need. *Pharmacotherapy* 40(5),) 379–381.

Løkke, A & Sørensen, P (2014) Theory Testing Using Case Studies. *The Electronic Journal of Business Research Methods Volume* 12(1), 66–74.

Millward, P (2011) *The Global Football League: Transnational Networks, Social Movements and Sport in the New Media Age.* Basingstoke. Palgrave Macmillan.

Millward, P (2017) World Cup 2022 and Qatar's Construction Projects: Relational Power in Networks and Relational Responsibilities to Migrant Workers. *Current Sociology* 65(5), 756–776.

Mythen, G & Walklate, S (2008) Terrorism, Risk and International Security: The Perils of Asking "What If?". *Security Dialogue* 39, 221–241.

Numerato, D (2018) *Football Fans, Activism and Social Change.* London. Routledge.

Parnell, D, Widdop, P, Bond, A & Wilson, R (2020) COVID-19, Networks and Sport. *Managing Sport and Leisure*, 1–7.

Roche, M (2000) *Mega-Events and Modernity: Olympics and Expos in the Growth of Global Culture.* London. Routledge.

Roche, M (2017) *Mega-Events and Social Change: Spectacle, Legacy and Public Culture.* Manchester. Manchester University Press.

Rookwood, J (2020) The Politics of ConIFA: Organising and Managing International Football Events for Unrecognised Countries. *Managing Sport and Leisure* 25(1–2), 6–20.

Rothan, HA & Byrareddy, SN (2020) The Epidemiology and Pathogenesis of Coronavirus Disease (COVID-19) Outbreak. *Journal of Autoimmunity* 109, 102433.

Rowe, D (2020) Subjecting Pandemic Sport to a Sociological Procedure. *Journal of Sociology* 56(4), 704–713.

Sky News (2021) Euro 2020: Angela Merkel tells Boris Johnson she is 'very concerned' number of fans at Wembley could be 'a bit too much'. *Sky News.* Available from: https://news.sky.com/story/euro-2020-angela-merkel-tells-boris-johnson-she-is-very-concerned-the-number-of-fans-at-wembley-could-be-a-bit-too-much-12347320 (Accessed 14 July 2021).

The FA (n.d.) A very special Euro. Available from: https://www.thefa.com/competitions/uefa-euro-2020/a-euro-for-europe (Accessed 14 July 2021).

The Independent (2021) Michel Platini's 'Zany' Idea Could Provide an Unforgettable Summer of Football. *The Independent.* Available from: https://www.independent.co.uk/sport/football/michel-platini-uefa-aleksander-ceferin-italy-rome-b1862547.html (Accessed 14 July 2021).

Tsoukala, A (2009) *Football Hooliganism in Europe: Security and Civil Liberties in the Balance.* Basingstoke. Palgrave.

UEFA (2005) *Good Practices for Safe and Secure Major Sporting Events: Experiences and Lessons from UEFA EURO 2004.* Den Haag. COT Institute for Safety and Crisis Management.

UEFA (2020) UEFA postpones EURO 2020 by 12 months. Available from: https://www.uefa.com/insideuefa/about-uefa/news/newsid=2641071.html (Accessed 27 May 2020).

UEFA (n.d.) *UEFA EURO 2020: Tournament Requirements.* Nyon. UEFA. Available from: https://www.uefa.com/MultimediaFiles/Download/EuroExperience/competitions/General/01/95/21/41/1952141_DOWNLOAD.pdf. (Accessed 17 July 2019).

Urry, J & Larsen, J (2011) *The Tourist Gaze 3.0.* London. Sage.

Webber, D.M (2022) Towards an 'Everyday' Cultural Political Economy of English Football: Conceptualising the Futures of Wembley Stadium and the Grassroots Game. *New Political Economy* 27(1), 47–61.

WHO (2020) Coronavirus. Available from: https://www.who.int/health-topics/coronavirus#tab=tab_3 (Accessed 27 May 2020).

Yin, RK (1994) *Case Study Research: Design and Methods* [2nd Edition]. Thousand Oaks, CA. Sage.

Zedner, L (2009) *Security*. London/New York. Routledge.

Chapter 1

The Dynamic Nexus between Sport, Mega-Events and Security

A Socio-Historical Sketch

Introduction

This chapter contextualizes the relationship between sport mega-events (SMEs) and security and places this complex pair within a socio-historical frame. It does so by examining key concepts, contemporary cases and external trends that collectively explain mega-events' intensified securitizations and their social significance. This is completely necessary in order to understand *why* SMEs and their cities, in the post-9/11 epoch, have become characterized by the application of novel surveillance technologies, globally networked security practices and the militarization of urban spaces. Currently, every mega-event will produce a display of 'total' (Bennett and Haggerty, 2011: 1), 'ring of steel' (Coaffee and Wood, 2006) or 'spectacular' (Boyle and Haggerty, 2009) security where control must not merely be achieved, but actively exhibited. Although the relationship between SMEs and security has been increasingly appreciated by academics in recent years (Boyle and Haggerty, 2009, 2012; Cleland, 2019; Giulianotti and Klauser, 2010; Pauschinger, 2020), the chapter contends that there are still some important gaps in the literature that this book will set out to fill. These relate to the construction of security in different event-specific contexts and the meanings of 'security' when applied to modern-day mega-events.

At the time of writing, it is nearly two decades since Horne and Manzenreiter (2006) predicted that security issues would advance to the very forefront of SMEs. Such prediction has proved accurate. Security issues are undoubtedly located at the frontiers of every contemporary SME. Notwithstanding, the securing of every mega-event differs in terms of their rationales, respective risk profiles and security cultures. Ultimately, broader and external trends impact every mega-event's security planning, delivery and what occurs when the mega-event's days are over and security practices, technologies or methods occasionally remain as 'security legacies' (Giulianotti and Klauser, 2010).

Structurally, this chapter begins with a brief overview of the sociology of mega-events. Then it provides a contextualization and review of the literature on mega-event securitization. This is placed in context of, and seen through the filter of Beck's (1992) influential risk society thesis. This is followed by a discussion of

DOI: 10.4324/9781003258445-2

three existing concepts – security field, networks and legacies – that are crucial as conceptual tools for an understanding of how SME security is increasingly standardized and constructed *pre-event* and remaining *post-event*.

The sociology of sport mega-events: Between spectacles, legacies and politics

Globalization processes and the economic restructuring of cities in Western societies during the twentieth century were crucial in increasing the attractiveness of mega-event housing as a catalyst for urban economic regeneration and growth (Roche, 1992). In the twenty-first century, hosting an SME is considered extremely prestigious because such events possess high levels of economic, cultural and political significance (Doidge et al., 2019; Horne, 2007; Preuss, 2007; Roche, 2000). SMEs are true spectacles. They are broadcasted worldwide and assigned extensive media coverage (Bourdieu, 1998). Given the enormous symbolic, political and social values attached to mega-events, Roche (2000, 2017) – a pioneer in the field – quickly recognized the importance of an academic study dedicated to mega-events. Prior to, but predominantly after Roche's seminal work, academics from a wide array of backgrounds have appreciated the social significance of mega-events. This has given life to an intriguing body of academic work that examines various social, cultural, political and financial aspects of mega-events. Considering mega-events' undisputed local, national and international importance, the social study of mega-events has steadily progressed and turned towards new pathways.

A complete overview of those aspects of mega-events that have been approached academically cannot be provided here. However, scholarly research in the social sciences has commonly been legacy centred (Preuss, 2007). Prior to this widespread interest in mega-events' socio-economic legacies, Roche (1992) observed that the field was dominated by narrow economic approaches concerned with financial impact studies. Indeed, mega-events are normally hosted for their alleged wider and positive post-event impacts or legacies. Therefore, much appreciated academically are specific mega-events and their (in)ability to act as catalysts for urban regeneration (Essex and Chalkley, 1998; Gold and Gold, 2011; Watt, 2013) and tourism impacts during and post-event (Weed, 2006). Mega-events' impact on local residents and communities in host cities, regions or countries are also commonly examined (e.g., Lin, 2013). Others investigate the political economies of SMEs (Boykoff, 2014; Horne and Manzenreiter, 2006) whilst recent years have seen an intensified interest in host countries' strategic deployment of SMEs as vessels to acquire 'soft power' in the international system (see Brannagan and Giulianotti, 2015).

As Yu et al. (2009: 391) maintain, these wide-reaching strands of research are invaluable and provide an insight 'into the roles of SMEs as catalysts for promoting socio-economic, urban, political or cultural outputs'. However, they assert that there is one important element of SMEs that has been allocated relatively limited critical attention, namely, the manifold of security issues. The dynamic SME/security *nexus*, although given more recognition over recent years (Cleland, 2019; Giulianotti and Klauser, 2012), undoubtedly represents an area that has the potential to grow further in line with new security-related developments. Resultantly, this chapter now delves into the emerging debates and concepts related to mega-events' securitization.

Security and sport mega-events in a risk society: Historical events and social change

Mega-events have for long been surrounded by security issues or tensions. Historically, even the first Olympic Games in Athens, in 1896, 'were a stage for military tension between the host nation and Turkey' (Atkinson and Young, 2008: 201). However, since then, SMEs occurring in contemporary societies have come to boast extensive media and social media coverage. They are symbolic, politicized and spectacular occasions visited by large crowds (Roche, 2000; Sugden, 2012). Partly for these reasons, mega-events also represent 'spectacular targets' (Coaffee and Wood, 2006).[1] Whereas heightened security and safety concerns before contemporary mega-events can be traced back to the 1960s (Houlihan and Giulianotti, 2012), the consensus is that the terrorist attack at the 1972 Olympics in Munich represents the first watershed moment in this context.

This attack, perpetrated by the Palestinian terrorist group Black September against Israeli athletes in the Olympic Village, resulted in 17 deaths and would elevate mega-event safety and security concerns (Boykoff, 2016; Fussey and Coaffee, 2011; Galily et al., 2015; Giulianotti and Klauser, 2012; Whelan, 2014). As Boykoff (2016: 114) notes, '[t]he terrorist attack in Munich was a pivotal point in Olympic history. Ever since, terrorism has been a major concern, and host cities have ramped up security measures to prevent attacks'. After 1972, security planning became increasingly centralized in the organization of mega-events (Coaffee et al., 2011). This was reinforced by the Centennial Park bombing, where two people were killed, during the 1996 Olympics in Atlanta (Cleland and Cashmore, 2018). However, it should also be mentioned that the stadium disasters of the 1980s, including the Heysel and Hillsborough tragedies (Scraton, 2016), hardened the nexus between security and sporting event attendance and led to safety-led legislations, security-related and social changes in the world of football (Turner, 2021). These tragedies, separately and collectively, have acted as 'sobering reminder of the public safety risks' associated with mega-events (Roche, 2017: 131). In addition to what has happened within the 'sport universe', the social and political shifts and developments well beyond sport have also impacted the securitization of SMEs greatly.

Following sociologist Ulrich Beck's (1992, 2009) pathbreaking (world) risk society thesis, the present-day globalized societies are characterized by the individual, local and global management and mitigation of transnational and often manufactured 'risks' induced by the modernity. Beck (1992: 19) observed that '[m]ore and more aspects of our lives are framed by an awareness of the dangers confronting humankind'. Beck named this epochal change 'reflexive modernization' as it symbolized a break from the industrial society. Fundamentally, the increasing array of human-made or manufactured risks – as opposed to 'natural hazards' – has potentially catastrophic consequences and must be addressed under conditions of uncertainty and limited 'methods of insurance' (Mythen and Walklate, 2008: 224).

Such threats have little respect for the borders of nation states and may include, for example, transnational terrorism, climate change and nuclear accidents. Yet, as Beck (2016: 43) reminded us, '[g]lobal risk is not global catastrophe', but rather the 'anticipation of catastrophe' and the 'day-to-day sense of insecurity that we can no longer accept'. Hence, global risk requires action and intervention politically, scientifically and technologically, as well as in day-to-day settings. Upon his reflections on the 9/11 attacks, Beck (2002) further observed how transnational terrorism had come to represent a powerful illustrator of the 'world risk society'. He noted that the terrorist attacks underlined the limitations to state insurance and 'rational calculations' (p. 43). In the political sphere, thus, Beck remained adamant that 'the hidden central issue in world risk society is *how to feign control over the uncontrollable*' (p. 41, original emphasis).

As Cleland (2019) and Toohey and Taylor (2008) demonstrate, Beck's (1992, 2002, 2009) theories are highly relevant and applicable to the study of security, risk and sport. The central tenets of Beck's risk society thesis may be identified in Olympic security planning (Toohey and Taylor, 2008). Moreover, under the conditions of omnipresent uncertainty that exceed into sport:

> [G]overnments, security agencies and sports governing bodies have implemented well-funded and resourced risk management strategies to confront the threat of terrorism to create a safe environment for those competing and watching.
>
> (Cleland, 2019: 150)

As such, upon proceeding, Beck's theories on risk should be considered as key touchstones for this book and its sociological inquiry into mega-event security. Furthermore, other scholars have also pointed towards the constant, yet problematic pursuit for 'safety' (Bauman, 2005) and 'security' (Zedner, 2003, 2009) as defining features of modern societies. Especially the 9/11 terrorist attacks and general threat posed from transnational terrorism have undeniably added to such pronounced preoccupation with 'security', 'safety' and risks'. As Zedner (2009: 2) points out, the 'attacks of 9/11 and the Bali, Madrid and London bombings have kept security at the foreground of public concern'. As completely central to this book, these external shifts and events and the subsequent wider trends have also brought security issues and logics to the foreground of mega-events (Atkinson and Young, 2012; Clavel, 2013) where threats and risk are widely anticipated.

It has been suggested that, following the 9/11 attacks and the global 'war on terror', the most prominent domain of mega-event expansion *vis-à-vis* financial costs and personnel has been within security and risk management (Giulianotti and Klauser, 2010). This is demonstrated by the elevated security costs and budgets for post-9/11 SMEs, compared to those taking place before 2001. This, again, must be seen in light of increasingly pre-emptive and precautionary approaches to security in response to the terrorist threat (Coaffee and Wood, 2006; Zedner, 2009) in modern risk societies. Consequently, this has underlined the need to respond efficiently, sufficiently and appropriately before and during SMEs.

To add some context: at the last Summer Olympics prior to 9/11 in Sydney in 2000, the security budget was in the region of US\$179 million (Sugden, 2012: 419). Four years later, US\$1.5 *billion* were allocated to the security costs for the 2004 Athens Summer Olympics. At the 2012 Summer Olympics in London, the expenditures reportedly reached US\$1.9 billion (Giulianotti, 2013). The number of active security-related personnel has also increased rapidly. At the mentioned Munich Olympics in 1972, the number of security staff was 2,130. Three decades later, in Athens, 41,000 people were actively maintaining or contributing to security (Toohey and Taylor, 2008: 463).

Such numbers indicate the social significance of security operations at SMEs. And, as Giulianotti (2013: 96) puts it, 'such enormous expenditure is in itself worthy of close examination'. Throughout the 2000s and 2010s, enormous security budgets have remained the norm, whilst other tragic incidents have elevated security fears ahead of SMEs. For example, the 7/7 bombings in London took place only 24 hours after the English capital won the hosting rights for the 2012 Summer Olympics (Coaffee and Wood, 2006). In April 2013, the Boston Marathon was targeted in a terrorist attack. Then, in November 2015, a terrorist attack took place just outside *Stade de France* in Paris, whilst France played against Germany in an international match (Cleland and Cashmore, 2018). The heightened threat levels subsequently led to the enforced state of emergency in France during Euro 2016 (Goldblatt, 2019). In that sense, SMEs have been targets for terrorists. Yet, mega-events' security operations are also impacted by powerful sets of external trends and incidents that will be discussed next.

Security operations, practices and measures at post-9/11 mega-events have become increasingly standardized (Galily et al., 2015; Pauschinger, 2020; Yu et al., 2009). The heightened security focus and extraordinary measures taken are therefore not only event-specific, although the objective levels of risk vary from event to event considering the host countries' or cities' very distinctive geopolitical, social and cultural dynamics (Pauschinger, 2020; Wong and Chadwick, 2017). Therefore, as Bennett and Haggerty (2011: 1) submit, '[e]ach mega-event now exhibits a "total security" effort akin to planning and deployment in times of war'. Hence, host countries' ability to guarantee and construct security has now become a prerequisite for being awarded the prestigious mega-event hosting rights. The construction and governance of security, notwithstanding, remain extremely complex and necessary to critically approach.

Precautionary security governance and complex security issues

As mentioned, security operations related to SMEs have, due to their scale, been described as warfare like undertakings. Yu et al. (2009) argue that the 2008 Olympics in Beijing was the largest peacetime security operation in history. Four years prior, a similar phrase was employed to describe the Athens Olympics (Wilson, 2004, cited in Toohey and Taylor, 2008). It has even been maintained that wars have been waged with less planning and coordination than some mega-events (Ryan, 2002, cited in Boyle and Haggerty, 2012). Such descriptions are in themselves important because they illuminate SME security operations' immensity in contemporary societies.

Presently, mega-event security planning and deployment encompass new security strategies, infrastructures, surveillance technologies and policing tactics (Armstrong et al., 2017; Coaffee et al., 2011; Cleland, 2019; Lauss and Szigetvari, 2010; Sugden, 2012; Whelan, 2014). The assemblages of security ultimately demonstrate the increasingly blurry distinctions between civilian/military, war/law enforcement and internal/external security relations (Klauser, 2017). Somewhat paradoxically, all this occurs amid local residents' everyday lives and in public spaces and urban areas (Fussey, 2015) that are converted into concealed lockdown zones and 'surveillant assemblages' (Haggerty and Ericson, 2000) fixed on social and crowd control.

Hence, Boyle and Haggerty (2009) argue that every host city attempts to, and is expected to emulate or excel its predecessors by creating 'spectacular security' and creating a subjective sense of 'security' that, simultaneously, facilitates fertile conditions for mega-event consumption. Further, organizers, authorities and security agencies must make precautionary efforts to account for the most 'unthinkable' scenarios. This feeds into the mentioned 'security spectacle', which transmits spectacular images of preparedness (ibid.). However, despite this emphasis on an exhibition of 'spectacular' or 'total security', it is also crucial that increased securitization of SMEs, ideally, does not obstruct the spirit of the sporting events and actions (Boyle and Haggerty, 2009; Coaffee et al., 2011) or deters international event tourists (Pauschinger, 2020). Fundamentally, the show must be allowed to go on. Based on his ethnographic work at mega-events hosted in Brazil, Pauschinger (2020: 122) builds upon this and argues that Brazil's security spectacles could be conceptualized as a selective and permeable 'security of camouflage' that served to masquerade the wider, 'brutal, oppressive, warlike police missions' in the city's favelas and non-event spaces.

Hence, event organizers, security agencies and authorities that convey spectacular images of a façade of security also have the incentive to keep security as invisible and discreet as possible, to avoid extensive perceptions of fear and insecurity from being created through overt and powerful displays of security or deployed militarized tools (Boyle and Haggerty, 2009; Clavel, 2013; Coaffee et al., 2009). More broadly, this connects with one of Zedner's (2003: 163) security paradoxes, holding that '[s]ecurity promises reassurance but increases anxieties'. Zedner notes that, ironically, by providing visible reminders of the threats that have been secured against, insecurity levels may actually be exacerbated. Buzan (1991: 37) describes this as self-destructive efforts to achieve security and a recent example of this includes the security operation before the 2016 Olympics in Rio de Janeiro, Brazil, which relied heavily upon military forces to counter insecurities, but rather contributed to increase violence in the securitized urban areas (Azzi, 2017). As such, it can be argued that the security at SMEs should, ideally and (somewhat) idyllically, be neatly balanced between being spectacular, yet not *too* spectacular (Boyle and Haggerty, 2009).

Having observed the expansion of security governance at SMEs, Giulianotti and Klauser (2010) provided an important research agenda with emerging issues and potential social scientific theoretical approaches compatible with the study of SME security. In addition, three types of risk categories are broken down. These, by no means an all-encompassing list of the potential risks and hazards present before or after SMEs, are (i) terrorism, (ii) spectator and political violence and lastly (iii) poverty, social division and urban crime (ibid.). Historically, these represent the most prominent mega-event threats. Yet, as South Korea's Pyongyang Winter Olympics in 2018 served as a reminder of state or cyber conflict can also threaten an event's prospects for achieving security (Rowe, 2019). Besides, threats to SMEs must be viewed in context of the mass crowds they attract. Recent years have seen crowds targeted in terrorist attacks (Coaffee et al., 2009), by criminals, or impacted by outbreaks of supporter violence or fan and law enforcement clashes (Millward, 2009).

Contemporary SMEs attract thousands of fans – with and without stadium tickets. Hence, stadiums are not the only spaces that must be sufficiently secured. Commonly, fans without match tickets congregate to watch matches, consume and socialize in erected fan zones (Hagemann, 2010; Kolyperas and Sparks, 2018).[2] Fan zones, again, can be site for disorder and clashes (Millward, 2009) and have themselves become interesting entry points for empirical examinations of security and surveillance at contemporary mega-events (Klauser, 2011a; Lee Ludvigsen, 2021) since they represent one joint in the wider SME security strategy. In fan zones, Lauss and Szigetvari (2010) write, the visiting supporters are 'governed by fun' through activities, consumption and monitoring that collectively allow for containment and highly choreographed crowd control.

This illuminates the important links between security, social control and consumption at mega-events. As Giulianotti and Klauser (2010) argue, there is a need for examinations of how security and its related policies inter-connect with mega-events' commodification processes. This relates to how consumption hubs like fan zones are secured (Klauser, 2017) and how security practices and policies serve to assist the construction of the ideal conditions in which consumption practices can thrive (McGillivray et al., 2020). The political economy and neoliberal rationalities inherent to SMEs emphasize creation of spectacles and aesthetic environments (Silk, 2014), and scholars find reinforcing links between security practices and event owners' or commercial partners' aspirations to maximize profits from the mega-events (Eick, 2011; Eisenhauer et al., 2014). Therefore, the need to secure is ostensible. Yet, it is also bound to aesthetic desires, as Chapter 2 discusses further.

It is clear that the security governance of mega-events can serve as a mirror for wider trends apparent in the modern world. In fact, drawing upon Debord's (1977) *Society of Spectacle*, Boyle and Haggerty (2009) remind us that mega-events' spectacular security practices are shaped by external security and surveillance dynamics. Hence, each mega-event represents an *entrée* or a window for contemporary analyses of securitization and surveillance and can 'offer important lessons about local and global processes' (Boyle and Haggerty, 2009: 271). Reinforcing this perspective, Tsoukala (2016) holds that security practices at SMEs cannot be disassociated from the broader security contexts in modern risk societies.

One pronounced way through which these arguments can be demonstrated is through the shifting modes of security assessments to counter transnational terrorism threats. These emerged in a post-9/11 world (Mythen and Walklate, 2008) and have become embedded in mega-event securitizations (Boyle and Haggerty, 2012; Cleland, 2019). Accordingly, risk assessments taken under conditions of uncertainty are now guided by the question 'what if?', instead of 'what was?', or 'what is?' (Mythen and Walklate, 2008). Drawing upon Beck's (1992) aforementioned scholarship, Mythen and Walklate (2008: 234) write that:

> This climate of not knowing enough – and, moreover, knowing about not knowing enough – has had a visible impact on the authority of security institutions. So far as regulating terrorism is concerned, there has been a palpable shift towards futurity in practices of risk analysis and the language of governance [...] The new calculus [of risk] does not assess the future by focusing on the past [...] *Instead, security assessments are direct by the question: 'What if?'.* (emphasis added)

In security domains, this again 'translates into policies that *actively* seek to prevent situations from becoming catastrophic at some indefinite point in the future' (Aradau and Van Munster, 2007: 105, original emphasis). As transplanted into the universe of sport, this means that SME security assessments also are increasingly informed and moulded by such precautionary thinking which influences the ways through which mega-event planners and security agencies secure events (Boyle and Haggerty, 2009). A result of this is the 'continuous reiteration in official circles that security planners must "think outside the box"' (ibid.: 260) when dealing with a number of unknowns including terrorism. This casts light on a central touchstone of this book, which is that security at SMEs operates in concert with, and not in isolation from, wider security contexts, assessments and trends.

The above analytical relation remains vital to this book, which not only anchors itself in these perspectives but also utilizes an SME – Euro 2020 – as a portal to enhance our understanding of security beyond the worlds of football and sport. The fact that security operations and assemblages at modern SMEs are being frequently portrayed as 'quasi-war' operations occurring in peacetime and involving clusters of international agencies and actors (Boyle, 2011) underpins the logic and strengths of employing an SME as a site of analysis for conceptually or empirically exploring security practices, meanings and security more generally in the present-day world.

To be clear, the importance of a continued study of the mega-event and security relationship is unequivocally agreed-upon. Though, for years it was a neglected relationship. As recently as in 2008, Toohey and Taylor (2008) described that the lack of conducted and published research on 'terrorism' and SMEs as surprising. Then, following some pioneering scholarship, the field has grown substantially (Boyle and Haggerty, 2009; Cleland, 2019; Cleland and Cashmore, 2018; Fussey, 2015; Giulianotti and Klauser, 2010, 2012; Pauschinger, 2020). Predominantly, however, security governance in relation to 'terrorism' has been in focus. Moreover, case studies are commonly related to the Olympics (e.g., Armstrong et al., 2017; Boykoff, 2020; Boyle and Haggerty, 2009) and to a lesser extent the World Cup or the European Championships. To be sure, it should still be clear that Olympic security has received less academic examination compared to other elements of the Olympics (Spaaij, 2016), and the study of mega-event securitization *still* presents new avenues for critical examination (Giulianotti and Klauser, 2010).

Not uncommonly, existing research often addresses Olympic-related (counter-) terrorism. This relationship has often been studied from afar and media-focused (Spaaij, 2016; Spaaij and Hamm, 2015). Whilst representing important scholarship, these also illuminate the manifold of largely untouched avenues that exist, which researchers could examine to – as called for – broaden and widen the scope of the critical mega-event securitization project (Giulianotti and Klauser, 2010, 2012). For example, by referring back to Giulianotti and Klauser's (2010) risk categories, there is undoubtedly scope for an enhanced focus on spectator violence,[3] poverty, crime and social division and how these are instrumental in an event's powerful securitization.

With the Olympic-terrorism nexus largely covered, it has been argued that 'critical social scientific analysis needs to move beyond common-sense reporting of such [terrorism] incidents' (Giulianotti and Klauser, 2012: 312). In that sense, it is argued here that more holistic analyses of SME security are needed, especially as new threats emerge (Cleland and Cashmore, 2018). Concurrently, such argument can be synthesized with the argument for examinations of SMEs not as confined to the Olympics or the World Cup (Müller, 2015) and Giulianotti and Klauser's (2010) more general research agenda in which social researchers were urged to critically unpack and investigate the diverse effects of SME securitization. SMEs are not securitized solely to account for or pre-empt 'real' or 'perceived' terrorism threats, because the securing of SME spaces and the associated social ramifications relate to a series of security threats (i.e., pandemics), issues, rationales and aims.

This must be understood in relation to how different security threats, on occasions, are collectively addressed under the banner of security (see Divišová, 2019).

For example, 'hooligans' or a host city's crime rates can contribute vastly to an SME's securitized milieus (Wong and Chadwick, 2017). However, existing studies approaching 'crime' and 'hooliganism' as security threats are limited compared to those studies focused on Olympic terrorism. The preoccupation with 'terrorism' in relevant scholarship is unsurprising. Arguably, 'terrorism' remains the one threat that can cause largest emotional and physical harm, and 'terrorism' concerns are, as discussed below, usually fuelled by the media's catastrophe forecasting coverage of potential 'terrorism' (Atkinson and Young, 2012). According to Galily et al. (2015), it also remains inevitable that the terrorism concerns at SMEs will continue and perhaps increase as the world's interconnectedness continues to grow.

Against this backdrop, it remains important to dedicate some attention to the mediation of security and threats. For Pierre Bourdieu (1998: 81), mega-event spectacles like the Olympics are 'produced twice'. First, this includes 'the actual event in the stadium', the sports event. Second, it involves reproduction of 'the first [event] in images and commentary', the media event (ibid.). Security at mega-events, similarly, is twofold. It is enforced or negotiated physically in stadiums and event cities. Concurrently, security threats or measures may be reproduced through images, press reports and commentaries. Media discourses and coverage before and during mega-events can essentially reinforce the perceived need to secure and the subjective perceptions of (in)security related to SMEs.

Generally, the modern media plays a prominent role in framing social problems (Stevens and Vaughan-Williams, 2014; Tsoukala, 2008). Broadly, the media also has the capacity to mould public perceptions of safety and security to a degree where they may stop corresponding with the social realities (Atkinson and Young, 2012) or security on an objective level. Occasionally, this enables the context where 'the perception of threat is a greater problem than the threat itself' (Zedner, 2009: 23). The construction of a social problem per se may be as important as its 'reality'. Especially so, when the 'power to construct lies […] with one side' (Pearson and Sale, 2011: 161). Indeed, this is confirmed by the discursive framing of potential Olympic-related terrorism, as explored by Atkinson and Young (2012: 289), who argue that mega-events represent 'fabricated zones of risk' and that the media was acting 'catastrophe-forecasting' and 'fear brokering' before the Olympic Games in the immediate post-9/11 period (between 2002 and 2006). Furthermore, in relation to the prospects or threats of spectator violence, Poulton (2005: 41) argues that media versions of violent supporters commonly paint a picture of 'mindless animals', but fail to give any 'in-depth analysis into the root of football-related disorder'. Media discourses of mega-event related security issues may thus amplify subjective insecurities. Though, they do not necessarily assist any deepened understanding of the social security realities.

The mass mediation of terrorism and other, potential disorder before SMEs is perhaps unsurprising. As Bauman (2005) observed, displays of those threatening our personal safety have now become the mass media's key asset. However, Taylor and Toohey (2015: 379) underline that 'there is a low risk of an actual terrorism incident occurring during an event'. Spaaij (2016: 456) tracks incidents of Olympic-terrorism and concludes that SMEs are 'quite safe with regard to terrorism'.[4] Threats to SMEs, like elsewhere in societies, are characterized by a dual nature. They are sometimes real, since they materialize (e.g., Munich, 1972 and *Stade de France*, 2015). They are also occasionally socially constructed or imagined, rather than 'real' (Atkinson and Young, 2012). Thus, terrorism risks are never completely non-existent, but must be placed in context.

Notwithstanding, the preoccupation with 'terrorism' in existing scholarship translates into substantial research gaps to fill concerning other and diverse security threats. Football mega-events like the European Championships are, for example, arguably more associated with issues of public disorder and supporter violence (Jennings and Lodge, 2011). And indeed, the potential and actual transgressive behaviour by fans, historically and presently, is constructed as a social threat requiring extra punishments, wide-reaching surveillance and expansion of legal powers (Spaaij, 2013).

Essentially, mega-event securitization is a multifaceted phenomenon. And, as this chapter argues, based on the existing research, there is scope for more inclusive, holistic and comparative analyses. This is compatible with mentioned directions for researchers (Cleland and Cashmore, 2018; Giulianotti and Klauser, 2010, 2012; Yu et al., 2009) and would allow for progressively understanding the wider social implications of SME securitization in both contemporary societies and more specific sporting contexts. As Yu et al. (2009: 392) argue, 'very few academic works have provided critical accounts of the wider social implications of the massive security efforts surrounding SMEs'. Hence, to fully understand these 'wider social implications', it is necessary to engage with the wider spectrum of expected and unexpected security threats and issues. Subsequently, this would enable even more holistic and diverse analyses of mega-event securitization.

Consequently, this argument and this chapter's discussion of security governance at SMEs serve to illuminate the observable research gaps. These undeniably serve to reinforce the contention that mega-events present new fields for a critical study of security (Giulianotti and Klauser, 2010). First, it becomes evident that researchers should commit to holistic analyses of event-specific 'security' and seek to empirically examine the processes that assist the construction of 'security' and the far-reaching and (in)direct effects caused by the securitization of multiple threats, populations and behaviours. This involves 'terrorism', but also 'crime', 'violence' and infectious diseases, which all represent 'threats' in the mega-event settings and require (or are used as justification for) the large volumes of planning, resources and capital invested into security efforts. Secondly – and inter-connectedly – in order to fill lacunas in the literature, it is required to increasingly examine the *social implications* of the enormous security operations that take place in the name of a mega-event. As will be returned to in Chapter 2, this relates to the social meanings of 'security' and exactly 'whom' (or 'what') security practices or policies tend to include or exclude Moreover, some of the social impacts or ramifications of mega-event security operations include what is commonly referred to as security fields, legacies (Giulianotti and Klauser, 2010) and knowledge networks

(Boyle, 2011). These concepts should be seen in context of the globalization of security and security-related knowledge (Bauman, 2005; Bigo, 2008; Tsoukala, 2009). Now, they represent integral components in the bidding and housing phases of mega-events and the overarching standardization of SME security.

Security fields, networks and legacies

To guide and assist our understanding of the social, spatial and transnational dynamics of mega-event securitizations, this section maps out three key conceptual tools – security field, security legacies and security networks – that can be mobilized and that all derive from the pre-existing literature (Boyle, 2011; Giulianotti and Klauser, 2010). Whilst these conceptual tools, in various ways, are inherently inter-linked, they must also be unpacked on their own. First, Giulianotti and Klauser (2010: 57) draw from Bourdieusian sociology and suggest that the security field is a 'a specific, security-defined social space, which contains objective, game-like relationships that are played out between various "players" (or stakeholders)'. However, the security fields of SMEs may be contested domains, whereas its stakeholders – or security 'players' – may include:

> local people and residents, visiting spectators, police officers, government officials, local authority officials, local business people, nongovernmental and community-based organizations, sports officials, national and local politicians, private security companies, journalists, and other commentators. (ibid.)

Importantly, given the wide scope of stakeholders that are present in an SME's security field, it is noted that every stakeholder will occupy different levels of 'power' within this field. This is particularly central to this book's approach, whereby wider stakeholder groups (i.e., other commentators, journalists) – and in particular football fan networks – are viewed as *present* and *important* actors in the SME security field and thereby necessary to provide a voice and to account better for, than what the existing literature has done to date. This also corresponds with Cleland et al.'s (2018) and Turner's (2021) relational sociological studies of collective actions in football. In their views, organized fan networks must be seen as connected to the sport's wider organizational structures. The security field concept allows for critically approaching the intersecting social worlds of mega-event security and football. In these social spaces, fan representatives, general fans and journalists – to name a few – are deeply embedded as actors that can bring about social change (Cleland et al., 2018; Numerato, 2018; Turner, 2021).

Then, in the current era, security-based networks 'transcend borders, time and space' (Zedner, 2009: 62). As Bigo (2008: 19) writes, policing systems are 'structured in differentiated networks'. As such, the concept of 'security knowledge networks' (Boyle, 2011) remains extremely relevant. This refers to the shifting linkages in-between security actors that enable the transnational movement of mega-event security expertise across times and spaces. Essentially, this explains how security-related practices and policies move from one mega-event place to another, through transnational partnerships and collaborations between security agencies, sport governing bodies, technology firms and consultants (ibid.). Indeed, Clavel (2013: 76) even suggests that mega-events comprise 'laboratories' in which transnational security collaborations are fostered and tested.

Central to a security knowledge network is the movement of expertise and knowledge. Here, the literature on 'policy transfer' and 'lesson-drawing' should be consulted (Boyle, 2011; Dolowitz and Marsh, 1996; Rose, 1991). In a nutshell, policy transfer and lesson-drawing explain how knowledge, best practices and policies from the past are transferred and/or applied in new spatial and temporal settings. For Rose (1991), there are five primary ways of drawing upon lessons. These include 'copying', which refers to 'using practice elsewhere literally as blueprint', and 'emulation', which not only adopts a particular programme, but also adapts for 'national circumstances' (p. 21). Moreover, 'hybridization' combines elements from two different places; 'synthesis' 'combine familiar elements from programmes in effect in three or more different places', and finally, 'inspiration' is used to refer to the deployment of other programs as an 'intellectual stimulus for developing a novel programme' (p. 22). In a globalized world, as McCann (2011) writes, the urban transfers of policy knowledge occur on a transnational context. Following this, learnt lessons, knowledge and policies that have been successfully employed in different settings are imported into new contexts.

This raises questions concerning *how* knowledge is transferred in the mega-event context. As the relevant literature finds, this could, *inter alia*, be through specific transnational networking activities in an event's build-up (Boyle, 2011; Klauser, 2011a). As Klauser (2011a) finds, the transfer of fan zone related 'best practices' between the Germany World Cup in 2006 and Euro 2008 in Switzerland and Austria involved exchanges between security stakeholders in conferences, workshops and gatherings. Whilst these may compose the 'key relational sites that are central to the process of teaching and learning about policy' (McCann, 2011: 120), lessons can also come from handbooks, manuals, guidelines and by 'reading policy documents about policies in other places' (ibid.: 112; see also Lauermann, 2016). Despite this, Klauser (2011a: 3305) crucially reminds us that 'the questions of how security policies circulate between mega-events have been widely ignored so far' (Klauser, 2011a: 3305). Therefore, as security policies and practices are (re-) circulated through security knowledge networks, one central question remains to examine how these are activated or indeed remain in-between mega-events.

Finally, the idea of a security legacy remains important to outline briefly, although it should be seen as connected with the mentioned security field and knowledge networks. Boyle and Haggerty (2009: 265) write that '[m]ega-events foster a legacy of knowledge, networks and habits that have a bearing on the lives of considerably more individuals than those in attendance'. A 'security legacy', therefore, is the 'range of security-related strategies and impacts which continue to have significance beyond the life of the sport event' (Giulianotti and Klauser, 2010: 53–54).

As mentioned, legacies and legacy promises are central to most mega-events (Roche, 2017). Given the limited timespan of SMEs and their humongous financial costs, their cities and organizers will not uncommonly stress their positive post-event legacies (i.e., increased tourism, new infrastructures, sporting participation). Increasingly, however, legacies have become intertwined with mega-events' security operations. More generally, security practices are likely to have immediate and long-term implications (Crawford and Hutchinson, 2016), and this remains the reality within the worlds of sport and football, too. Importantly, SMEs may also act as *the* catalyst for new security or surveillance tools, practices or technologies that are transferred onto other spheres of modern-day public life (Boyle and Haggerty, 2009).

Essentially, Giulianotti and Klauser (2010: 54) advance six security legacy typologies. In short, these involve technologies, new security practices, governmental policies and new legislations, externally imposed social transformations, generalized changes in social and trans-societal relationships and urban redevelopment. However, despite the significant growth of security complexes at post-9/11 SMEs, it is also important to acknowledge that security legacies do not represent a novel trend. For example, Boykoff (2020) points out that military equipment used to secure the 1984 Olympic Games in Los Angeles later was deployed in the 'war on drugs' and gangs. Hence, the 'weapons purchased for the Olympics are not boxed up and returned to sender at the conclusion of the Games; they become part of everyday policing moving forward', Boykoff (2020: 22) warns us.

Upon proceeding, the concept of a security legacy remains important for at least two principal reasons. Firstly, it represents a stark reminder of the fact that the social, political and geographical implications of mega-event security exceed the mega-event's more modest timespan (usually, a mega-event's sporting actions last for about 3–5 weeks). However, security legacies still tend to be 'underplayed by host cities and nations, especially during the bidding process' (Houlihan and Giulianotti, 2012: 716). Second, as hinted upon, this demonstrates how SMEs are employed as time-specific and high-profile sites and moments to test new surveillance technologies, security partnerships and strategies that sometimes extend into other policing and urban contexts that are not necessarily sports-related or fixed. In the present-day societies, increasingly preoccupied by the management of risk (Beck, 1992) and pursuit of security (Zedner, 2009), this is a phenomenon that should not be ignored or deemed insignificant. Notwithstanding, whereas security legacies must be considered a key concept in the academic vocabulary and study of mega-event security governance, it has still been subject to limited empirical research to date.

Conclusion

This chapter offers an appraisal of the existing literature on the relationship between SMEs and security in modern risk societies. Importantly, it argues for and sheds a light on the sociological importance of a continued and comparative scholarship in this field. As situated within a socio-historical frame predominantly spanning from 1972 to the present-day, this chapter has contextualized the dynamic mega-event/security nexus. This contextualization was complemented by a discussion of Beck's (1992) risk society, and the growing literature, which examines specific trends, cases and facets of contemporary mega-event securitizations, including the wider shift towards precautionary security principles (Boyle and Haggerty, 2009; Mythen and Walklate, 2008) and the discursive framing of security threats (Atkinson and Young, 2012). Then, the chapter unpacks three key concepts: security field, legacies and knowledge networks. These will work as conceptual touchstones and relations as this book advances. Overall, the chapter has argued that in spite of the growing academic interest in mega-event securitizations, there are still some important research gaps remaining, which this book sets out to address. Every mega-event's security planning and delivery remain unique, multifaceted and will have diverse social implications (Armstrong et al., 2017; Fussey, 2015; Pauschinger, 2020). Furthermore, increasingly standardized security templates are globally assembled but uniquely delivered locally (Pauschinger, 2020). As argued here, unexplored terrain exists *vis-à-vis* how security is constructed through processes of lesson-drawing, knowledge exchange (Boyle, 2011; Klauser, 2011a) and future-leaning precautionary assessments (Boyle and Haggerty, 2012; Mythen and Walklate, 2008) under the exceptional geographical and political circumstances that Euro 2020's multi-host country format warranted and was delivered within.

Giulianotti and Klauser (2010) called for a continued commitment to the critical study of mega-event security governance. They encouraged researchers to come up with transnational mega-event case studies in order to ensure a sustained and comparative study of security issues in different contexts. Similarly, Klauser (2011b: 133) argues that researchers should 'undertake detailed and comparative empirical investigations into how different types of events, in different cultural contexts, both resemble and differ from each other'. More recently, Pauschinger (2020: 109) emphasized the importance of examining how security measures 'are implemented and adapted to host cities that already present high levels of urban security challenges'. All this has profound implications for this book's rationale and this chapter's main argument. It is maintained that comparative, holistic and empirical understandings of diverse SME securitizations still are required. Particularly so, when the mega-event format in itself is as inherently transnational and networked as Euro 2020. This informs the aforementioned key research question this book sets out to explore relating to the processes, assessments, activities and policies that served to assist the construction of security and safety in the case of Euro 2020. Such question refers to the multiple dimensions of 'security': its *construction*, articulated *meanings* and expressed *perceptions* of it. An engagement with these facets can therefore facilitate an exploration of wider security developments that, as discussed, dictate, inform and impact a mega-event's security, in the unprecedented mega-event format of Euro 2020.

Notes

1 Interestingly, this is also increasingly depicted in popular culture and cinematic representations. For example, *The Dark Knight Rises* (2012), *The Brothers Grimsby* (2016) and *Manhunt: Deadly Games* (2020).
2 Elsewhere, fan zones are sometimes referred to as 'public viewing areas' or 'fan parks'. They are closed-off, open air spaces with giant screens that show football matches and provide activities for fans.
3 Indeed, studies on 'hooliganism' exist in large numbers. Some have even argued that 'hooliganism' has been 'over-researched' (Marsh et al., 1996: 1). What I argue is that there is more scope for exploring how 'hooliganism' impacts mega-event securitizations and their logics. Existing studies on 'hooliganism' predominantly pursue a theoretical explanation of 'hooliganism', describe 'hooligan culture' from the 'inside' or the policing of 'hooligans' in domestic leagues or international tournaments. See, for instance, Giulianotti (1995), Armstrong (1998), Spaaij (2007) and Stott and Pearson (2007).
4 Spaaij (2016) employs the *Global Terrorism Database* and identifies 22 cases of Olympic-related terrorism.

Bibliography

Aradau, C & Van Munster, R (2007) Governing Terrorism through Risk: Taking Precautions, (Un)Knowing the Future. *European Journal of International Relations* 13(1), 89–115.

Armstrong, G (1998) *Football Hooligans: Knowing the Score*. Oxford. Berg.

Armstrong, G, Giulianotti, R & Hobbs, D (2017) *Policing the 2012 London Olympics: Legacy and Social Exclusion*. London. Routledge.

Atkinson, M & Young, K (2008) *Deviance and Social Control in Sports*. Champaign, IL. Human Kinetics.

Atkinson, M & Young, K (2012) Shadowed by the Corpse of War: Sport Spectacles and the Spirit of Terrorism. *International Review for the Sociology of Sport* 47(3), 286–306.

Azzi, V (2017) Security for Show? The Militarisation of Public Space in Light of the 2016 Rio Olympic Games. *Contexto Internacional* 39(3), 589–607.

Bauman, Z (2005) *Liquid Life*. Cambridge. Polity.

Beck, U (1992) *Risk Society: Towards a New Modernity*. London. Sage.

Beck, U (2002) The Terrorist Threat: World Risk Society Revisited. *Theory, Culture & Society* 19(4), 39–55.

Beck, U (2009) *World at Risk*. Cambridge. Polity.

Beck, U (2016) *The Metamorphosis of the World*. Cambridge. Polity.

Bennett, CJ & Haggerty, KD (2011) Introduction: Security Games: Surveillance and Control at Mega-Events. In C.J. Bennett & K.D. Haggerty (eds) *Security Games: Surveillance and Control at Mega-Events*. Abingdon. Routledge, 1–19.

Bigo, D (2008) Globalized (In)Security: The Field and the Ban-Opticon. In D. Bigo & A. Tsoukala (eds) *Illiberal Practices in Liberal Regimes*. Paris. L'Harmattan, 10–48.

Bourdieu, P (1998) *On Television*. Translated by P. Ferguson. New York. New York Press.

Boykoff, J (2014) *Celebration Capitalism and the Olympic Games*. London/New York. Routledge.

Boykoff, J (2016) *Power Games: A Political History of the Olympics*. London. Verso.

Boykoff, J (2020) *Nolympians: Inside the Fight against Capitalist Mega-Sports in Los Angeles, Tokyo and Beyond*. Nova Scotia. Fernwood.

Boyle, P (2011) Knowledge Networks: Mega-Events and Security Expertise. In C.J. Bennett & K.D. Haggerty (eds) *Security Games: Surveillance and Control at Mega-Events*. Abingdon. Routledge, 169–184.

Boyle, P & Haggerty, KD (2009) Spectacular Security: Mega-Events and the Security Complex. *International Political Sociology* 3(3), 57–74.

Boyle, P & Haggerty, KD (2012) Planning for the Worst: Risk, Uncertainty and the Olympic Games. *British Journal of Sociology* 63(2), 241–259.

Brannagan, PM & Giulianotti, R (2015) Soft Power and Soft Disempowerment: Qatar, Global Sport and Football's 2022 World Cup Finals. *Leisure Studies* 34(6), 703–719.

Buzan, B (1991) *People, States and Fear* [2nd edition]. Hertfordshire. Harvester Wheatsheaf.

Clavel, A (2013) Armed Forces and Sports Mega Events: An Accepted Involvement in a Globalized World. *Sport in Society* 16(2), 205–222.

Cleland, J (2019) Sports Fandom in the Risk Society: Analyzing Perceptions an Experiences of Risk, Security and Terrorism at Elite Sports Events. *Sociology of Sport Journal* 36(2), 144–151.

Cleland, J & Cashmore, E (2018) Nothing Will Be the Same Again after the Stade de France Attack: Reflections of Association Football Fans on Terrorism, Security and Surveillance. *Journal of Sport and Social Issues* 42(6), 454–469.

Cleland, J, Doidge, M, Millward, P & Widdop, P (2018) *Collective Action and Football Fandom: A Relational Sociological Approach*. New York. Palgrave.

Coaffee, J & Wood, DM (2006) Security Is Coming Home: Rethinking Scale and Constructing Resilience in the Global Urban Response to Terrorist Risk. *International Relations* 20(4), 503–517.

Coaffee, J, Fussey, P & Moore, C (2011) Laminated Security for London 2012: Enhancing Security Infrastructures to Defend Mega Sporting Events. *Urban Studies* 48(15), 3311–3327.

Coaffee, J, O'Hare, P & Hawkesworth, M (2009) The Visibility of (In)security: The Aesthetics of Planning Urban Defences against Terrorism. *Security Dialogue* 40(4–5), 489–511.

Crawford, A & Hutchinson, S (2016) Mapping the Contours of "Everyday Security": Time, Space and Emotion. *British Journal of Criminology* 56, 1184–1202.

Debord, G (1977) *Society of the Spectacle*. Cambridge. Zone Books.

Divišová, V (2019) Euro 2016 and Its Security Legacy for Football Supporters: A Conceptual Blurring of Hooligans and Terrorists? *Soccer & Society* 20(5), 757–769.

Doidge, M, Claus, R, Gabler, J, Irving, R & Millward, P (2019) The Impact of International Football Events on Local, National and Transnational Fan Cultures: A Critical Overview. *Soccer & Society* 20(5), 711–720.

Dolowitz, D & Marsh, D (1996) Who Learns What from Whom? A Review of Policy Transfer Literature. *Political Studies* 44, 343–357.

Eick, V (2011) "Secure Our Profits!" The FIFA™ in Germany 2006. In C. Bennett & K. Haggerty (eds) *Security Games: Surveillance and Control at Mega-Events*. New York. Routledge, 87–102.

Eisenhauer, S, Adair, D & Taylor, T (2014) FIFA-isation: Spatial Security, Sponsor Protection and Media Management at the 2010 World Cup. *Surveillance & Society* 11(4), 377–391.

Essex, SJ & Chalkley, BS (1998) The Olympics as a Catalyst of Urban Renewal: A Review. *Leisure Studies* 17(3), 187–206.

Fussey, P (2015) Command, Control and Contestation: Negotiating Security at the London 2012 Olympics. *The Geographical Journal* 181(3), 212–223.

Fussey, P & Coaffee, J (2011) Olympic Rings of Steel: Constructing Security for 2012 and Beyond. In C.J. Bennett & K.D. Haggerty (eds) *Security Games: Surveillance and Control at Mega-Events*. Abingdon. Routledge, 36–54.

Galily, Y, Yarchi, M & Tamir, I (2015) From Munich to Boston, and from Theater to Social Media: The Evolutionary Landscape of World Sporting Terror. *Studies in Conflict & Terrorism* 38(12), 998–1007.

Giulianotti, R (1995) Participant Observation and Research into Football Hooliganism: Reflections on the Problems of Entrée and Everyday Risks. *Sociology of Sport Journal* 12(1), 1–20.

Giulianotti, R (2013) Six Security Legacies of Major Sporting Events. *ICSS Journal* 1(1), 95–101.

Giulianotti, R & Klauser, F (2010) Security Governance and Sport Mega-Events: Toward an Interdisciplinary Research Agenda. *Journal of Sport and Social Issues* 34(1), 48–60.

Giulianotti, R & Klauser, F (2012) Sport Mega-Events and "Terrorism": A Critical Analysis. *International Review for the Sociology of Sport* 47(3), 307–323.

Gold, JR & Gold, M (2011) *Olympic Cities: City Agendas, Planning, and the World's Games, 1986–2016*. London/New York. Routledge.

Goldblatt, D (2019) *The Age of Football: The Global Game in the Twenty-First Century*. London. Macmillan.

Hagemann, A (2010) From the Stadium to the Fan Zone: Host Cities in a State of Emergency. *Soccer & Society* 11(6), 723–736.

Haggerty, KD & Ericson, RV (2000) The Surveillant Assemblage. *British Journal of Sociology* 51(4), 605–622.

Horne, J (2007) The Four "Knowns" of Sports Mega-Events. *Leisure Studies* 26(1), 81–96.

Horne, J & Manzenreiter, W (2006) An Introduction to the Sociology of Sports Mega-Events. *Sociological Review* 54(2), 1–24.

Houlihan, B & Giulianotti, R (2012) Politics and the London 2012 Olympics: The (In)Security Games. *International Affairs* 88, 701–717.

Jennings, W & Lodge, M (2011) Governing Mega-Events: Tools of Security Risk Management for the FIFA 2006 World Cup in Germany and London 2012 Olympic Games. *Government and Opposition* 46(2), 192–222.

Klauser, F (2017) *Surveillance & Space*. London. Sage.

Klauser, F (2011a) The Exemplification of "Fan Zones": Mediating Mechanisms in the Reproduction of Best Practices for Security and Branding at Euro 2008. *Urban Studies* 48(15), 3202–3219.

Klauser, F (2011b) Commonalities and Specificities in Mega-Event Securitisation: The Example of Euro 2008 in Austria and Switzerland. In C.J. Bennett & K.D. Haggerty (eds) *Security Games, Surveillance and Control at Mega-Events*. London. Routledge, 120–136.

Kolyperas, D & Sparks, L (2018) Exploring Value Co-creation in Fan Fests: The Role of Fans. *Journal of Strategic Marketing* 26(1), 71–84.

Lauss, G & Szigetvari, A (2010) Governing by Fun: EURO 2008 and the Appealing Power of Fan Zones. *Soccer & Society* 11(6), 737–747.

Lauermann, J (2016) Made in Transit: Mega-Events and Policy Mobilities. In N.B. Salazar, C. Timmerman, J. Wets, L.G. Gato & S. Van den Broucke (eds) *Mega-Event Mobilities: A Critical Analysis*. London. Routledge, 90–107.

Lee Ludvigsen, JA (2021) Between Security and Festivity: The Case of Fan Zones. *International Review for the Sociology of Sport* 56(2), 233–251.

Lin, Q (2013) A Critical Review of Social Impacts of Mega-Events. *The International Journal of Sport and Society* 3, 57–64.

Marsh, P, Fox, K, Carnibella, G, McCann, J & Marsh, J (1996) *Football Violence in Europe*. Amsterdam. The Amsterdam Group.

McCann, E (2011) Urban Policy Mobilities and Global Circuits of Knowledge: Toward a Research Agenda. *Annals of the Association of American Geographers* 101(1), 107–130.

McGillivray, D, Duignan, MB & Mielke, E (2020) Mega Sport Events and Spatial Management: Zoning Space across Rio's 2016 Olympic City. *Annals of Leisure Research* 23(3), 280–303.

Millward, P (2009) Glasgow Rangers Supporters in the City of Manchester – The Degeneration of a 'Fan Party' into a 'Hooligan Riot'. *International Review for the Sociology of Sport* 44(4), 381–398.

Müller, M (2015) What Makes an Event a Mega-Event? Definitions and Sizes. *Leisure Studies* 34(6), 627–642.

Mythen, G & Walklate, S (2008) Terrorism, Risk and International Security: The Perils of Asking "What If?". *Security Dialogue* 39, 221–241.

Numerato, D (2018) *Football Fans, Activism and Social Change*. London. Routledge.

Pauschinger, D (2020) The Permeable Olympic Fortress: Mega-Event Security as Camouflage in Rio de Janeiro. *Conflict and Society* 6(1), 108–127.

Pearson, G & Sale, A (2011) "On the Lash" – Revisiting the Effectiveness of Alcohol Controls at Football Matches. *Policing and Society* 21(2), 150–166.

Poulton, E (2005) English Media Representation of Football Related Disorder: "Brutal, Short-Hand and Simplifying"? *Sport in Society* 8(1), 27–47.

Preuss, H (2007) The Conceptualisation and Measurement of Mega Sport Event Legacies. *Journal of Sport & Tourism* 12(3–4), 207–228.

Roche, M (1992) Mega-Events and Micro-Modernisation: On the Sociology of the New Urban Tourism. *British Journal of Sociology* 43, 563–600.

Roche, M (2000) *Mega-Events and Modernity: Olympics and Expos in the Growth of Global Culture*. London. Routledge.

Roche, M (2017) *Mega-Events and Social Change: Spectacle, Legacy and Public Culture*. Manchester. Manchester University Press.

Rose, R (1991) What Is Lesson-Drawing? *Journal of Public Policy* 11(1), 3–30.

Rowe, D (2019) The Worlds That Are Watching: Media, Politics, Diplomacy and the 2018 PyoengChang Winter Olympics. *Communication & Sport* 7(1), 3–22.

Ryan, P (2002) *Olympic Security: The Relevance to Homeland Security*. Salt Lake City. The Oquirrh Institute. Cited in Boyle, P & Haggerty, KD (2012) Planning for the Worst: Risk, Uncertainty and the Olympic Games. *British Journal of Sociology* 63(2), 241–259.

Scraton, P (2016) *Hillsborough: The Truth*. Edinburgh. Mainstream.

Silk, M (2014) Neoliberalism and Sports Mega-Events. In J. Grix (ed) *Leveraging Legacies from Sports Mega-Events*. Basingstoke. Palgrave, 50–61.

Spaaij, R (2007) Football Hooliganism as a Transnational Phenomenon: Past and Present Analysis: A Critique – More Specificity and Less Generality. *The International Journal of the History of Sport* 24(4), 411–431.

Spaaij, R (2013) Risk, Security and Technology: Governing Football Supporters in the Twenty-First Century. *Sport in Society* 16(2), 167–183.

Spaaij, R (2016) Terrorism and Security at the Olympics: Empirical Trends and Evolving Research Agendas. *The International Journal of the History of Sport* 33(4), 451–468.

Spaaij, R & Hamm, MS (2015) Endgame? Sports Events as Symbolic Targets in Lone Wolf Terrorism. *Studies in Conflict and Terrorism* 38(12), 1022–1037.

Stevens, D & Vaughan-Williams, N (2014) Citizens and Security Threats: Issues, Perceptions and Consequences beyond the National Frame. *British Journal of Political Science* 46, 149–175.

Stott, C & Pearson, G (2007) *Football "Hooliganism": Policing and the War on the 'English disease'*. London. Pennant Books.

Sugden, J (2012) Watched by the Olympics: Surveillance and Security at the Olympics. *International Review for the Sociology of Sport* 47(3), 414–429.

Taylor, T & Toohey, K (2015) The Security Agencies' Perspective. In M.M. Parent & J.L. Chappelet (eds) *Routledge Handbook of Sport Event Management*. New York. Routledge, 373–396.

Toohey, K & Taylor, T (2008) Mega Events, Fear, and Risk: Terrorism at the Olympic Games. *Journal of Sport Management* 22(4), 451–469.

Tsoukala, A (2008) Boundary-Creating Processes and the Social Construction of Threat. *Alternatives* 33, 137–152.

Tsoukala, A (2009) *Football Hooliganism in Europe: Security and Civil Liberties in the Balance*. Basingstoke. Palgrave.

Tsoukala, A (2016) Asymmetric Power Relations (Athens 2004). In V. Bajc (ed) *Surveilling and Securing the Olympics: From Tokyo 1964 to London 2012 and Beyond*. Basingstoke. Palgrave, 275–296.

Turner, M (2021) The Safe Standing Movement: Vectors in the Post-Hillsborough Timescape of English Football. *The Sociological Review* 69(2), 348–364.

Watt, P (2013) It's Not for Us. *City* 17(1), 99–118.

Weed, M (2006) Olympic Tourism? The Tourism Potential of London 2012. *E-Review of Tourism Research* 4(2), 51–57.

Whelan, C (2014) Surveillance, Security and Sports Mega Events: Toward a Research Agenda on the Organisation of Security Networks. *Surveillance & Society* 11(4), 392–404.

Wilson, S (2004) IOC Close a Deal for Cancellation Insurance. Cited in Toohey, K & Taylor, T (2008) Mega Events, Fear, and Risk: Terrorism at the Olympic Games. *Journal of Sport Management* 22, 451–469.

Wong, D & Chadwick, S (2017) Risk and (In)security of FIFA Football World Cups – Outlook for Russia 2018. *Sport in Society* 20(5), 583–598.

Yu, Y, Klauser, F & Chan, G (2009) Governing Security at the 2008 Beijing Olympics. *The International Journal of the History of Sport* 26(3), 390–405.

Zedner, L (2003) Too Much Security? *International Journal of the Sociology of Law* 31, 155–184.

Zedner, L (2009) *Security*. London/New York. Routledge.

Chapter 2

The Meanings and (Re)productions of Security

Introduction

As has been established now, present-day mega-events are securitized moments. As Chapter 1 emphasized, mega-event security has been impacted by a series of external and internal developments. For this reason, countries, security planners, organizers and sports' governing bodies seek to secure their mega-events and competitions. Establishing or facilitating for security and public safety – by diminishing insecurity – are often the assumed, underlying aims of mega-event security operations. However, despite representing a particularly contested concept, limited academic discussion has taken place concerning what 'security' means or refers to in the worlds of sport and football. This chapter will revisit and critically rethink the concept and grammar of 'security' and its implications at sport mega-events (SMEs). The chapter does this by outlining and following the lead of three key insights from the subfield of critical security studies which, albeit distinctive, share a broad commitment to challenging and question the traditional and historically hegemonic assumptions around security practices, measures and definitions (see Peoples and Vaughan-Williams, 2010).

Then, drawing mainly from manually analyzed documentary data speaking to Euro 2020's securitization and the extant literature, this chapter explores how security is constructed through the desired reproduction of so-called 'good' or 'best practices'. However, this trend, when approached critically, also provides us with stark indications of the meanings of 'security' insofar this opens up questions concerning whom that may have the ability or power to define security. The chapter also discusses how contemporary security practices and policies at SMEs intersect with the commercial aspirations of the relevant event owners and their official partners and licensees. Security-related policies as applied to mega-events, it is argued, not only serve to provide objectively and subjectively safe spaces for event visitors, athletes, VIPs and official partners from pre-defined security threats. They may also work to facilitate for commercially fertile spaces in which the consumption of football can be sustained and prosper when assisted by powerful processes of what Giulianotti (2011) calls 'securitized commodification', whereby mechanisms of social control and commercial strategies reinforce each other in contemporary sporting spaces.

DOI: 10.4324/9781003258445-3

Situating critical security studies in the universe of sport

The security complexes at mega-events have undergone huge transformations over the past years. Indeed, Grix (2013: 26) suggests that the securitization of sport 'has even given rise to a new academic subdiscipline'. It can reasonably be claimed that the existing literature has successfully addressed the logics and rationales that lie behind the security complexes associated with SMEs, such as the post-1972 or post-9/11 developments and the consequent need to secure mega-events (Chapter 2). Notwithstanding, as Whelan (2014: 396) writes, 'very few have actually addressed [...] what to secure from'. Moreover, the efforts to secure spaces automatically instigate questions about what is being secured and for which reasons (Barnard-Wills et al., 2012). Engaging with and unpicking such questions may also produce an understanding of what 'security' means in the context of SMEs, and it concurrently remains imperative to ask whom or what that is provided *with* security as security referent objects. Questions that should guide critical discussions of security at mega-events include 'for which exact purposes?' and 'what are the effects?'. In this vein, I seek to illuminate here the potential for intersections and cross-fertilization between sports studies and critical security studies and these approaches' reading of security.

A basic but necessary starting point is the concept of 'security' which, to this point, has been frequently referred to. Simultaneously, it must be acknowledged that this book and this specific chapter do not seek to redefine 'security', but rather, to critically rethink and discuss the concept's diverse meanings in the sporting universe. First, as Zedner's (2009: 10) contends, 'security is too big an idea to be constrained by the strictures of any single discipline'. This implies that the academic study of security should be inter-disciplinary in its nature and approaches. Second, security is also commonly described as an 'essentially contested' (Baldwin, 1997; Herington, 2012) and 'problematical' concept (Cottey, 2007) that means 'different things to different people in different places and at different times' (Croft and Vaughan-Williams, 2017: 22). Therefore, formulating an agreed-upon definition is complicated because the 'nature of security defies [the] pursuit' of exactly this (Buzan, 1991: 16).

For Cottey (2007: 6), the 'meaning of security is [...] open to a variety of different interpretations [...] In a general sense, security – being secure – implies the absence of threats or a lack of vulnerability'. Likewise, Booth (2005: 21) highlights that a standard definition of 'security' typically equates it with 'the absence of threats'. As Cottey (2007) highlights, within international politics, the term 'security' has often been viewed in realist terms of war, peace and the protection of national territories. Or, as Walt (1991: 212) writes, 'the threat use and control of military force'. Intellectually, the traditional and state-centric perspectives of security dominated security studies until 1990. And, in traditional security thinking, the nation state has typically figured as security's primary referent object (Browning and McDonald, 2011). However, since the 1990s, there

38 The Meanings and (Re)productions of Security

have been important developments and advances in the study of security. Peoples and Vaughan-Williams (2010) characterize one of these shifts as the shift from 'traditional' to 'critical' approaches to security. Yet, as they remind us, '[t]here is no singular definition of what it means to be critical in security studies' (p. 1). Such reminder remains important here. Whilst the below account provides a basic overview of three insights that regularly are located within critical security studies, this cannot outright be considered as a 'monolithic area' of study (ibid.).

Notwithstanding, the available perspectives from critical security studies are still yet to be made the most of in the study of security in sport. That is despite Giulianotti and Klauser's (2012) call for the employment of critical approaches and perspectives found within International Relations to the study of SME security and terrorism. They argue for a turn towards critical terrorism studies which indeed carry some similarities with critical security studies, particularly in their critical approach to conventional assumptions in the more mainstream fields. However, there are primarily three approaches, or schools of thought, that will be provided an overview of next that influence this chapter's commitment to a critical engagement with the concept of security. That includes securitization theory (Copenhagen School), Critical Theory (Welsh School) and international political sociology (Paris School) (see Peoples and Vaughan-Williams, 2010). Whilst providing a full-scale account of these approaches is beyond this chapter's remit, these will now be outlined briefly *vis-à-vis* their key features and how they may enhance a critical reading of sport's securitization.

First, this book has already deployed the term 'securitization' and referred to 'securitized' mega-events. *Securitization theory* is associated with the 'Copenhagen School's' social constructivist theorization of the securitization process (Buzan et al., 1998). Analytically, an 'issue' becomes a *security* issue when it is securitized through a discursive speech act by, for example (but not exclusively), state leaders, elites or politicians.[1] In this performative process, a political issue is taken beyond the established rules and processes of 'normal politics'. An issue is framed or constructed as a security threat to a referent object whose survival is supposedly at stake. This discursive practice – subject to a receiving audience's acceptance – allows for extreme security measures to be taken to address the relevant threat (ibid.). For Floyd (2007), the three key steps of a successful securitization involve the identification of existential threats (a securitizing move), emergency action and convincing the audience. Following this, security can be understood as a 'social and intersubjective construction' (ibid.: 329) and a self-referential procedure that invites exceptional measures to ensure survival. Such view of security is ultimately negative. The 'danger of "security" as understood by the Copenhagen School is that it allows governments to suspend legal constraints and democratic principles in the name of security' (Hanrieder and Kreuder-Sonnen, 2014: 333). Consequently, and at a basic level, this conception of security may assist analyses of how mega-event threats are discursively constructed to subsequently justify the deployment of extraordinary security measures. In a mega-event context, the framework may also be mobilized to consider the 'perceived threats, representations of danger [and] the thing declared endangered' (Bernhard and Martin, 2011: 23).

Second, the *international political sociology* of the 'Paris School' draws upon Bourdieu's concepts of 'habitus' and 'field' and 'fuses a concern with discourses of security and constructions of danger with a focus on security *practices*' (Peoples and Vaughan-Williams, 2010: 69, original emphasis). In an era where 'external' and 'internal' security agencies are increasingly entangled in the same fields and dealing with the same threats, this approach's focus is often directed at the social relations between security professionals, including the police, private security actors, border control agencies and intelligence actors in a globalized world (Bigo, 2002). Moreover, the Paris School is concerned with 'how security and insecurity are mutually constituted through elite knowledge and routinized bureaucratic practices' (Browning and McDonald, 2011: 240). Hence, as applied to sport, this critical lens can for example help us better understand how the provision of security for one group of people or in a specific space may lead to the *in*security of other groups or spaces, and how the transnationalization of security practices is based upon networks, social relations, power dynamics and existing bureaucratic structures in the blurry fields of (in)security.

Third, the 'Welsh School' work within the tradition of Frankfurt School's *Critical Theory* and adopts a normative approach to the study of security which equates security with human emancipation (Floyd, 2007). This centrality of 'emancipation' borrows from the Frankfurt School's intellectual premises and its traditions speaking to social change and resistance (Aradau, 2004). Central to this project is the rejection of the state as the primary referent object of security. In short, this approach maintains that individuals should figure as the primary referent object of security and be emancipated from what/whom constrains their security (Booth, 1991; Peoples and Vaughan-Williams, 2010).[2] The positioning of individuals as security referent objects is central and 'provides the conceptual shift that allows these perspectives to take their place as central elements of any comprehensive understanding of security' (Krause and Williams, 1997: 46). Whilst the Welsh School's agenda is wide and famously relate to 'broadening', 'deepening', 'extending' and 'focusing' security studies (see Wyn Jones, 1999), it is particularly this approach's commitment to a critical investigation of security issues in specific places – such as mega-events and their places and cities – that informs this chapter and my approach.

As must be reiterated at this stage, these approaches and understandings of security are largely distinctive and bound to different intellectual aims (Peoples and Vaughan-Williams, 2010: 9–11). Despite this, there is still an argument to be made that 'the more unified the critical schools of security are, the stronger an alternative they can offer to the mainstream of security studies' (Floyd, 2007: 336). Further, the Case Collective (2006) – a network of researchers of contemporary security – have argued for potential cross-fertilization between the critical approaches to security. So, the overview above is not tied to subsequent aspirations of theory testing, nor to settle epistemological debates, but simply to

40 The Meanings and (Re)productions of Security

outline these insights as analytical relations or starting points. My key argument here is first that these critical approaches and theoretical strands are yet to be fully utilized in the study of SME security governance and concurrently yet to be cross-fertilized with insights and interpretations from the sociology of sport (exceptions here include Tsoukala, 2009 and Bernhard and Martin, 2011). Then, if one is committed to examine and better understand what contemporary mega-events secure from (Whelan, 2014), what is being secured (Barnard-Wills et al., 2012) and what the effects are, the critical approaches to security may, separately and collectively, represent valuable tramlines in the engagement with such questions. That is because one commonality is that the critical approaches to security, 'in different ways, refute the idea that security has a constant or definitively settled meaning and content that can be taken for granted' (Peoples and Vaughan-Williams, 2010: 2).

As stated, consulting the critical security studies lexicon is also compatible with the call for utilizing insights from International Relations in the study of mega-event security (Giulianotti and Klauser, 2012). So, to summarize, the public 'experience and perceive (in)security in a plurality of ways and contexts' (Jarvis and Lister, 2012: 172). Moreover, the 'contestedness of "security" arises naturally as the meaning of security is not an ontological given, but changes across time' (Floyd, 2007: 333). Such integral points can be exported to the realm of sport. However, as previously remarked in relation to Olympic security, many authors 'do not probe the central concept of security' (Bernhard and Martin, 2011: 22). This is problematic, and in that respect, it is as timely as it is sociologically important to rethink the meanings, traditional assumptions and implications of the concept 'security' in the world of sport. Indeed, such stance formulates a base for the remainder of this chapter.

Reproducing security paradigms

The construction of security, situated at the core of this book, is one of the key tasks for mega-event host cities in the modern world. Upon a reading of relevant policy documents, including UEFA's (n.d.) publicly available '*UEFA EURO 2020 Tournament Requirements*', it becomes evident that, in Euro 2020's context, bidders and what later became appointed host cities were guided to adapt practices and policies originating from previous sporting events. In relation to this chapter's aim of critically examining the meanings of 'security', such circular trend remains highly important because it accurately demonstrates both the mobility and standardization of mega-event security and the relational reproduction of security that occur in-between event-specific contexts where pre-established security standards and templates 'migrate from one host city to the next' (Pauschinger, 2020: 109).

This connects well with Klauser's (2017) assertation holding that policy handbooks, guidelines and standardized norms may serve as mechanisms that, individually or in tandem, enable the transnational circulation and reproduction of mega-event specific policies and practices. For example, in the hosting requirements for Euro 2020's bidders (UEFA, n.d.), what is commonly referred to as 'good practice/s' emerged as a dominant term (employed 29 times overall). Furthermore, this document also referred the Euro 2020 bidders to a 217-page long document published following Euro 2004 in Portugal titled '*Good practices for safe and secure major sporting events: experiences and lessons from UEFA EURO 2004*' (2005). Essentially, this in itself gives a powerful glimpse into how security-related policies and practices are informally stored, transferred and imported between events.

For example, UEFA (n.d.) stated that the relevant authorities – those responsible for providing security and taking the necessary measures in the host countries – had to comply with 'the UEFA Safety and Security Regulations and other identified good practices' (UEFA, n.d., Sector 6: 3). Bidders, and those that eventually were appointed hosts, were also encouraged to make 'use of all existing international agreements, recommendations and good practices relating to the organisation of international sports events' to enable, *inter alia*, border security and intelligence-sharing practices (ibid., Sector 6: 8). In distinctive ways, these mechanisms connect with the existing research (Klauser, 2011, 2012, 2017) and make it suggestable that Euro 2020, at a pre-event stage, exemplified the reproduction of existing lessons and that 'the hosting of sport mega events […] push towards the reproduction of previously tested and subsequently standardized best-practice models' (Klauser, 2012: 1043). Seemingly, the recirculation of good or best practice models constituted an underlying base for the subsequent steps in Euro 2020's security planning and implementation (Chapters 3 and 4). Yet, this also initiates important, reflexive questions – discussed towards this section's end – regarding what exactly constitutes so-called good practices, whom that defines it, and how standardized templates may be applied in extraordinary event contexts like Euro 2020 encompassing multiple diverse security cultures.

As Stead (2012: 104) writes, the 'concept of best practice (or good practice) is rife in European policies and programs'. This entails the fields of urban and spatial planning (McCann, 2011; Stead, 2012), which mega-events undeniably overlap with (Lauermann, 2016). Also, in the context of football policing and security, the terms 'good' or 'best practice' are common. For instance, Tsoukala et al. (2016: 170) note how the '[e]xchange of "best practice" policies in policing and security throughout the EU and Council of Europe nations' is a typical measure of the pan-European responses to 'hooliganism' and in football policing. Furthermore, Klauser (2011) documents the mechanisms through which Euro 2008 organizers reproduced best practices speaking to fan zone security and surveillance from the 2006 World Cup in Germany.

Although 'mega-event planning is a highly mobile industry' (Lauermann, 2016: 97), the desire to use measures that have proved efficient elsewhere is not unique to SMEs and may be identified in other urban development or policy settings. Such desire can also be analyzed in relation to the public policy concept of 'lesson-drawing' (McCann, 2011; Rose, 1991). It is well established that policy makers and nation states learn from counterparts elsewhere when facing a 'common problem' (Rose, 1991: 4). Such a 'common problem' may, in this book's context, be understood as the need to plan and secure mega-events. Hence, at a basic level, a lesson is 'knowledge that is instructive, a conclusion about a subject drawn after the fact from observation or experience' (ibid.: 7). Lesson-drawing thus entails the adoption of knowledge originating from past spatial and temporal settings for the application in, and the improvement of, current programmes and policies (ibid.). In a way, this can explain the emphasis on good practices in documentary form, whilst this points towards processes of lesson-drawing as central to Euro 2020's security planning. Seemingly, one primary lesson was Euro 2004 (as one manual reflects on), which presented an 'available experience elsewhere' that was 'attractive because of evidence that it has been effective' (ibid.: 7).

Regarding the meanings of 'good practices', a rigid line must be drawn between 'good practice' and 'requirements'. Before Euro 2020, requirements were a 'must have' whilst 'good practices' were described as 'nice to have' (UEFA, n.d., Sector 3: 2). Whilst somewhat vague, this allows for an interpretation of 'good practices' in themselves as not formally nor legally required, but encouraged – thus representing those 'less coercive mechanisms' (Klauser, 2017: 118) that ensure the circulation of SME security policies. 'Good practice' has also been previously defined as the 'effective methods or innovative practices that contribute to the improved performance of an organisation and are widely accepted as "good" by other peer organisations' (UEFA, 2005: 18). Elsewhere, the Council of Europe (2016: 9) defines it as 'tried and tested measures […] proven to be effective in one or more States, which can be implemented in other countries or other sports'. What remains crucial here, however, is that these definitions imply a *retrospective* element and suggest that good practices, in this context, represent ideal, security-related lessons that can assist future mega-events or football matches. Such lessons are beneficial to draw upon by 'copying', 'emulating' or using as 'inspiration' (Rose, 1991: 22) and the practices' proven records render them 'good'.[3]

In relation to mega-event security, 'good practices' can therefore be seen as one broad and time/space diffuse 'security legacy' (Giulianotti and Klauser, 2010) and the document evaluating the Euro 2004 experience may be interpreted as an informal guide for future hosts, with its evidence-based knowledge and learnt lessons. Indeed, even the handbook from 2004 states that the description of good practices may assist the future planning of safety and security and that Euro 2004 similarly made 'extensive use of knowledge acquired at past events' (UEFA, 2005: 41). Whilst the transfer of knowledge may occur through site visits, guided tours, exchange programs and conferences, lessons can also be transferred through ideas, legal documents, handbooks, existing guidelines and plans (Klauser, 2011). More broadly, as McCann (2011) points out, the circulation of policy knowledge may be shaped by the consultation of existing policy documents and more mundane items like brochures.

In the context of the Olympic Games, Fussey et al. (2011) draw upon Bauman's 'liquid security' and argue that 'transferable paradigms operate as a form of "liquid

The Meanings and (Re)productions of Security   43

security", where a shared *lingua franca* of defensible motifs coalesces into strategies that generate securitized spaces dissociated from their geographical contexts' (Fussey et al., 2011: 61, original emphasis). As suggested, event owners typically push hosts towards the reproduction of best-practice models (Klauser, 2011) and 'transferable paradigms' and, in distinctive ways, the Euro 2020 case reinforces the idea of how learning from past 'successes' or 'failures' constitutes crucial elements of mega-event security planning (Boyle, 2011; Boyle et al., 2015; Klauser, 2011, 2012). The reference to and encouragement to reproduce 'good practice' and existing lessons demonstrate that hosts, security planners and agencies had to consider and adapt retrospective logics by also asking *'what was?'* – not merely *'what if?'* (cf. Mythen and Walklate, 2008) – so that formal and informal knowledge could be recirculated ahead of Euro 2020 (as elaborated on in Chapter 3).

However, the apparent and desired reproduction of security still raises some critical and practical questions. First, this speaks to power relations: whom that sits with the power to pre-define what constitutes exemplars of good, best or indeed bad practices. Or, in a security context, whom – as Bigo (2008) writes – that are positioned to classify threats and broadly determine what 'security' *is*. The transfer of policy knowledge does not occur within a vacuum or an 'apolitical space' (Boyle, 2011: 170), whereas 'mega-event cities face pressure to implement standardised policy models' (Lauermann, 2016: 93). Host countries, as the 'adopters of best practices' (McCann, 2011: 109), were pushed towards the reproduction of standardized templates (see Klauser, 2011) and are usually are expected to adapt to and guarantee the requirements of the Union of European Football Associations (UEFA) before and during European Championships (see Włoch, 2012). This speaks to how mega-event owners, representing 'powerful global governors' (ibid.: 298), in pre-event settings, have the ability to pre-define – even in documentary form – what represents examples of security best practice. Further, although this carries an assumption that good practices are 'good' for all hosts, this may not always be the case. Notwithstanding, this is significant. And in the wider global order, this represents an important shift whereby sports' governing bodies, representing international organizations, pre-define security practices and securitize issues that sovereign states –in their role as host nations – are pushed towards or must sufficiently address.

Second, despite the desired learning and adaption of established practices, there are still a wide range of uncertainties attached to each event where 'maximum security' commonly is promised 'under conditions of radical uncertainty' (Boyle and Haggerty, 2012: 243). Indeed, the modern world is characterized by uncertainty and past tests cannot longer account for the rapid and unpredictable changes in circumstances (Bauman, 2005: 1). Specific to Euro 2020's hosting format, this also meant that best practices and policies from the past events were now desired in 13 (later 12 and 11) unique cultures of security with varying risk profiles and levels of mega-event staging experience. However, 'security' or 'security threats' cannot be objectively defined (Bigo, 2008). Ultimately, states may diverge on what composes a security issue and the 'appropriate means for ameliorating it'

(Sperling, 2010: 13). The eventual 11 host countries translated into the same number of national cultures of security in which not only the understandings of security and threat were likely to differ, but also what constituted good practices for the construction of security.

Fundamentally, whilst it is not denied here that there are security practices that, on the whole, are regarded as efficient, all this goes to highlight the very limitations of security-related knowledge and practices before mega-event staged in novel contexts. Thus, such *copy and paste* like processes have spatio-temporal implications and limitations. So, to summarize, in relation to the critical examination of security meanings before and at SMEs, what is reaffirmed here is how security is largely pre-defined, standardized, relational and framed in terms of past events. Then, how the reproduction of promoted security templates – even in documentary form – is desired *before* host countries even were selected.

Securitized commodification and spatial implications

In the attempt to critically approach the meanings of security at SMEs further, it is necessary to zoom in on the connections between security-related policies and processes of commodification. This subsequently provides an insight into the socio-spatial logics, dynamics and footprints of mega-event securitization. Concerning the intersection between security and the political economy in sport and modern urban settings, Giulianotti (2011) describes this as 'securitized commodification'. Following this, security-focused policies (that *may* be deemed to represent best practice) – that increasingly are reproduced in new event milieus – can also be analyzed in light of the neoliberal influences in global sport (Andrews and Silk, 2012; Boykoff, 2020).

As a slippery term, the extension into untapped markets lies at the core of 'neoliberalism', as one form of economic liberalism (Mudge, 2008). SMEs, owing much to their global popularity, therefore attract enormous interest from global corporate sponsors that chase revenue streams *via* sponsorship, association and visibility. In a way, this explains why, as one stakeholder said to me, 'when you get there [the mega-event fan zone], it's all about sponsors and showcasing the relationship with the tournament and expensive beer' (Stakeholder 8). Against the background of (hyper-)commercial expansions, mega-event security, when designed and implemented, can become a tool that ensures individuals' objective safety, but simultaneously facilitates for 'clean sites' (Klauser, 2012) or cleansed event environments (Roche, 2000), which mega-event owners and their partners and licensees intend to establish in and around fan zones, stadiums and in the wider host cities, free for 'disruptive' elements like vendors or unofficial products (Pearson, 2012).

As Klauser (2012: 1043) observes in the case of Euro 2008, UEFA created 'a patchwork of "clean sites" [...] for its official partners' advertisement and merchandise to be displayed'. Ahead of Euro 2020, 'clean sites' were also referred to in UEFA's (n.d.) tournament requirements document. For instance, it was stated that 'any stadium at which a UEFA EURO 2020 match will be played, together with all other facilities within the outer security zone or otherwise required to comply with the clean site principle' (UEFA, n.d., Sector 1: 4). Whilst this demonstrates, in part, the desired recirculation of the 'clean site' policy (from 2008 and onwards, see Klauser, 2012), it also illustrates how these logics are in place several years before the relevant mega-event is staged, and how hosts must agree to such requirements.

Essentially, what such principle ensures is that official partners and licensees of the relevant event are granted a monopoly to brand, showcase and offer their products. Two oft-cited examples of how this relates to security policies and occurs in practice at modern-day SMEs are the two cases of, first, over 1,000 Dutch fans, which, upon entering the stadium, were told to remove their trousers at the 2006 World Cup in Germany because they 'bore the insignia of a beer company (Bavaria) that was not sponsoring the event' (Giulianotti, 2013: 101). Second, a family at the cricket World Cup in South Africa that 'was ejected from a stadium after opening a soft drink produced by the main market rival of a tournament sponsor' (ibid.). As Hagemann's (2010) reflections from the Euro 2008 in Austria and Switzerland suggests, security searches in the official fan zones were not only enforced under the banner of public safety and security. They also worked to prevent the introduction of 'external sources' that could compromise the sponsors' monopoly (e.g., printed t-shirts, flyers, food and drinks) (ibid.). This again intersects with strategies to prevent 'ambush marketing' and to ensure brand protection (Pearson, 2012). Similarly, at the 2006 World Cup, Eick (2011: 93) noted that '[e]ven selling sausages became a security issue'. It is important to underline that the above-mentioned events were staged at different times and are administered by different sport governing bodies. Yet, broadly, what can be seen is that sponsors, brands and licences are secured and protected insofar the spaces they operate or are present in are cleansed and sanitized – as aided by security-related policies or practices – in order to avoid disruption from rival brands and to maintain the 'spirit of consumption' (Boyle and Haggerty, 2009: 265) at SMEs. Significantly, these linkages make it appropriate to speak of 'securitized commodification' (Giulianotti, 2011).

An argument may be made that recirculated security practices and policies relate to the central idea of creating lucrative, tamed and clean environments. This enables mega-events to occur within delineated and consumer-oriented lagoons of security. Indeed, Silk (2014: 54) reminds us that 'the political and economic rationalities of neoliberalism emphasise spectacular SMEs that centre on the production of aesthetic environments'. Further, existing research shows an inter-play between securitization and aesthetical considerations (Barnard-Wills et al., 2012; Coaffee et al., 2009). The dimension of aesthetic securitization also applies to beyond the 'obvious' mega-event spaces before and during mega-events. For example, Kennelly (2015) finds how security measures related the 2010 Olympics in Vancouver intersected with city cleansing and the sanitization of spaces, amplifying the marginalization of homeless youth in the city. Here, the

46 The Meanings and (Re)productions of Security

concept of 'corporate kettling' is also useful, since it explains the process where 'physical geography, security measures [...] combine to direct and manoeuvre people into spaces of transnational consumption' (Giulianotti et al., 2015: 132). Essentially, this may perpetuate inequalities in urban settings, and even more so *if* such practices are rendered 'good', circulated and consequently applied to new mega-event cities.

And so, this chapter began by stressing the need to deepen our understanding of security meanings at mega-events. In any critical examination of the concept of 'security' at SMEs, the links between commercialism and security should be accounted for. There is no doubt that security policies and practices are implemented for objectives of public safety and managing security. Arguing against that would be both cynical and unfair. However, at the same time, mega-event security policies can also, as existing examples show, serve to protect business-related interests and thereby enhance the corporate attractiveness, although neoliberal policies of course seldom are signposted as such. Arguably, this is the reality in global sport too. Here, neoliberal agendas are covertly normalized and perpetuated to maintain the current order of sport's political economy (Boykoff, 2020). Crucially, all this speaks to the *duality* of meanings and purposes of present-day mega-event security.

Securing people, spaces and festivity

The term 'security' is contentious and can be exploited. As Kennelly (2015: 9) maintains, '[w]hile the chimera of safety makes for persuasive public rhetoric, an important question to be asked is "safety for whom"'. Others highlight that:

> [A]ttempts to secure space against terrorism or other associated risks and national hazards raise questions about what exactly is being secured and for what purposes [and which] populations or activities are included or excluded from a space.
>
> (Barnard-Wills et al., 2012: 92)

This invites critical discussion, and by drawing from UEFA's (n.d.) mentioned tournament requirements for Euro 2020 hosts, this section engages with these questions. The key rationale behind repeatedly using this document is because mega-event bidding documents give insight into processes of security, mobility and hospitality several years before relevant the mega-event actually begins, which concurrently speaks to the pre-emptive nature of such documents (see Bulley and Lisle, 2012).

Pre-event, UEFA (n.d., Sector 6: 9) required appointed hosts to develop plans to protect 'target groups' including the 'general public, teams, VIPs, sponsors, media, officials and security personnel, and protection for all official sites within the theatre of operations'. The requirements also mentioned an accreditation policy that – when applied – would serve to 'prevent unauthorised access of people

The Meanings and (Re)productions of Security   47

and objects to official sites, e.g. stadiums, hotels, training facilities, fan zones and other UEFA EURO 2020 sites' (ibid.). As such, those in need for protection were distinctively framed years in advance of the event's commencement and also encompassed official sponsors and licensees, as discussed above. The subjects to be provided with security were, as Klauser (2017: 73) observes, categorized according to occupation into target groups and risk categories. Here, subjective processes of social sorting and classification occur (Lyon, 2007), and one's allocated category determines whether one has authorized or unauthorized access to the securitized event spaces.

Whilst these are precautionary processes of categorization, they are also inherently fluid. For example, by this logic, if a supporter – who is secured upon entering a stadium – gains access to a secured space for which the same supporter is not accredited to – for example, the VIP lounges or the players' changing rooms – the same supporter that initially was secured immediately becomes secured against (consider for example a pitch invader). Being 'secured' is thus pre-defined, but spatially dependent, conditional or subject to change. The French anthropologist Marc Augé (1995), writing on globalized and accelerated 'non-places' devoid of historical roots or identity, argued that the users of these spaces – in order to prove themselves as generic, admissible individuals – were always required to prove their innocence. For instance, by verifying their identity by providing identification, boarding cards, tickets or paying tollbooths. Indeed, and as applied to a relevant real-life scenario, this was captured by the TV cameras at Euro 2020 when Portugal star Cristiano Ronaldo – who has won the prestigious *Ballon d'Or* five times – was stopped by a security guard who demanded to verify Ronaldo's identity before he could follow his teammates into the team's changing rooms inside the *Puskás Aréna* in Budapest. Following a check of Ronaldo's personalized lanyard, his access was granted.[4] Such accreditation policies – assisting security aims – are commonly found inside stadiums, around stadiums and in fan zones. They are often implemented at cultural festivals too, where e-tickets, lanyards, colour-coded wristbands and bar code scanning – as the 'markers of categorization' – mean that 'the conveyor belt of categorisation and containment is set in motion' and serve to determine individuals' access to segregated and privileged event spaces (Flinn and Frew, 2014: 428). Hence, without meaning to conflate a stadium, a fan zone or a mega-event with an Augean 'non-place', a resembling logic *vis-à-vis* authorization and access may be identified. Access to the socially constructed, categorized and secured spaces is subject to appropriate accreditations. These again are directly linked to one's allocated category which, to a degree, is based upon one's innocence (cf. Augé, 1995).

Furthermore, it may be seen how festivity and welcoming atmospheres were framed in terms of security. One key task for Euro 2020's hosts was related to: 'Creating a welcoming atmosphere for foreign visitors is crucial to minimising public order risks and to making the tournament a great national and football occasion' (UEFA, n.d., Sector 6: 4). This is noteworthy, as it suggests a potential link between the welcoming atmospheres and minimized public order risks.

48 The Meanings and (Re)productions of Security

This in itself is perhaps unsurprising. As Klauser (2010) observes in the context of another SME; the Olympics. Security operations here are designed:

> [N]ot only to physically secure the games, but also to create a hospitable environment, a climate of joy; in short, a jointly inhabited "Olympic atmosphere". To achieve this aim, toxic elements and people, as well as bad news and attempts at undermining, had to be kept out [to ensure] a sense of physical and psychopolitical security and togetherness. (p. 334)

This speaks to the governance of space. The pursued environment – 'a climate of joy' – reflects those of theme parks (see Roche, 2000: 135–138) and relies upon 'safe' and 'hospitable' atmospheres. This relates to what one interviewee commented, namely that 'if you are in a festive celebratory environment, your emotions are all heightened towards enjoying yourself and not being scared or worried or concerned' (Stakeholder 1). Moreover, the ideal environment should be characterized by a façade of 'order' and 'stability', which means that 'exceptions' and 'phenomena' that do not generate, or challenge this, 'fall outside these idealized categories' (Fussey et al., 2012: 264).

Security and atmospheres are related, and for Adey (2014) security is atmospheric. Increasingly, he notes, atmospheres are becoming a 'security dispositif', whilst security is becoming attuned to 'affective atmospheres'. Atmospheres are powerful forces that – compared to people or concrete places – are far more intangible, subjective and occasionally perceived as being 'in the air'. Normally, atmospheres are seen as crucial to mega-events that, by their very nature, are collectively memorized and spectacular moments (Roche, 2000). Atmospheric dimensions feed into the mega-event 'spectacle' and contribute to the festivalization of urban public space (Klauser, 2012). In the case of Euro 2020, it seems that host cities were encouraged to assemble a festive and welcoming atmosphere that remained undisrupted by both external and internal 'undesirables'. Nonetheless, such interrelations between security-related policies and commodification processes have implications.

Whilst supporters 'accept the need for security initiatives' (Cleland and Cashmore, 2018: 466), some will feel that excessive security can enhance an oppressive atmosphere (Cleland, 2019; Cleland and Cashmore, 2018). The balancing-act required to 'secure' atmospheres – to prevent their oppressive dimensions – connects with Zygmunt Bauman's (2005) writings on the trade-off between 'security' and 'freedom'. Bauman's (2005) 'freedom' may here be read as the freedom to enjoy the event without oppressive atmospheres. As Bauman continues, a fully satisfying security-freedom balance is rarely achieved. Accordingly, when 'freedom is missing, security feels like a slavery or prison' (ibid.: 36). Yet, when security is missing, freedom can 'hardly be exercised', whereas an 'increase in freedom may be read as a decrease of security and vice versa' (ibid.).

Balancing the security/atmosphere couplet is highly important in order not to 'disrupt the circuits of capital and consumption' (Boyle and Haggerty, 2009: 264).

As such, an oppressive atmosphere – as directly opposed to a welcoming one – can be seen as potentially incompatible with its desired global corporate attractiveness partly derived from atmospheres. This simultaneously touches the surface of how security becomes a 'means of both physical protection and macro-spherical assurance and insulation', which opposes a 'supposedly unitary inside to a threatening outside' (Klauser, 2017: 87). The pre-event discourses and requirements can thus extend the linkages between security and festivity loaded atmospheres. Ultimately, this meant that the latter was framed as a subject to be secured. Naturally, this relates to hosts' obligation to provide public safety, but it may also be linked back to the desire to ensure continuous visitor flows and the event's commercial value (McGillivray et al., 2020) and how, as one stakeholder I interviewed said, 'they [UEFA] want to create a visual spectacle as well, on their media streams' (Stakeholder 9). Moreover, on another level, spreading images of a festive tournament can also be considered a political message to those seeking to threaten or disrupt the event. Such outward message can articulate that real or perceived threats would not succeed in deterring the enjoyment nor the state from its way of life (Divišová, 2019). As such, this section demonstrates the pre-defined objects and subjects that were framed in *need for* security and the social and spatial implications of these pre-emptive processes.

Specific and general security threats

Having addressed whom or what that was to be secured ahead of Euro 2020, this final section deals with the central question of whom or what Euro 2020 was secured against as framed security threats. As may be extracted from the existing literature, contemporary security operations at modern SMEs are normally related to the prevention of 'terrorism' (Armstrong et al., 2017; Atkinson and Young, 2012; Boyle and Haggerty, 2012), the policing and regulation of 'hooligans' (Tsoukala, 2009) and urban crime control (Giulianotti and Klauser, 2010; Pauschinger, 2020). Hence, as expected 'terrorism' and 'criminal activity' were also framed as potential security threats host countries would have to consider pre-event (see UEFA, n.d., Sector 6: 5–6). It was also noted that: 'The host population has a major role to play and should be reassured that the overwhelming majority of visiting supporters will not be hooligans but football-loving tourists' (UEFA, n.d., Sector 6: 4). Noteworthy here, 'hooligans' were framed as a social group from which the public needed reassurance would merely be a minority across Euro 2020's cities. However, no definition of the term is provided despite the term's legal and definitional vagueness, which means that there is no established, universal definition available of the term (Rookwood and Pearson, 2010). Further, and interestingly, an 'epidemic', which became the very real and primary threat to Euro 2020, was merely mentioned once in the policy document (UEFA, n.d., Sector 6: 9). The shift from endemic threats (like 'hooliganism', 'crime' and 'terrorism') towards the sudden, epidemic threat is of course highly significant and captured as it unfolded in Chapters 5 and 6. Further, it is naturally interesting

50 The Meanings and (Re)productions of Security

whether epidemics will be allocated more space in future bid books ahead of SMEs in light of COVID-19.

Notwithstanding, there are particularly two elements of the framed security threats above that warrant a discussion. First, a number of the outlined threats, including 'terrorism', 'epidemics' and other emergencies or disasters, are inherently uncontrollable risks with large-scale consequences. This may be seen in light of the defining features of Beck's (1992, 2002) risk society thesis, which maintains that 'uncontrollable risk is now irredeemably and deeply engineered into all the processes that sustain life in advanced societies' (2002: 46). One of these processes includes security, and as mentioned, this has increasingly called for future-oriented security logics to inform security planners and analysts that are central in the securing of mega-events (Boyle and Haggerty, 2012). Second, and inter-relatedly, those subjects or objects that were formulated as (potential) security issues demonstrate the impact of external security developments on a mega-event's securitization. This renders it impossible to fully distinguish the general security context from the event-specific security context. Here, Tsoukala's work on European 'counter-hooliganism' is useful. She writes that:

[E]ach of the phenomena included or to be included in the security threats continuum has become a specific threat, following the criminalisation or harsher punishment of some of its aspects or even control of its deviant characteristics, while simultaneously becoming a general threat, owing to the absence of any delimitation of the threat itself.

(Tsoukala, 2007: 7)

Borrowing from this, it seems appropriate to argue that the threats to Euro 2020 represented both 'specific threats' and 'general threats'. To provide some elaboration on such perspective: those adversaries, groups or actions that are securitized in the mega-event landscape resonate accurately with what is secured against elsewhere, in the broader society, by politicians, elites and security officials (Bigo, 2008). Thus, these are also general threats. For example, the threats of 'terrorism', 'crime', 'anti-social behaviour' and 'health issues' also represent general threats that are securitized and in the 'everyday life' (Rushton, 2011; Stevens and Vaughan-Williams, 2016). Yet, these are embedded into – and acquire specific meanings – when secured against as threats in sport.

This, again, has monumental implications for the meanings of 'security', which this chapter has investigated. 'Security', in Euro 2020's case, must be seen as referring to the presence and well-being of 'good inflows' and contemporaneous absence or concealment of 'bad inflows'. At mega-events, 'good inflows' are encouraged. These may include athletes, officials, workers, joyful atmospheres and enthusiastic supporters. Consequently, these become the subjects to be provided with security. In contrast, pre-defined 'bad inflows' – for example, epidemics, 'hooligans', 'terrorists', 'criminals' or 'protesters' – have to be secured against and, as far as possible, refused entry (see Fussey, 2015; Klauser, 2017) or be mitigated. Overall,

The Meanings and (Re)productions of Security   51

this goes to demonstrate how the array of pre-defined threat before Euro 2020 depended largely on international, local and situational security contexts and indeed historical relations and occurrences.

Conclusion

This chapter has advocated for, and adopted, critical approaches to the concept of 'security'. Although the critical approaches to security are non-uniform (Peoples and Vaughan-Williams, 2010), they still provide diverse tools and collectively represent a broader commitment to the questioning of established definitions of security (i.e., as the 'absence of threats') and traditional security assumptions tightly knitted to the nation state's security (Browning and McDonald, 2011). In the SME context, this chapter therefore challenges some of the conventional assumptions attached to this highly contested concept (Zedner, 2009). Predominantly, this is done through a close reading of documentary data, including the security requirements for Euro 2020's bidders (UEFA, n.d.) and by drawing upon insights offered from pre-existing mega-event case studies (Eick, 2011; Hagemann, 2010; Klauser, 2012). This documentary data should be considered the public and formal security-related discourses in Euro 2020's context, because such documents set out the parameters of security several years before the event even took place.

Significantly, the emphasis on good security practices, whose reproduction is desired, demonstrates how the idealized security is largely based upon standardized templates from past events. This chapter also reaffirms the links between 'security' and so-called 'clean' spaces or environments. Hence, in addition to providing public safety and security for those individuals, organizations or spaces framed in need for this, the tested practices and requirements may also enable the 'conditions within which consumption practices can flourish' (McGillivray et al., 2020: 283). Hence, *vis-à-vis* the under-researched meanings of 'security' at mega-events, this encapsulates how security-related policies – as set out for hosting right bidders and holders – have both operational, aesthetic, and commercial purposes (see Giulianotti, 2011). As discussed more generally and then with specific reference to Euro 2020, security appears multidimensional and meant that individuals, spaces and the current political economy of sport were provided protection throughout and beyond the modern-day mega-event landscapes.

This chapter therefore connects with and builds upon Chapter 1's examination of the rise of mega-event security complexes. More distinctively, it produces a discussion of what exactly security before Euro 2020 could mean, as set out in advance documentary format. Yet, it also sheds a light on the 'migratory nature of mega-event planning' (Lauermann, 2016: 100) with specific reference to how security was to be (re-)constructed and implemented on policy level. Notwithstanding, it must still be acknowledged that those pre-defined security issues, apparent in the documentary form years in advance, did not necessarily correspond with what or whom spectators or the general public eventually would consider as threating upon attending or being impacted by Euro 2020. Further, important questions still

52 The Meanings and (Re)productions of Security

remain surrounding how security, on a more practical level, would be implemented to ensure a safe Euro 2020. Some of these questions are addressed in the next chapter, which focuses on the merger between retrospective and future-oriented security logics in SME security. Collectively then, this and the upcoming chapter will further advance our understanding of how mega-event security is impacted by processes, assessments and activities related to policy recirculation and precautionary governance principles, as embedded into Euro 2020.

Notes

1 However, some argue that Bourdieu's (1991[1982]) concept of 'cultural capital' is essential in order to perform a speech act, as a speech act is not merely a question of linguistics. It also depends on the 'social position of the enunciator' (Buzan et al., 1998: 46).
2 As Booth (1991: 319) writes, the 'litmus test concerns the primary [security] referent object: is it states, or is it people? Whose security comes first?'.
3 Importantly, 'good practice/s' as used by UEFA (n.d.) are not strictly security-related, but used in other contexts too, including technology.
4 This episode, which received much media attention, can be seen at https://www. youtube.com/watch?v=Dq-IHaDPsHA (YouTube Video, accessed 3 July 2021).

Bibliography

Adey, P (2014) Security Atmospheres or the Crystallisation of Worlds. *Environment and Planning D: Society and Space* 32(5), 834–851.

Andrews, DL & Silk, ML (2012) *Sport and Neoliberalism: Politics, Consumption, and Culture.* Philadelphia. Temple University Press.

Aradau, C (2004) Security and the Democratic Scene: Desecuritization and Emancipation. *Journal of International Relations and Development* 7(4), 388–413.

Armstrong, G, Giulianotti, R & Hobbs, D (2017) *Policing the 2012 London Olympics: Legacy and Social Exclusion.* London. Routledge.

Atkinson, M & Young, K (2012) Shadowed by the Corpse of War: Sport Spectacles and the Spirit of Terrorism. *International Review for the Sociology of Sport* 47(3), 286–306.

Augé, M (1995) *Non-Places: Introduction to an Anthropology of Supermodernity.* London. Verso.

Baldwin, D (1997) The Concept of Security. *Review of International Studies* 23(1), 5–26.

Barnard-Wills, D, Moore, C & McKim, J (2012) Introduction: Spaces of Terror and Risk. *Space and Culture* 15(2), 92–97.

Bauman, Z (2005) *Liquid Life.* Cambridge. Polity.

Beck, U (1992) *Risk Society: Towards a New Modernity.* London. Sage.

Beck, U (2002) The Terrorist Threat: World Risk Society Revisited. *Theory, Culture & Society* 19(4), 39–55.

Bernhard, D & Martin, AK (2011) Rethinking Security at the Olympics. In C.J. Bennett & K.D. Haggerty (eds) *Security Games, Surveillance and Control at Mega-Events.* London. Routledge, 20–35.

Bigo, D (2002) Security and Immigration: Towards a Critique of the Governmentality of Unease. *Alternatives* 27(1), 63–92.

Bigo, D (2008) Globalized (In)Security: The Field and the Ban-Opticon. In D. Bigo & A. Tsoukala (eds) *Illiberal Practices in Liberal Regimes.* Paris. L'Harmattan, 10–48.

Booth, K (1991) Security and Emancipation. *Review of International Studies* 17(4), 313–326.

Booth, K (ed) (2005) *Critical Security Studies and World Politics*. London. Lynne Rienner Publishers.

Bourdieu, P (1991[1982]) *Language and Symbolic Power*. Cambridge. Harvard University Press.

Boykoff, J (2020) *Nolympians: Inside the Fight against Capitalist Mega-Sports in Los Angeles, Tokyo and Beyond*. Nova Scotia. Fernwood.

Boyle, P (2011) Knowledge Networks: Mega-Events and Security Expertise. In C.J. Bennett & K.D. Haggerty (eds) *Security Games: Surveillance and Control at Mega-Events*. Abingdon. Routledge, 169–184.

Boyle, P & Haggerty, KD (2009) Spectacular Security: Mega-Events and the Security Complex. *International Political Sociology* 3(3), 57–74.

Boyle, P & Haggerty, KD (2012) Planning for the Worst: Risk, Uncertainty and the Olympic Games. *British Journal of Sociology* 63(2), 241–259.

Boyle, P, Clement, D & Haggerty, KD (2015) Iterations of Olympic Security: Montreal and Vancouver. *Security Dialogue* 46(2), 109–125.

Browning, C & McDonald, M (2011) The Future of Critical Security Studies: Ethics and the Politics of Security. *European Journal of International Relations* 19(2), 235–255.

Bulley, D & Lisle, D (2012) Welcoming the World: Governing Hospitality in London's 2012 Olympic Bid. *International Political Sociology* 6(2), 186–204.

Buzan, B (1991) *People, States and Fear* [2nd Edition]. Hertfordshire. Harvester Wheatsheaf.

Buzan, B, Wæver, O & de Wilde, J (1998) *Security: A New Framework for Analysis*. London. Lynne Rienner Publishers.

Case Collective (2006) Critical Approaches to Security in Europe: A Networked Manifesto. *Security Dialogue* 37(4), 443–487.

Cleland, J (2019) Sports Fandom in the Risk Society: Analyzing Perceptions an Experiences of Risk, Security and Terrorism at Elite Sports Events. *Sociology of Sport Journal* 36(2), 144–151.

Cleland, J & Cashmore, E (2018) Nothing Will Be the Same Again after the Stade de France Attack: Reflections of Association Football Fans on Terrorism, Security and Surveillance. *Journal of Sport and Social Issues* 42(6), 454–469.

Coaffee, J, O'Hare, P & Hawkesworth, M (2009) The Visibility of (In)security: The Aesthetics of Planning Urban Defences against Terrorism. *Security Dialogue* 40(4–5), 489–511.

Cottey, A (2007) *Security in the New Europe*. Basingstoke. Palgrave Macmillan.

Council of Europe (2016) Convention on an Integrated Safety, Security and Service Approach at Football Matches and Other Sports Events. Council of Europe Treaty Series No. 218. Strasbourg. Council of Europe.

Croft, S & Vaughan-Williams, N (2017) Fit for Purposes? Fitting Ontological Security Studies "into" the Discipline of International Relations: Towards a Vernacular Turn. *Cooperation and Conflict* 52(1), 12–30.

Divišová, V (2019) Euro 2016 and Its Security Legacy for Football Supporters: A Conceptual Blurring of Hooligans and Terrorists? *Soccer & Society* 20(5), 757–769.

Eick, V (2011) Secure Our Profits!" The FIFA™ in Germany 2006. In C. Bennett & K. Haggerty (eds) *Security Games: Surveillance and Control at Mega-Events*. New York. Routledge, 87–102.

Flinn, J & Frew, M (2014) Glastonbury: Managing the Mystification of Festivity. *Leisure Studies* 33(4), 418–433.

54 The Meanings and (Re)productions of Security

Floyd, R (2007) Towards a Consequentialist Evaluation of Security: Bringing Together the Copenhagen and the Welsh Schools of Security Studies. *Review of International Studies* 33(2), 327–350.

Fussey, P (2015) Command, Control and Contestation: Negotiating Security at the London 2012 Olympics. *The Geographical Journal* 181(3), 212–223.

Fussey, P, Coaffee, J, Armstrong, G & Hobbs, D (2011) *Securing and Sustaining the Olympic City: Reconfiguring London for 2012 and Beyond.* Aldershot. Ashgate.

Fussey, P, Coaffe, J, Armstrong, G & Hobbs, D (2012) The Regeneration Games: Purity and Security in the Olympic City. *The British Journal of Sociology* 63(2), 261–284.

Giulianotti, R (2011) Sport Mega Events, Urban Football Carnivals and Securitised Commodification: The Case of the English Premier League. *Urban Studies* 48(15), 3293–3310.

Giulianotti, R (2013) Six Security Legacies of Major Sporting Events. *ICSS Journal* 1(1), 95–101.

Giulianotti, R & Klauser, F (2010) Security Governance and Sport Mega-Events: Toward an Interdisciplinary Research Agenda. *Journal of Sport and Social Issues* 34(1), 48–60.

Giulianotti, R & Klauser, F (2012) Sport Mega-Events and "Terrorism": A Critical Analysis. *International Review for the Sociology of Sport* 47(3), 307–323.

Giulianotti, R, Armstrong, G, Hales, G & Hobbs, D (2015) Global Sport Mega-Events and the Politics of Mobility: The Case of the London 2012 Olympics. *The British Journal of Sociology* 66(4), 118–140.

Grix, J (2013) The Risks and Rewards of Hosting Sports Mega-Events. *ICSS Journal* 1(1), 22–27.

Hagemann, A (2010) From the Stadium to the Fan Zone: Host Cities in a State of Emergency. *Soccer & Society* 11(6), 723–736.

Hanrieder, T & Kreuder-Sonnen, C (2014) WHO Decides on the Exception? Securitization and Emergency Governance in Global Health. *Security Dialogue* 45(4), 331–348.

Herington, J (2012) The Concept of Security. In M. Selgelid & C. Enemark (eds) *Security Aspects of Infectious Disease Control: Interdisciplinary Perspectives.* Ashgate. Farnham, 7–25.

Jarvis, L & Lister, M (2012) Vernacular Securities and Their Study: A Qualitative Analysis and Research Agenda. *International Relations* 27(2), 158–179.

Kennelly, J (2015) "You're Making Our City Look Bad": Olympic Security, Neoliberal Urbanization, and Homeless Youth. *Ethnography* 16(1), 3–24.

Klauser, F (2010) Splintering Spheres of Security: Peter Sloterdijk and the Contemporary Fortress City. *Environment and Planning D: Society and Space* 28, 326–340.

Klauser, F (2011) The Exemplification of "Fan Zones": Mediating Mechanisms in the Reproduction of Best Practices for Security and Branding at Euro 2008. *Urban Studies* 48(15), 3202–3219.

Klauser, F (2012) Interpretative Flexibility of the Event-City: Security, Branding and Urban Entrepreneurialism at the European Football Championships 2008. *International Journal of Urban and Regional Research* 36(5), 1039–1052.

Klauser, F (2017) *Surveillance & Space.* London. Sage.

Krause, K & Williams, MC (1997) From Strategy to Security: Foundations of Critical Security Studies. In K. Krause & C.M. Williams (eds) *Critical Security Studies: Concepts and Cases.* Minneapolis. University of Minnesota Press, 33–60.

Lauermann, J (2016) Made in Transit: Mega-Events and Policy Mobilities. In N.B. Salazar, C. Timmerman, J. Wets, L.G. Gato & S. Van den Broucke (eds) *Mega-Event Mobilities: A Critical Analysis.* London. Routledge, 90–107.

The Meanings and (Re)productions of Security   55

Lyon, D (2007) *Surveillance Studies: An Overview*. Cambridge. Polity.

McCann, E (2011) Urban Policy Mobilities and Global Circuits of Knowledge: Toward a Research Agenda. *Annals of the Association of American Geographers* 101(1), 107–130.

McGillivray, D, Duignan, MB & Mielke, E (2020) Mega Sport Events and Spatial Management: Zoning Space across Rio's 2016 Olympic City. *Annals of Leisure Research* 23(3), 280–303.

Mudge, S (2008) What Is Neo-Liberalism? *Socio-Economic Review* 6(4), 703–731.

Mythen, G & Walklate, S (2008) Terrorism, Risk and International Security: The Perils of Asking "What If?". *Security Dialogue* 39, 221–241.

Pauschinger, D (2020) The Permeable Olympic Fortress: Mega-Event Security as Camouflage in Rio de Janeiro. *Conflict and Society* 6(1), 108–127.

Pearson, G (2012) Dirty Trix at Euro 2008: Brand Protection, Ambush Marketing and Intellectual Property Theft at the European Football Championships. *Entertainment and Sports Law Journal* 10(1), 1–12.

Peoples, C & Vaughan-Williams, N (2010) *Critical Security Studies: An Introduction*. London/ New York. Routledge.

Roche, M (2000) *Mega-Events and Modernity: Olympics and Expos in the Growth of Global Culture*. London. Routledge.

Rookwood, J & Pearson, G (2010) The Hoolifan: Positive Fan Attitudes to Football 'Hooliganism'. *International Review for the Sociology of Sport* 47(2), 149–164.

Rose, R (1991) What Is Lesson-Drawing? *Journal of Public Policy* 11(1), 3–30.

Rushton, S (2011) Global Health Security: Security for Whom? Security from What? *Political Studies* 59(4), 779–796.

Silk, M (2014) Neoliberalism and Sports Mega-Events. In J. Grix (ed) *Leveraging Legacies from Sports Mega-Events*. Basingstoke. Palgrave, 50–61.

Sperling, J (2010) National Security Cultures, Technologies of Public Goods Supply and Security Governance. In E.J. Kirchner & J. Sperling (eds) *National Security Cultures: Patterns of Global Governance*. Oxon. Routledge, 1–18.

Stead, D (2012) Best Practices and Policy Transfer in Spatial Planning. *Planning Practice and Research* 27(1), 103–116.

Stevens, D & Vaughan-Williams, N (2016) *Everyday Security Threats: Perceptions, Experiences, and Consequences*. Manchester. Manchester University Press.

Tsoukala, A (2007) Security Policies & Human Rights in European Football Stadia. *CEPS CHALLENGE Paper* 5, 1–20.

Tsoukala, A (2009) *Football Hooliganism in Europe: Security and Civil Liberties in the Balance*. Basingstoke. Palgrave.

Tsoukala, A, Pearson, G & Coenen, PT (2016) Conclusions: Social Control at the Expense of Civil Liberties and Human Rights. In A. Tsoukala, G. Pearson & P.T. Coenen (eds) *Legal Responses to Football 'Hooliganism' in Europe*. The Hague. Springer, 169–178.

UEFA (2005) *Good Practices for Safe and Secure Major Sporting Events: Experiences and Lessons from UEFA EURO 2004*. Den Haag. COT Institute for Safety and Crisis Management.

UEFA (n.d.) *UEFA EURO 2020: Tournament Requirements*. Nyon. UEFA. Available from: https://www.uefa.com/MultimediaFiles/Download/EuroExperience/competitions/General/01/95/21/41/1952141_DOWNLOAD.pdf (Accessed 17 July 2019).

Walt, SM (1991) The Renaissance of Security Studies. *International Studies Quarterly* 35(2), 211–223.

Whelan, C (2014) Surveillance, Security and Sports Mega Events: Toward a Research Agenda on the Organisation of Security Networks. *Surveillance & Society* 11(4), 392–404.

Włoch, R (2012) UEFA as a New Agent of Global Governance: A Case Study of Relations between UEFA and the Polish Government against the Background of the UEFA EURO 2012. *Journal of Sport and Social Issues* 37(7), 297–311.

Wyn Jones, R (1999) *Security, Strategy, and Critical Theory*. London. Lynne Rienner.

Zedner, L (2009) *Security*. London/New York. Routledge.

Chapter 3

Between Retrospective and Futuristic Processes of Security

Extending the 'Troika of Security'

Introduction

In this book's endeavour to examine which processes, activities and policies that assisted the construction of security before Euro 2020 – representing an ideal example of the football world – this chapter delves deeper into the above questions. This chapter will add empirical layers to Chapter 2, which touched upon security reproductions as pushed for in documentary form and precautionary logics to mitigate pre-defined (yet inherently uncontrollable) security threats. Theoretically, this chapter leans upon literature on security governance in the twenty-first century (Boyle and Haggerty, 2012; Mythen and Walklate, 2008) and public policy transfer (McCann, 2011; Rose, 1991). I intend to revisit a concept – the 'troika of security' – which I originally conceptualized elsewhere (Lee Ludvigsen, 2020).[1] However, the remainder of this chapter will elaborate on and update this concept by locating football fans, fan activities and fan networks more centrally within this framework than previously. Therefore, the aims of reflecting on, and extending the conceptual reach and worth of the 'troika of security', lie at this chapter's core.

Regarding the terminology here, a 'troika' implies a set of threes that, in some capacity, work together. The three processes collectively making up the 'troika' include lesson-drawing, institutional memory and precautionary logics. Together, the convergence of these processes can aid our understanding of the construction of security before Euro 2020, it is argued (ibid.). The sociological value of such contention is associated with how modern-day mega-events' future-oriented and recirculation-based security are identified in a new event setting. The construction of security can be appropriately analyzed as the merger between *futuristic* (precautionary logics) and *retrospective* (lesson-drawing and institutional memory) processes that remain both local and global in nature and possess distinctive strengths and limitations. In essence, this chapter reflects on how the past is consulted, and how the future – as far as possible – must be predicted. The latter comes as a reflexive consequence of the uncertainty and uncontrollable threats surrounding each mega-event (cf. Beck, 1992).

In some sections, this chapter remains principally focused on London as one Euro 2020 host city. This can be justified since London, after all, was the city

DOI: 10.4324/9781003258445-4

58 Between Retrospective and Futuristic Processes of Security

with the highest number of fixtures (eight games). Whilst drawing from stakeholder interviews, discourses deriving from documentary data and press releases, the chapter also draws heavily upon insights from the existing literature. This remains important to acknowledge for at least two key reasons. First, although scant research has focused on the creation of security prior to Euro 2020 *per se*, retrospective and futuristic modes of security have figured centrally in the extant scholarship (Boyle, 2011; Boyle and Haggerty, 2009, 2012; Klauser, 2012). Second, because it can be inherently complicated to 'conclusively identify security planners' main concerns' (Bernhard and Martin, 2011), the insights offered by pre-existing literature may weigh up for some of the challenges related to pre-event security research. Though, in the context of earlier literature, this chapter pays closer attention to fan networks' roles, the importance and meanings of institutional memory and, naturally, the new event context of Euro 2020. It also calls into question and problematizes the use of precautionary principles and recirculated security policies with specific reference to the heterogeneous yet significant social group of football fans.

Revisiting the 'troika of security': The touchstones and an overview

It is necessary first to briefly map out the processes, logics and discourses that constitute the 'troika of security' framework and its theoretical and conceptual touchstones. Theoretically, the chapter's sociological roots are informed by current perspectives on 'security' and 'risk' governance in the twenty-first century which again draw largely upon and reinterpret the seminal work of Ulrich Beck (Mythen and Walklate, 2008, 2016; see Chapter 1). Simultaneously, this reflects a broader call within critical security studies for engagement with 'risk-based and threat-based interpretations of (in)security' (Case Collective, 2006: 468–469). The 'troika' also borrows central ideas from the public policy literature on lesson-drawing and policy transfer, which is concerned with how lessons from elsewhere are drawn upon in new settings by institutions (Dolowitz and Marsh, 1996; Rose, 1991).

With respect to the wider relevance, the futuristic and retrospective modes of securing that the troika captures have a distinctive political significance in the post-9/11 world and may speak to broader trends in the pursuit of security. First, the concept covers the contentious shift towards future-oriented and speculative 'what if?' questions, which increasingly dictate the pursuit of security in an epoch of transnational terrorism threats (Mythen and Walklate, 2008; Chapter 1). Here, potential security threats must constantly be screened, contemplated and anticipated *before* any incidents have occurred. As Mythen and Walklate (2016: 1111) highlight:

> The logic of anticipatory risk, a future-centric logic – which prioritizes predictive horizon scanning for upcoming attacks – has increasingly informed the making of tiers of legislation over the last two decades [...] The preemptive moment takes place prior to anything having happened and thus

occurs at a point at which threats may be inexact and uncertain. This anticipatory logic of risk seeks not so much to prevent an occurrence through the interpretation of past incidents but to pre-empt the unravelling of emergent events in relation to the horizon of projected futures.

Under such circumstances, the providers of security – security agencies and officials – must increasingly subscribe to speculative precautionary thinking (Boyle and Haggerty, 2012) and attempt to imagine risks and 'scenarios that appear low in probability but high in consequence' (Betts, 2002: 49). As embedded into the mega-event context, this becomes increasingly necessary given that the broader post-1972 and post-9/11 security landscapes have had profound impacts on how mega-events are secured. As Stakeholder 1 said, 'In fact, when you talk to the police in London, their operations are more about counter-terrorism than they are about disorder'. This serves as a powerful reminder of how mega-event security efforts largely revolve around mitigation of unpredictable terrorism threats.

Although security officials, agencies and organizers, to a degree, must attempt to speculate about potential worst-case scenarios, there is one important paradox here: to actually plan for such scenarios is 'epistemologically and practically impossible' (Boyle and Haggerty, 2012: 241) given the unpredictability of terrorism threats and the inherent limitations to security assessments.[2] Here, Beck's (2009) concept of *nichtwissen*, referring to 'non-knowledge', becomes relevant because it explains how emerging security threats must be responded in the absence of complete knowledge and estimates. In that respect, the security providers, as Zedner (2009: 126–127) highlights, 'operate in conditions of considerable uncertainty' and 'imperfect information'. Concurrently, it remains vital here to abstain from a conflation of mega-event security operations and governance with counter-terrorism strategies. Whilst the two overlaps, they are not synonymous. Partly for this reason, and in the context of the abovementioned limitations to futuristic thinking, mega-event security must also be largely based upon retrospective assessments.

Lesson-drawing is one form of policy transfer. It relates to the adoption of lessons deriving from other sources and settings. By searching in the past, not only what *worked* is learnt but also what not to repeat (see Dolowitz and Marsh, 1996; Rose, 1991). And so, processes of learning and lesson-drawing can be located in contemporary security governance (Klauser, 2011). This creates the foundations for what Molnar et al. (2019) call failure-inspired learning, which impacts contemporary policing and security planning. Furthermore, writing on the stockpiling of supplies as a security device, in relation to (imagined) worst-case scenarios, Folkers (2019: 497) highlights that 'stockpiles seek to assemble a repertoire of stuff in the present that matches and thereby neutralizes what the future might have in "in store"'. In the climate of not knowing what the future holds, the 'stockpiling' of existing knowledge, policies and practices thus partly compensate for not knowing. To a degree, Folker's argument has a transferable and analytical value and can be applied to mega-events, where practices and lessons drawn from past events, essentially, are 'stockpiled' and then used. Consequently, this has 'a securing effect in the present', even when the anticipated future 'never comes to fruition' (Folkers, 2019: 497). Despite this, when pre-existing templates or lessons are transferred onto new contexts, there are no guarantees they will be effective within new national circumstances (Rose, 1991).

All this helps us understand Molnar et al.'s (2019: 119) argument holding that processes of learning occur alongside the 'imagination of potential worst-case scenarios as a significant driver in the scope of scale of mega-event security'. Such contention remains central. Ultimately, this is a contention that the 'troika of security' empirically realizes and captures in Euro 2020's pre-event context. Learning from the past – represented in the troika by institutional memory and lesson-drawing – operates triangularly and intersect with the future-leaning precautionary logic. To enable the highest standards of 'security' for visiting fans, event consumers and spaces, the three are required, adapted and adhered to. As the empirical account demonstrates, these three components were integral to Euro 2020's security pre-planning (see Lee Ludvigsen, 2020) which sought to secure the tournament from the range of pre-defined yet unpredictable and largely uncontrollable threats (Chapter 2). To empirically sharpen the contours of these components, the next subsections will briefly review the processes of lesson-drawing, institutional memory and precautionary logics as situated in Euro 2020's pre-event context.

Lesson-drawing

As Chapters 1 and 2 discuss, the domain of mega-event security remains relevant for the identification of lesson-drawing processes and mechanisms that circulate best practice paradigms. This in itself is not a new trend, but one that it remains imperative to devote critical attention as a *continuing* global trend. Boyle and Haggerty (2009: 268) remind us that mega-events incorporate 'lessons learned and best practices gleaned from other events and real-world experience'. Klauser (2011, 2017) also investigates how expert conferences, exercises and progress monitoring represent spaces and tools that ensure the circulation of security practices and policies before mega-events. Before Euro 2020 too, a number of meetings, conventions and exercises were frequently announced publicly. As argued, these transnational knowledge exchange platforms and networking events facilitated for transnational lesson-drawing processes.

In December 2016, an *ad hoc* Euro 2020 working group was established by the Council of Europe's Standing committee of the Spectator Violence Convention, and reportedly, this group first met up in Paris in February 2017 (Council of Europe, 2017). Then, between 2018 and 2019, the group met up bi-annually for consultative visits in Euro 2020 host cities Baku, Budapest, Bilbao and Rome. The programme also included peer-review exercises in two other host cities: London and Amsterdam (Council of Europe, n.d.). Following the Amsterdam peer-review exercise, a press release stated that the exercise's aim was to 'promote dialogue between police match commanders' in Euro 2020 hosts cities 'in light of good practices enshrined in the Saint-Denis Convention and the 2015

Recommendation of the Standing Committee' (Council of Europe, 2019a). In attendance on the above-mentioned consultative visits were security experts, Union of European Football Associations (UEFA) representatives, representatives from national football associations and observers of the convention, like Football Supporters Europe (FSE) and SD Europe (Council of Europe, 2019a). The Council of Europe (n.d.) also reported that the working group would meet in December 2021, *after* Euro 2020, to reflect on good practices emanating from the competition, illustrating how such activities extend beyond the event-specific timeframes and how generated knowledge extent to future events.

Concerning the Bilbao visit in February 2019, Stakeholder 2 noted that there were primarily two aspects of the three-day long visit: 'The first aspect is presentations by local authorities, in this case the Basque government and Bilbao's local authorities, police, fire services, health and also stadium authorities of Bilbao. Second part was a practical observation'. The practical observation took place during Athletic Bilbao's home game against Barcelona in the Spanish Premier Division and allowed the stakeholders in attendance to reflect on the experience and security infrastructures and the local agencies to demonstrate their own contingencies and strategies (see FSE, 2019).[3] Beyond working group meetings, other events centred around knowledge exchange reportedly took place. This included a Euro 2020 advisory group on legal issues in Paris, March 2019 (Council of Europe, 2019b) and a Euro Stadium Operator Workshop in April 2019 (UEFA, 2019).

Essentially, the number of workshops, peer-reviews and consultative visits gives us a glimpse of how networking events facilitate for lesson-drawing and sharing processes. Seemingly, lessons were drawn from *inter alia* domestic leagues, specific games, security experts and local agencies. For the transnational movement of policy and lessons, global networks remain important as assistive vehicles (Stone, 2004). The activities accounted for above illustrate how practices of security and safety were shared across 'different bureaucracies' (Bigo, 2002: 75) linked together in football's governance and security management. However, as Stone (2004: 550) argues, although the actors of lesson-drawing are commonly considered to be 'elites' or 'officials', the 'agents of lesson-drawing and policy transfer' are not confined to 'official' agencies. As can be seen in Euro 2020's pre-planning, there was a variety of actors involved in the working group, including international organizations, football associations, fan networks, stadium managers and security experts. Moreover, following each consultative visit, evaluative reports containing specific action plans were produced by the Council of Europe's committee, in order to inform the organizers and members of the convention (FSE, 2019).[4]

As argued, Euro 2020's pre-event conventions, peer-reviews, meet-ups and observations provided spaces for lesson-drawing to occur and organizations to learn from each other. The aims of the mentioned transnational networking events seemed tied to assisting the upcoming security and safety delivery at Euro 2020. This account may therefore answer how, when, by whom and from whom previous lessons were drawn. Further, it accurately demonstrates the transnational movements of mega-event security knowledge (Boyle, 2011). Though, there

62 Between Retrospective and Futuristic Processes of Security

are certain caveats attached to this discussion. First, COVID-19 impacted the dynamics of lesson-drawing immensely, as Chapter 6 reflects on. Then, given the secrecy surrounding 'security', it is possible that some networking events or exercises may have taken place without being publicly announced. This book draws from publicly announced meetings, their subsequent press releases, documents and accessible stakeholders. Hence, whilst it may not provide a *complete* picture; it still provides a high-quality portrait of the repertoire of lesson-drawing platforms and spaces, and emerging networks of expertise before Euro 2020.

Institutional memory

The second component of the 'troika of security' is the institutional memory stored within the relevant organizations, which is utilized to assist the securing or policing of an upcoming event. The nature of institutional memory is retrospective, as implied by 'memory'. Yet, it should not be conflated with lesson-drawing. As a starting point, it is useful to briefly unpack what institutional memory is. For Seifert (2007), institutional memory is the stored knowledge within a relevant organization and based on post-event analysis. The knowledge is stored and then taught or narrated across the organization onto its new members. As such, institutional memory may be interpreted as more locally based than global lesson-drawing processes. As Seifert argues, institutional memory can reduce 'the likelihood of repeating past mistakes and increases the accuracy of perception by transferring insights from similar incidents from similar incidents of the past to current responders' (p. 114). Meanwhile, Hardt (2018: 8) writes, 'organizations that develop institutional memory are less likely to repeat strategic error' and impact an organization's ability to reform crisis management operations.

To use London as a relevant example, the city's experience with major sporting events and cultural festivals was considered by some interviewees to be instrumental to the staging of a successful Euro 2020. London has long traditions of hosting SMEs. Recent events included the 2012 Olympics, single *Tour de France* stages, the Wimbledon Tennis Championship and the 2013 Champions League final. London is, of course, also the site of hundreds of Premier League fixtures each season. For the upcoming security efforts associated with Euro 2020, the institutional memory of relevant organizations such as the FA, the Metropolitan Police and local authorities was thus seen as instrumental, as illustrated by the below quotes:

> It is kind of like an *institutional memory* as well [assisting the pre-planning and delivery], and that's there in somewhere like London, but it might not be there in somewhere like, I don't know... Budapest. (Stakeholder 2, emphasis added)

> London is very, very used to hosting big events, the Met [Metropolitan Police] have got matches up at Wembley every odd week. They're really, really good at what they do. (Stakeholder 1)

> London has an enormous amount of experience [...] The scenes in London last night [for a Football League trophy final, March 2019] were extraordinary,

and London can cope with pretty much anything that is thrown at it from that point of view. (Stakeholder 3)

Significantly, relevant organizations in London involved in the securing of mass events were considered to possess the relevant experience which was obtained from previous encounters with mass sporting or cultural events. Such past experiences inform organizations' and institutions' institutional memory (Rose, 1991), which partly explains the sentiment that London possessed an 'enormous amount of experience'. Despite the London-specific comments above, it remains important here, as Stakeholder 7 emphasized, that all the Euro 2020 hosts are 'used to in their own way to organize big matches'. This implies that the available institutional memory relevant to the policing of football matches and staging of mega-events was not specific to London organizations, but expected to be found across Euro 2020's hosts who, despite varying level of mega-event experience, regularly stage large-scale one-off matches or domestic games.

Coupled with the lesson-drawing processes discussed above, institutional memory formulates one of the processes assisted the securing of Euro 2020. However, it remains important to highlight that despite the retrospective references of the stakeholders – emphasizing the importance of 'what was' – past tests are not in themselves sufficient to ensure future security. Neither can past tests prevent institutional *memory loss*. O'Grady (2019: 457) reminds us that although security often is premised by acting on memories, habits and routines, each security performance also 'embody difference in each recurrence'. Partly for that reason, future-oriented modes of security governance cannot be eschewed.

Precautionary logics

The presence of precautionary principles in the construction of security came to the fore already in Chapter 2, where it was discussed how the security-related tournament requirements called for the appointed hosts to acknowledge a range of security issues defined by their uncertainty, exemplified by health issues and terrorism (UEFA, n.d., Sector 6). Predominantly, the precautionary logics situated in the 'troika of security' emerge from the documentary data and pre-existing scholarship (Boyle and Haggerty, 2009, 2012). Concurrently, the precautionary *logic* must not be conflated with precautionary security *measures* that, fundamentally, can be notoriously hard to evidence in pre-event settings.

Ultimately, the 'troika' captures the need for organizers and host cities' relevant authorities to remain reactive, flexible and adapt to external global events. Indeed, the ever-changing dynamics of the international system and its security fields were also referred to in interviews. For instance, one interviewee stated that:

The Olympics back in 2012, when the environment was quite different, I don't think the terrorist threat was a strong as it is now. And the Olympics was a global event and they kept it right so there was a huge amount of work done [...] I think there's probably going to be an awful lot of police that we don't see, that we don't even know are there [...] terrorism is going to be the main focus, not dealing with disorder. (Stakeholder 1)

What is significant here, is the 'quite different' environment in London's 2012 Olympics to that environment expected at Euro 2020. For example, between 2012 and Euro 2020, sporting events were targeted in terrorist attacks in Paris (2015) and Boston (2013). In European football, the *Stade de France* bombing led to large-scale changes as 'security and surveillance became an ever more important form of event and crowd management in football' (Cleland and Cashmore, 2018: 456). The interviewee's quote epitomizes how there *are* developments between events (for example, changing threat levels) that place restrictions on the retrospective facets of mega-event security.

Notwithstanding, it was not solely the potential terrorist threats that were touched upon as extremely unpredictable by interviewees. It was highlighted that uncertainty originating from mass crowds of football fans could place restrictions on the recirculated templates or agencies' institutional memory. This becomes apparent in the passage below:

JL: How important is experience when it comes to 2020, in terms of housing so many fans?

STAKEHOLDER 3: [...] I remember Euro '96 and London 2012, for comparable events. London '96 had six matches in London, same as this time, and *it was a slightly different situation then,* because fewer people travelled from abroad. I think the same is true at 2012, in that ... although a lot of people came, *it wasn't the standard football crowd.* [...] *We don't know who's coming to London.* (emphasis added)

What is especially interesting to point out here is that whilst my question focused on *past* experiences, the stakeholder's answer still touches upon the uncertainty that still would remain before and during Euro 2020. With reference to previous and comparable mega-events – Euro 1996 and the 2012 Olympics – one may view how the situation again was framed as 'slightly different' at those events. Whilst the Olympics were heavily visited, it seemingly did not attract a 'standard football crowd', which suggests that football crowds are associated with higher levels of uncertainty than Olympic visitors. This is illustrated by outbreaks of 'hooliganism' at previous football mega-events, including Euro 2016, and the rivalry that exists between some fan groups, even in international football. Interestingly, although London's experience of mega-event housing was considered to be unprecedented, each mega-event also brings about a whole set of new uncertainties that relate to changing threat levels, risk profiles and the nature of the present crowds. In Euro 2020's case, the latter is accurately demonstrated by the discourses surrounding the Scottish supporters' – or the 'Tartan Army's' – trip to London, for Scotland's fixture against England, and the 'storming' of Wembley during the final, which are both discussed in Chapter 6.

So, despite existing paradigms based on past events, international security contexts remain unpredictable and dynamic. This means security stakeholders must contemplate 'a broad spectrum of catastrophic *futures*' (Boyle and Haggerty, 2012: 246, emphasis added). Yet, such future-orientation is not merely to thwart terrorism threats. At football mega-events, this also relates to the uncertainties related to attending crowds. Typically, football fans are divided into pre-defined categories based on the supposed 'risk' they pose by policing actors. Whilst this may be based on the fans' previous history or behaviour in football contexts, the reality is that fans arriving at an SME without intentions of causing problems, due to the emergence of a 'social identity', may end up in conflict with other fans or the police (Stott and Pearson, 2007). Hence, the perceived unpredictability of football crowds and crowds more generally feed into the ever-presence of uncertainty prior to SMEs, in addition to terrorism threats. Together with other external risks like health issues or natural disasters, this explains the identified precautionary logics that must guide mega-event security.

The presence of fan networks: A 'two-way process'

The independent fan networks, FSE and SD Europe, were present at several networking events and active members of the Euro 2020 working group. First, this should be seen in the context of the convention signed in 2016 emphasizing the need for including supporter voices into sporting event planning (see Numerato, 2018). Second, it can also be viewed as related to the increased prominence of non-state actors and organizations in the transnational networking activities before SMEs (Boyle, 2011). The interview accounts provided an interesting insight into the nature of fan networks' roles in the mentioned networking events and build-up prior to Euro 2020.

For context, organized fan networks or associations have become increasingly active stakeholders in modern football and its governance (Hill et al., 2018). Across Europe, fan networks composed of football fans mobilize to bring about social change through civic engagement with political issues (Numerato, 2018). So, in context of security- and safety-related issues in European football, FSE and SD Europe have, since 2009 and 2016, respectively, held an observer status on the Council of Europe Standing Committee of the Convention on Spectator Violence and regularly participate on consultative visits (FSE, 2019; Numerato, 2018: 75). In May 2018, FSE's observer status was also prolonged for three more years, as the network reiterated its 'commitment to the work of this essential European body' (FSE, 2018). FSE is a democratically organized and pan-European fan network which is also 'recognized as an association of supporters' by UEFA and beyond the football world by the Council of Europe (Cleland et al., 2018: 169). When asked about what this observer role encompassed in practice, one interviewee summarized this neatly:

> There are two aspects to it. One is information sharing and that's a two-way process. It's just as important that we like… do stakeholders in football know

what the fans are thinking? And they let us know what the security services and local authorities are thinking. The second part is actual practical observation. (Stakeholder 2)

The first element worth noticing here is the two-way information exchange, between fan representative on the one hand, and sport governing bodies, security services and local authorities on the other. Second, the practical observation element here speaks to how policy circulation involves 'fact-finding trips' where delegations – including FSE or SD Europe – can 'learn firsthand from their peers' (McCann, 2011: 118) about potential advantages or disadvantages of particular policy models or practices. For example, as FSE (2019) reflected on following the Bilbao visit, there were concerns regarding the 'often-belligerent approach' used by the Spanish police 'when it comes to foreign football supporters, though it must be noted that the Basque regional and municipal police do not seem to have the same record in recent years'. The information sharing and observation aspects are, to a degree, inter-connected and allow for fan networks to feed back to the Council of Europe, UEFA and relevant agencies their own perspectives on the practicalities of security.

Accordingly, the recognition was also a crucial measure and the working group inclusion of FSE and SD Europe meant that these networks' representatives could work closely with local authorities and exchange information, opinions and knowledge and ultimately influence how Euro 2020 was secured:

> Just on 2020, I know that the work has already started. I know the Met Police are talking to FSE. They won't want it to go wrong. They want it to be an overwhelmingly successful event. (Stakeholder 1)

> We [FSE] attend regular meetings with stakeholders at major tournaments well in advance of events like 2020, which will be a particularly difficult tournament for members due to it being shared by so many different countries. (Stakeholder 4)

> Now, we're members of this Euro 2020 working group. We [SD Europe] have this remit. It is our role. So, we started promoting the [SLO] role a lot more at national team level and with the results we have seen, several national associations make appointments. (Stakeholder 7)

As can be seen, the inclusion of fan networks into the Euro 2020 working group and Standing Committee was seen as positive, and as Stakeholder 1 noted, the planning and dialogue started early (the interview was conducted in January 2019). Stakeholder 7 elaborated by commenting that SD Europe's promotion of the Supporter Liaison Officer (SLO) role for international teams increasingly had proved fruitful and that SLOs, for example, were used at the 2019 Women's World Cup in France and for Sweden's national team before Euro 2020. Essentially, SLOs are designated individuals working to enhance team/supporter relations and dialogue between the police, security, football organizations and fans (see Chapter 4 for a discussion of the implementation of SLOs). To date, however, SLOs have predominantly been employed in club football, with some tentative deployment in international football. As Stakeholder 7 summarized it: 'So, we have gone from having no influence, no role, to now [have a role] through promotion of SLO's'. In a way, this captures the increased recognition of fan networks and their representatives in – and their integration into security- and policing-related matters in European football, as laid out in the convention. Here, fan networks are assigned specific tasks – exemplified above by SD Europe's promotion of the SLO role and SLO training – which can go to influence how football games and competitions are secured, policed and organized.

By returning to the lesson-drawing component of the 'troika', which commonly occurred through designated networking events and visits, it seems prudent to situate the relevant fan network and their representatives as important actors involved in these processes as regular dialogue partners that ensure 'information sharing' (Stakeholder 2), which have specific remits (i.e., as observers that monitor visits and proceedings, dialogue partners, promoting the SLO role), and which, through reflexive pressure, may bring about social changes to football cultures (Numerato, 2018). Whilst some of this will be returned to in Chapter 4, which focuses more specifically on fan networks and football policing, this section provides an empirical silhouette of the fan networks' presence and practical roles within the discussions and circuits of football mega-event security knowledge.

Problematic implications and impacts on fan cultures

Returning once again to the 'troika of security', this concept can explain the construction of mega-event security and may be transferable to other social contexts, including cultural events, protests or one-off football games, which possess a fixed duration and where security must be constructed (Lee Ludvigsen, 2020). Indeed, this is where the concept's primary sociological value lies. This, however, invites future research from scholars who may wish to adopt the concept's analytical relations or extend them. Whilst the conceptual usefulness of the 'troika' is important, it is also integral to warrant some critical discussion to the practical, political and problematic implications of the futuristic and retrospective dimensions that can be located within it. As argued, these may have huge implications for fans and fan cultures and thereby extend well beyond time-specific SMEs and onto the wider football world.

As Mythen and Walklate (2008: 236) acknowledge in their discussion on futurity, security and risk, 'true security cannot and should not depend on inflicting insecurity on another'. Such argument is largely compatible with the perspectives of the critical approaches to security discussed in Chapter 2. In a way, such argument illustrates the problematic implications of what is discussed above. Whilst the 'troika' may serve to explain how security providers and stakeholders work towards the idyllic conditions of 'optimal' security, a number of the processes that may be identified within the troika's three components are highly contested by the social groups impacted by the implemented policies or mechanisms of social control, such as football fans.

As documented, the reliance on precautionary measures like intrusive surveillance technologies (Sugden, 2012), securitized commodification in the desire for 'clean spaces' (Chapter 2), or implemented legislative changes (Divišová, 2019), can come at the cost of individuals' civil liberties and may lead to the socio-spatial exclusion of social groups (Armstrong et al., 2017; Kennelly, 2015). More generally, the adherence to precautionary principles in security governance may translate into the exceptional suspension of 'normal democratic freedoms' in the name of collective security (Zedner, 2003: 169).

Here, Divišová (2019) provides some recent and applied examples of how this may occur in relation to modern SMEs. Divišová argues that the exceptional terrorism threat posed to Euro 2016 in France, during the enforced state of emergency, allowed for minimal opposition to a precautionary 'counter-hooligan' law which, she argues, remained as a 'security legacy' in the French domestic football culture. Since the 'terrorist' and 'hooligan' threats, as Divišová writes, 'sometimes intermingle in the security considerations', the potential consequences of this are that '"[o]rdinary" football fans can [be] easily caught in the middle, and such an impact can outlive the championship for much longer' (p. 757). Hence, fans occupy a space in the 'middle' of the security efforts made to prevent 'terrorism' or 'hooliganism' – as subjects to be secured against. As Doidge et al. (2019: 712, original emphasis) remind us:

> As with the political discourses associated with SME security, these focus on the combined approach to tackle terrorism *and* hooliganism. In the process, football fans are seen not only as potential hooligans, but as potential terrorists.

The danger is when, as aforementioned, SMEs may become distinct moments for new legislation, technologies or policies that by their nature are precautionary measures for the control of pre-defined yet contested, uncertain and fluid 'security threats' – and then also implemented elsewhere, or in the general policing of football fans and cultures (see Chapter 6). This way, SMEs are initially influenced by wider security developments (Boyle and Haggerty, 2009). The need to secure is, notwithstanding, open for political exploitation (Zedner, 2009) whilst 'mega-events are very seductive' (Horne, 2007: 91). In some cases, then, SMEs become arenas for piloting new – often exceptional – modes of security. Sometimes, the exceptional legislation or security moments are transplanted onto 'everyday' spheres after the event (Kitchen and Rygiel, 2014) where they might become normalized.

As Tsoukala (2009: 133) asks, '[i]f civil rights can be sacrificed in the name of fighting terrorism, why not also in the name of fighting football hooliganism?'. Indeed, this became a reality with the blurred and overlapping 'counter-terrorism' and 'hooligan' legislation post-Euro 2016, which Divišová (2019) argues impacted 'ordinary' fans of French clubs, who then found themselves as defined threats to national security. As Doidge et al. (2019: 714) argue, '[t]ournaments are liminal spaces where traditional boundaries and rivalries can be temporarily dissolved, but there are lasting changes after the tournament through security and anti-hooliganism legislation'. This displays again how the relationship between 'security' and 'SME security' not only is inter-dependent but mutually reinforcing. 'Security' *elsewhere* impacts SMEs, and SMEs impact 'security' *elsewhere*, in form of everyday settings, fan cultures or future matches.

This relates to, *inter alia*, precautionary strategies and pre-emptive legislation. However, it is not solely this futuristic component of the 'troika' that possesses potential problematic implications and the potential to inflict insecurity on citizens and – in football's contexts – the fans. Whilst the retrospective elements, such as the recirculation of 'best practices' may be viewed by some as 'effective' for the construction and governance of security, this does not mean the same practices cannot be intrusive, counter-productive and, in fact, exacerbate perceptions of insecurity for some. Rather, it could simply mean that they are regarded as 'effective' by those with the power to define this and classify what 'security' *is* (Bigo, 2008; Chapter 2) and simultaneously 'define the sources of our insecurity' (Bigo, 2000: 94), such as the international organizations (like sport governing bodies), security officials, authorities or even the media who may legitimate security measures. Furthermore, the transfer of knowledge from one place to another may mean that security-related policies that are generally disliked or resisted by fan cultures are reproduced and transferred across times/spaces.

As research suggests, and as Chapter 4 delves deeper into, examples of this may include, repressive or disproportionate policing tactics, heavy-handed stewarding (Numerato, 2018), the policing of banners brought by fans to stadiums, or the protection from so-called pre-defined 'rival brands' or 'disruptive' political messages. Broadly, football supporters across Europe are still treated as a threat to public order and subject to pre-emptive legislation and policing strategies, but the policing of fans also draws largely upon so-called best practice (Tsoukala et al., 2016). The retrospective side of the 'troika' may therefore facilitate conditions for the (re)circulation of controversial strategies or legislation that seek to sustain those social control mechanisms that fans, as a wide and heterogeneous social group, are subjected to and actively resist across Europe (Numerato, 2018).

Against this backdrop, it is undoubtedly a welcome development that networks like FSE and SD Europe are granted observer statuses, a platform and a voice in the networking activities that occur before European Championships. As Doidge et al. (2019) point out, police repression is one of those issues that affect fans which FSE sets out to challenge, along with other issues of the game. Concerning the potential implications that the reproduction of policies or practices, disliked by attending fans and fan cultures, can have on spectators perceived security in addition to the findings of this chapter, it seems prudent to suggest that the inclusion of fan networks should be maintained for future events, so that fans – accepting the different typologies subordinated to this term (Giulianotti, 2002) – preserve

70 Between Retrospective and Futuristic Processes of Security

a say in security and policing planning and practice and the opportunity to raise specific concerns.

Furthermore, it can be argued that even the recirculation of knowledge and best practices must not be viewed as an unequivocally or unconditionally 'positive' exercise. Simply because these previously tested templates may not be considered as 'effective' by those at the receiving ends of security – the fans – who may end up feeling socially excluded, targeted or marginalized. Largely, this may be echoed in the context of the precautionary post-9/11 security logics that commonly have led to increased '*insecurity*' for specific social groups and individuals in the overarching quest for 'security' (Mythen and Walklate, 2008). For example, in the aftermath of the 2015 *Stade de France* attack, some fans found the increased presence of armed police at public sport venues to be intimidating, off-putting and to be contributing towards an 'oppressive atmosphere' (Cleland and Cashmore, 2018: 464).

Sociologically and politically, this remains relevant, and by returning to the 'troika of security', it is clear that the framework scratches the surface of the far more overarching and philosophical question: the trade-off between freedom and civil liberties, and security (Bauman, 2005; Tsoukala, 2009). The different processes adding up to the 'troika of security' therefore highlight and further validate the perspectives maintaining that mega-events' security efforts and practices and indeed their 'security legacies' can come at the cost of human rights, rights to privacy or civil liberties, as researchers have warned (Boykoff, 2020; Tsoukala, 2009). In many ways, these complex issues – fully identifiable in the football world – highlight and call into question the paradoxical and problematic elements that are inherent to most operations, efforts and projects in the present-day societies that are invoked in the name or under the aegis of 'security'. In that sense, it becomes potentially problematic when the retrospective and futuristic rationales subscribed to with the intention to secure the football world, instead come to make up a 'troika of *insecurity*', in which ordinary football fans are caught in the middle of, when the lines between security threat and referent object become hazy. This means that the 'troika' becomes increasingly dynamic as a conceptual framework as it not merely accounts for those producing security, but those impacted by the (un)intended ramifications of the securing efforts.

Conclusion

A recurring question within the academic field of mega-event security is which processes that assist the efforts to secure event-specific contexts. Such question also lies at this book's core. As sustained, despite the pronounced tendency of standardization, '[t]he pattern of securitization is […] likely to vary according to various structural and cultural factors' (Bennett and Haggerty, 2011: 13). Building on Chapter 2, this chapter has provided an examination of the more practical constructions of security before Euro 2020. The existing literature suggests that mega-event security governance is based upon the transfer of past templates

(Boyle, 2011). These are employed in tandem with the 'articulation of precautionary thinking' (Boyle and Haggerty, 2009: 261). This produces a foundation and building on such insights, this chapter discussed the coalescence of retrospective and futuristic security logics, activities and policies in Euro 2020's context. Previously, such investigation has mobilized my framework, the 'troika of security' (see Lee Ludvigsen, 2020). The 'troika of security' refers to the inter-play between lesson-drawing, the utilization of relevant agencies' institutional memory and precautionary logics, as embedded into mega-event security governance. As argued, these processes, separately and collectively, assisted the construction of security before Euro 2020 (ibid.).

Notwithstanding, this chapter has sought to revisit and critically extend my own concept. As Cleland et al.'s (2018: 183) powerful relational analysis demonstrates, '[f]ans are important stakeholders in football'. However, despite fans' and fan activities' importance in the socially constructed football world, it must be acknowledged that fans' position in the original 'troika of security' was not sufficiently reflected on in Lee Ludvigsen (2020). Resultantly, this chapter has been committed to locate football fans more centrally within this framework. Then, it called into question the problematic implications of merging futuristic/ retrospective modes of security. It can be argued that in a football mega-event securitization, football fans are not solely passive recipients of reproduced security policies, surveillance technologies or public order policing tactics. Whilst the broad nature of the term 'football fans' must be restated, fans and elements of fan cultures are subjects to be provided *with* security and simultaneously secured against as potential threats. This chapter paid critical attention to this, and the potential implications *if* exceptional security measures based on retrospective/ futuristic logics extend into new event-specific or 'everyday' settings. As argued, this is highly illustrative of the implications of security projects more generally in the present-day society. The chapter also shed a light on how fan representatives are stakeholders in the wider consultation and information sharing processes. This remains vital and shall be elaborated on in the next chapter, which examines pressing issues in the policing of European football, and continues to explore the roles of fan networks before, throughout and in-between mega-events as knowledge transfer actors. So, to summarize, within what I call the 'troika of security', this chapter's revisitation exercise has illuminated how fans are present as actors to be secured against as 'potential troublemakers' (Numerato, 2018: 15); stakeholders operating as information brokers (Cleland et al., 2018); and match-goers and event consumers to be provided with security.

Notes

1　This is an amended and updated chapter of an article previously published. In the previous article, I focused more on developing the original conceptual framework. Whilst some of the narratives and interview quotes remain similar, the chapter provides new discussions from the lens of football fans. A reprint of sections of this article has been permitted with the kind permission of the publisher, Taylor

& Francis Ltd (www.tandfonline.com). The original text is titled: 'The 'troika of security': merging retrospective and futuristic 'risk' and 'security' assessments before Euro 2020', Lee Ludvigsen, published in *Leisure Studies* 39(6) (2020), 844–858.

2 As argued by Betts (1978: 88), 'intelligence failures are not only inevitable, they are natural', partly because of human cognitive limitations leading to natural shortcomings in analysis and estimates.

3 However, Bilbao was later replaced by Seville as Spain's host city, in light of COVID-19.

4 See: https://www.coe.int/en/web/sport/monitoring-of-the-convention.

Bibliography

Armstrong, G, Giulianotti, R & Hobbs, D (2017) *Policing the 2012 London Olympics: Legacy and Social Exclusion*. London. Routledge.

Bauman, Z (2005) *Liquid Life*. Cambridge. Polity.

Beck, U (1992) *Risk Society: Towards a New Modernity*. London. Sage.

Beck, U (2009) *World at Risk*. Cambridge. Polity.

Bennett, CJ & Haggerty, KD (2011) Introduction: Security Games: Surveillance and Control at Mega-Events. In C.J. Bennett & K.D. Haggerty (eds) *Security Games: Surveillance and Control at Mega-Events*. Abingdon. Routledge, 1–19.

Bernhard, D & Martin, AK (2011) Rethinking Security at the Olympics. In C.J. Bennett & K.D. Haggerty (eds) *Security Games, Surveillance and Control at Mega-Events*. London. Routledge, 20–35.

Betts, RK (1978) Analysis, War, and Decision: Why Intelligence Failures Are Inevitable. *World Politics* 31(1), 61–89.

Betts, RK (2002) Fixing Intelligence. *Foreign Affairs* 81(1), 43–59.

Bigo, D (2000) Liaison Officers in Europe: New Officers in the European Security Field. In J. Sheptycki (ed) *Issues in Transnational Policing*. London. Routledge, 67–99.

Bigo, D (2002) Security and Immigration: Towards a Critique of the Governmentality of Unease. *Alternatives* 27(1), 63–92.

Bigo, D (2008) Globalized (In)Security: The Field and the Ban-Opticon. In D. Bigo & A. Tsoukala (eds) *Illiberal Practices in Liberal Regimes*. Paris. L'Harmattan, 10–48.

Boykoff, J (2020) *Nolympians: Inside the Fight against Capitalist Mega-Sports in Los Angeles, Tokyo and Beyond*. Nova Scotia. Fernwood.

Boyle, P (2011) Knowledge Networks: Mega-Events and Security Expertise. In C.J. Bennett & K.D. Haggerty (eds) *Security Games: Surveillance and Control at Mega-Events*. Abingdon. Routledge, 169–184.

Boyle, P & Haggerty, KD (2009) Spectacular Security: Mega-Events and the Security Complex. *International Political Sociology* 3(3), 57–74.

Boyle, P & Haggerty, KD (2012) Planning for the Worst: Risk, Uncertainty and the Olympic Games. *British Journal of Sociology* 63(2), 241–259.

Case Collective (2006) Critical Approaches to Security in Europe: A Networked Manifesto. *Security Dialogue* 37(4), 443–487.

Cleland, J & Cashmore, E (2018) Nothing Will Be the Same Again After the Stade de France Attack: Reflections of Association Football Fans on Terrorism, Security and Surveillance. *Journal of Sport and Social Issues* 42(6), 454–469.

Cleland, J, Doidge, M, Millward, P & Widdop, P (2018) *Collective Action and Football Fandom: A Relational Sociological Approach*. New York. Palgrave.

Council of Europe (2017) 1st T-RV Working Group Meeting on the Preparation of UEFA EURO 2020. Available from: https://www.coe.int/en/web/sport/newsroom/-/asset_publisher/x9nLQ8ukPUk9/content/1st-t-rv-working-group-meeting-on-the-preparation-of-uefa-euro-2020?inheritRedirect=false.

Council of Europe (2019a) Peer-review Exercise in Amsterdam, in the Run-up to UEFA EURO 2020. Available from: https://www.coe.int/en/web/sport/-/peer-review-exercise-to-amsterdam-in-the-run-up-to-uefa-euro-2020.

Council of Europe (2019b) Council of Europe Holds the 1st Meeting of the UEFA EURO 2020. Advisory Group on Legal Issues. Available from: https://www.coe.int/en/web/sport/-/council-of-europe-holds-the-1st-meeting-of-the-uefa-euro-2020-advisory-group-on-legal-issues.

Council of Europe (n.d.) Working Group EURO 2020. Available from: https://www.coe.int/en/web/sport/working-group-euro-2020.

Divišová, V (2019) Euro 2016 and Its Security Legacy for Football Supporters: A Conceptual Blurring of Hooligans and Terrorists? *Soccer & Society* 20(5), 757–769.

Doidge, M, Claus, R, Gabler, J, Irving, R & Millward, P (2019) The Impact of International Football Events on Local, National and Transnational Fan Cultures: A Critical Overview. *Soccer & Society* 20(5), 711–720.

Dolowitz, D & Marsh, D (1996) Who Learns What from Whom? A Review of Policy Transfer Literature. *Political Studies* 44, 343–357.

Folkers, A (2019) Freezing Time, Preparing for the Future: The Stockpile as a Temporal Matter of Security. *Security Dialogue* 50(6), 493–511.

FSE (2018) Council of Europe Standing Committee: Prolongation of FSE's Observer Status. Available from: https://www.fanseurope.org/en/news/news-3/1663-council-of-europe-fse-gains-observer-status-for-3-more-years.html.

FSE (2019) FSE Takes Part in Council of Europe Visit to Bilbao. Available from: https://www.fanseurope.org/en/news/news-3/1750-fse-takes-part-in-coe-visit-to-bilbao-en.html.

Giulianotti, R (2002) Supporters, Followers, Fans, and Flaneurs: A Taxonomy of Spectator Identities in Football. *Journal of Sport and Social Issues* 26(1), 25–46.

Hardt, H (2018) *NATO's Lessons in Crisis: Institutional Memory in International Organizations*. Oxford. Oxford University Press.

Hill, T, Canniford, R & Millward, P (2018) Against Modern Football: Mobilising Protest Movements in Social Media. *Sociology* 52(4), 688–708.

Horne, J (2007) The Four "Knowns" of Sports Mega-Events. *Leisure Studies* 26(1), 81–96.

Kennelly, J (2015) "You're Making Our City Look Bad": Olympic Security, Neoliberal Urbanization, and Homeless Youth. *Ethnography* 16(1), 3–24.

Kitchen, V & Rygiel, K (2014) Privatizing Security, Securitizing Policing: The Case of the G20 in Toronto. *Canada. International Political Sociology* 8(2), 201–217.

Klauser, F (2011) The Exemplification of "Fan Zones": Mediating Mechanisms in the Reproduction of Best Practices for Security and Branding at Euro 2008. *Urban Studies* 48(15), 3202–3219.

Klauser, F (2012) Interpretative Flexibility of the Event-City: Security, Branding and Urban Entrepreneurialism at the European Football Championships 2008. *International Journal of Urban and Regional Research* 36(5), 1039–1052.

Klauser, F (2017) *Surveillance & Space*. London. Sage.

Lee Ludvigsen, JA (2020) The 'Troika of Security': Merging Retrospective and Futuristic 'Risk' and 'Security' Assessments Before Euro 2020. *Leisure Studies* 39(6), 844–858.

McCann, E (2011) Urban Policy Mobilities and Global Circuits of Knowledge: Toward a Research Agenda. *Annals of the Association of American Geographers* 101(1), 107–130.

Molnar, A, Whelan, C & Boyle, P (2019) Securing the Brisbane 2014 G20 in the Wake of the Toronto 2010 G20: 'Failure-Inspired' Learning in Public Order Policing. *British Journal of Criminology* 59, 107–125.

Mythen, G & Walklate, S (2008) Terrorism, Risk and International Security: The Perils of Asking "What If?". *Security Dialogue* 39, 221–241.

Mythen, G & Walklate, S (2016) Counterterrorism and the Reconstruction of (In)Security: Divisions, Dualisms, Duplicities. *British Journal of Criminology* 56(6), 1107–1124.

Numerato, D (2018) *Football Fans, Activism and Social Change*. London. Routledge.

O'Grady, N (2019) Designing Affect into Security: Shared Situational Awareness Protocols and the Habit of Emergency Response. *Cultural Geographies* 26(4), 455–470.

Rose, R (1991) What Is Lesson-Drawing? *Journal of Public Policy* 11(1), 3–30.

Seifert, C (2007) Improving Disaster Management Through Structured Flexibility among Frontline Responders. In D.E. Gibbons (ed) *Communicable Crisis: Prevention, Response and Recovery in the Global Arena*. North Carolina. IAP, 137–168.

Stone, D (2004) Transfer Agents and Global Networks in the 'Transnationalization' of Policy. *Journal of European Public Policy* 11(3), 545–566.

Stott, C & Pearson, G (2007) *Football "Hooliganism": Policing and the War on the 'English disease'*. London. Pennant Books.

Sugden, J (2012) Watched by the Olympics: Surveillance and Security at the Olympics. *International Review for the Sociology of Sport* 47(3), 414–429.

Tsoukala, A (2009) *Football Hooliganism in Europe: Security and Civil Liberties in the Balance*. Basingstoke. Palgrave.

Tsoukala, A, Pearson, G & Coenen, PT (2016) Conclusions: Social Control at the Expense of Civil Liberties and Human Rights. In A. Tsoukala, G. Pearson & P.T. Coenen (eds) *Legal Responses to Football 'Hooliganism' in Europe*. The Hague. Springer, 169–178.

UEFA (2019) Stadiums to Be EURO Centrepiece. Available from: https://www.uefa.com/insideuefa/news/newsid=2601822.html (Accessed 29 May 2019).

UEFA (n.d.) *UEFA EURO 2020: Tournament Requirements*. Nyon. UEFA. Available from: https://www.uefa.com/MultimediaFiles/Download/EuroExperience/competitions/General/01/95/21/41/1952141_DOWNLOAD.pdf.

Zedner, L (2003) Too Much Security?. *International Journal of the Sociology of Law* 31, 155–184.

Zedner, L (2009) *Security*. London/New York. Routledge.

Chapter 4

Policing, Policy and Fan Networks

Introduction

As Cleland et al. (2018: 173–174) write, football fans are becoming 'increasingly aware that they are having similar shared experiences with fans across Europe. Increasing commercialization and changes to ownership, combined with changes to regulations and legislation, is affecting fans'. Not uncommonly, football fans will express their dissatisfaction with repressive security measures, the implementation of new technologies, policing and the wider criminalization of supporters on policy level or through the media (see Numerato, 2018). The policing of football fans remains an integral aspect of any football mega-event and its delivery. Here, as this chapter and Chapter 6 reflect on, Euro 2020 was no exception. More specifically, this chapter explores stakeholder perceptions of football policing across Europe, the pressing issues and the impact of the media ahead of Euro 2020. In addition, the chapter builds upon Chapter 3 and zooms in on how fan networks influence the policing and security planning before, during and after mega-events like Euro 2020.

Within the mentioned 'troika of security', fans play multiple and, at times, overlapping roles. This comes to fore again in this chapter, which focuses primarily on fan networks as stakeholders in the policing- and security-related consultation processes ahead of the European Championships. Two main arguments will be formulated over the course of this chapter. First, ahead of Euro 2020, the chapter argues that the stakeholders viewed the policing of fans as a critical and problematic issue despite clearly favouring policing approaches towards fans based upon interaction and de-escalation. Second, this chapter sheds a light on the practical implications of the greater recognition of fan networks as stakeholders in security and policing matters in European football governance and policies and within its associated 'security field' (Giulianotti and Klauser, 2010, see Chapter 1). As contended, the Euro 2020 exemplar powerfully demonstrates that fan networks and their representatives are important actors and transporters of knowledge *before*, *during* and *in-between* European Championships. Taken together, this is sociologically important because such arguments advance existing insights holding that fan networks and their representatives – accepting that fans compose

DOI: 10.4324/9781003258445-5

a heterogeneous social group – remain vital stakeholders in the football world, which can enhance, contest or foster social changes related to safety and security (Cleland et al., 2018; Numerato, 2018; Turner, 2020, 2021). This chapter yields new insight into this and begins by placing this firmly within the context of wider policy transformations in European football's governance.

Policy, recognition and participation: Policing and fan networks in the security field

As Tsoukala's (2009) influential work demonstrates, policies and repressive measures designed to control and respond to football 'hooliganism', from 1985 and onwards, have been addressed at both European Community and European levels and involved diverse stakeholders, including the Council of Europe, Union of European Football Associations (UEFA) and police forces. In this context, the concept of the 'security field' (Giulianotti and Klauser, 2010) – outlined in Chapter 1 – becomes a very useful relation. Essentially, the security and policing-related responses in European football emerge from a wider security field, in which one can locate organized fan networks and their representatives.

However, for contextual reasons, it is also prudent to briefly visit the extant literature on football policing. A body of research examines the operational policing of crowds and fans in various international and club football contexts (O'Neill, 2005; Stott et al., 2008; 2012; Stott and Reicher, 1998). This research provides theoretical and empirical explanations for football policing and fan-police interactions and includes O'Neill's (2005) fascinating ethnographic account of the social interactions between club fans and policing actors in Scotland. Other work explores the social-psychological dynamics between crowds and the police and uses the Elaborated Social Identity Model to understand crowd dynamics and power relations. For example, it is found that the crowds' perceptions of police legitimacy are linked to an absence of disorder in football contexts (Stott et al., 2008, 2012). Drawing from this, the policing of football fans can be largely considered a social process. This research has informed both policy and practice on a European level (Stott et al., 2008: 261). Yet, as Tsoukala (2009: 9) writes, the conclusions of this pioneering work 'have not been correlated with the current configuration of the political and security fields which the security officials under examination are operating'.

Here, Tsoukala (2007, 2009) and Spaaij (2013) help us conceptualizing 'counterhooliganism' and the wider security governance of football fans, by locating these trends within the broader realm of European cooperative turns within security and policing fields. As Spaaij (2013: 176) writes, '[c]ounter-hooliganism police cooperation networks have been on the increase ever since the 1985 European Convention on Spectator Violence and Misbehaviour at Sports Events'. Some the key developments following this include the collection, analysis and dissemination of intelligence and information before football matches and tournaments through pan-European networks like the National Football Information Points (NFIP).

Policing, Policy and Fan Networks 77

Besides, and most central to this book, existing lessons and 'best practice' paradigms related to policing, security and surveillance – deriving from previous European Championships, sport mega-events or single games – are regularly transferred through networks of expertise onto upcoming events (Chapter 2). This ensures a reproduction of tested measures, technologies and recommended techniques, which feed into modern-day mega-events' security apparatuses (Klauser, 2011). Moreover, Tsoukala's (2009) analysis of 'counter-hooliganism' in Europe reveals an increased convergence in the policing approaches, legal and policy responses, which entail cooperative and preventative measures and techniques across Europe.

Throughout EU and Council of Europe states, the exchange of 'best practice' remains a key feature of the legal and policing responses to 'hooliganism' (Tsoukala et al., 2016). Though, as scholars have emphasized, the quest for security in football may erode supporters' civil liberties and often proceed in the absence of a clear-cut definition of what 'hooliganism' actually means (Tsoukala, 2009; Tsoukala et al., 2016). In a way, these developments reinforce Spaaij's (2013: 176) suggestion that '[s]ecurity and risk management technologies at football matches are characterized by a high degree of internationalization and Europeanization' in the twenty-first century. Therefore, as central to this book, competitions like Euro 2020 device platforms for transnational information exchanges, consultation processes and knowledge transfers between the array of stakeholders – *not* as confined to law enforcements, security experts or security agencies – that are involved in some way in European football's security field and planning.

Hence, mobilizing Giulianotti and Klauser's (2010) security field concept allows us to conceptualize the width and presence of diverse stakeholders and their intra-relations around sport mega-events (SMEs). For decades, organized networks of fans have contested modern football's profound changes both domestically and transnationally (Turner, 2021; Webber, 2017). As mentioned, the recent years' developments demonstrate that certain fan networks advocating for supporter involvement in football's governance, increasingly, have become recognized partners herein by UEFA and the Council of Europe (Cleland et al., 2018; UEFA, 2012a). As Numerato (2018) writes, key institutional transformations in that respect involve the recognition of Football Supporters Europe (FSE) and SD Europe as observers, since 2009 and 2016, respectively, on the Council of Europe Standing Committee of the Convention on Spectator Violence (T-RV). Numerato notes that:

> Throughout their [FSE's and SD Europe's] participation in the Committee, the fans have the opportunity to contribute to discussions of the body, which monitors the application of the European Convention on Spectator Violence and Misbehaviour at Sports Events. Moreover, the FSE have been actively involved in the Pan European Football policing Training Project. The aim of the project was to develop innovative policing strategies, foster the communication of police with supporters and prevent escalation of conflicts.

The signature of the Council of Europe Convention on an Integrated Safety, Security and Service Approach at Football Matches and Other Sports Events could be understood as another significant institutional response to fans' transnational activism; the convention signed in 2016 emphasised the necessity of taking into consideration the perspective of supporters during the organisation of sport events. (p. 75)

Another highlighted institutional response to fan activism was the implementation of Supporter Liaison Officer (SLOs) since 2012/13. This development was 'heavily influenced' by SD Europe, which was 'appointed by UEFA to assist in the implementation process of the SLO role' (Stott et al., 2020: 198). SLOs are intended to operate as a 'a bridge' between clubs and fans, to enhance the dialogue between the two, and to build 'relationships not just with various fan groups and initiatives but also with the police and security officers' (UEFA, 2011: 10).

Institutionally, we spot a clearer recognition of fan networks or associations as legitimate stakeholders on modern fan issues including security. Chapter 3, for example, discussed fan networks' presence and roles at pre-event visits. However, as Cleland et al. (2018) highlight, recognition does not automatically equate with influence. Therefore, whilst FSE, for example, is recognized as a dialogue partner in security and policing matters before football mega-events, and although this provides an opportunity to influence decision-making, this does not guarantee that fan networks' voices are 'listened to' (p. 171). Numerato (2018: 92) also suggests that despite the intensification of fan activism, 'the impact of critical football fans on the culture of security [...] remains limited'. Giulianotti (2011), meanwhile, observes increased levels of formal opposition and resistance from fan cultures and associations. He also notes that whilst such criticism and resistance 'are not always successful', they still demonstrate the 'underlying concerns regarding the impact of security-focused social policies on the popular urban cultures and social freedoms of supporter formations' (p. 3307). This naturally opens up questions around how much influence fan networks have, how their representatives perceive their own influence, and what the observer status means in practice, and whether this is limited according to the relevant event context.

Thus, this section presents a breakdown of important institutional and policy developments within European-wide football policing and security. It analyses the trend whereby fan networks are increasingly recognized stakeholders in the organization of security and policing in European football and have a presence within the 'security field' (Giulianotti and Klauser, 2010). This book's earlier chapters and the wider literature also demonstrate that football presents a site for security-related cooperative practices, convergent responses to security issues and the transnational exchange of recommended 'best practices' concerning SME security and policing. To investigate this further, this chapter first seeks to examine how stakeholders voice their perceptions about European-wide football policing and describe the football policing experience across Europe. In doing so, it also explores the links between the policing of football fans and the media coverage before and during tournaments. Second, this chapter investigates how a set of stakeholders, some of whom represent fan networks, felt that their organizations impacted the exchange of 'good' or 'best practice' (see Chapter 2) within the pre-planning and arrangements of policing and security before Euro 2020, given their recognition *within* (i.e., by UEFA) and *beyond* (by the Council of Europe) the football world as dialogue partners.

Current issues and national variations

Commonly, the interviewed stakeholders articulated clear ideas of what constituted 'favourable' and 'less-favourable' policing approaches towards fans. With reference to Euro 2020's host countries, stakeholders made references to specific countries or contexts upon assessing the (less-)favourable models of football policing. For example, this comes to fore below:

> A low key [police] presence is favoured by supporters. Generally we find that German Police handle football matches better than most. They understand fan culture and are generally able to distinguish between behaviour which is good natured and that which is malicious. (Stakeholder 5)

The above quote effectively encapsulates the policing approach which the majority of interviewees favoured. The described approach bears a resemblance to one that is based on friendly interactions between most fans and the police on matchdays. More generally, 'low profile' policing is found to reduce or de-escalate conflict and aggression in domestic (Stott et al., 2008) and international football mega-event settings (Stott et al., 2007). In contrast, this stakeholder also provided insight into a *less*-favourable policing approach from the perspectives of the stakeholders. This referred to a less interactive and more confrontational approach which could prove potentially counter-productive:

> Policing style has a major impact on the atmosphere [and] an over aggressive style tends to create resentment and puts fans on edge creating an unpleasant and unwelcome atmosphere which is not enjoyable. (Stakeholder 5)

Essentially, this give us an insight into how vital the selected policing approaches towards football fans can be for the overall atmospheres. A disproportionate policing style may accordingly create a somewhat oppressive atmosphere described as 'unpleasant', 'unwelcome', 'not enjoyable' and fuelled with 'resentment'. In explaining this, the literature on the policing of crowds, protest and fans in club football can guide our sensemaking. In some situations, where stern or 'over-aggressive' approaches are taken towards crowds, this may impact the levels of disorder and transmit signals that disorder will occur (Gorringe and Rosie, 2008; Stott et al., 2012: 391). The signifiers of such approach can include the deployment or riot squads or gear, the absence of interaction and the engagement and the use of coercive force (Brechbühl et al., 2017). The danger, thus, is 'that policing interventions designed to control "risk" can actually initiate dynamics of "risk" escalation because of their impact on crowd psychology and dynamic' (Stott et al., 2018: 3). Here, the recommendations provided by Reicher et al. (2004: 570) are extremely relevant, because they suggest that the police should 'consider crowds as an opportunity and seek to enable them', to ensure that 'crowd members and their wider communities may cease to see the police as a problem' and to enable cooperation.

In this context, another stakeholder, who had attended a workshop with various security actors before Euro 2020, could tell me that a policing approach based on engagement with fans was favourable and expected in certain Euro 2020 host countries such as Dublin,[1] Glasgow and London:

> I mean, the words of the Chief Superintendent, who is going to be the Gold Commander in [host city], said '20 arrests are a failure', 'no arrests are a success'. So, that's always positive when you're hearing that from the outset. (Stakeholder 9)

Such account reinforces Stakeholder 5's reflections, who commented that: 'This [friendly approach] tends to be the case in Scotland most of the time however the experience in Europe varies quite significantly from country to country'. Importantly, it must be acknowledged that there are occasional inconsistencies between *expected* policing approaches and the realities. Yet these accounts remain important as they manifest two central themes that will be highlighted.

First, the accounts reaffirm the perceived strengths of an interaction-based policing approach that seeks to de-escalate potentially escalating situations and avoid adding extra resentment. Second, it was clear that stakeholders distinguished between favourable and unfavourable policing approaches to fans. However, extremely interestingly, in doing so, stakeholders commonly employed country-specific references to make their points. Of course, this is likely explained by the interviewees' own national backgrounds, but it is remarkable that certain countries seemed to be mentioned in relation to favourable exemplars of football policing (e.g., Scotland, Germany, Ireland, England and Denmark). Then importantly, other countries were seen as less exemplary due to the perceived different traditions in the policing of fans:

> Now, we're [England] quite lucky in the sense that unless we finish second in the group and go to the semi-final, all of our matches we'll be in Western Europe. Now, Rome is a little bit the exception there. The Italian police have a very different policing style [than] the UK policing style we're used to. The Irish policing style will not be that different [from the UK] and I think we have cause for optimism that the Danish policing style will also be quite similar. (Stakeholder 8)

In a way, this account accurately captures this section's emerging argument. The interviewed stakeholders largely pointed towards the football policing in Western and Northern European countries as relatively convergent (see Tsoukala, 2009) and hence favourable. The policing approaches expected in these countries did, accordingly, correspond with the favourable policing approaches based on interaction and de-escalation. Then, some stakeholders mentioned the football policing in for example Rome (Italy) and Seville (Spain) as the exceptions, which was less favourable due to high police visibility, large presence and lack of interaction:

> Spain [has] a pretty poor record when it comes to policing, particularly international fans. (Stakeholder 2)

> [In Seville, for Spain versus England] it was a standard situation, where you were locked in after the game. There was a large police presence to act as a deterrent. (Stakeholder 3)

However, although the stakeholders expressed clear ideas of what constituted favourable or unfavourable examples of football policing before Euro 2020, this did not mean that they saw the experience of policing and security as *unproblematic* across countries like England, Scotland or Ireland. Football-related security and policing commonly include privately hired stewards inside the stadia, and as Stakeholder 2 commented, 'Stewarding is far worse than the policing in English football. Far worse'. This echoes Numerato's (2018) findings. He notes how European 'fan activists criticised policing at football games and the inadequate role played by stewards [and that] stewards behaved as provokers who stimulated, rather than mitigated, conflicts on the terraces' (p. 15–16). Hence, despite the availability of favourable approaches, the policing of fans was still regarded a problematic and contested terrain.

Furthermore, and importantly, stakeholders also stressed that favoured policing approaches, despite being expected, were not necessarily fixed or static. Here, the impact of fan cultures emerged as central. Put simply: 'you don't know who's going to turn up' (Stakeholder 3). Indeed, the below conversation yields an insight into some of the challenges related to policing football mega-events possessing an international aspect:

JL: So, do you expect it to be quite similar to club football, so how the Premier League or FA Cup are policed? Will they adopt those measures in the Euros in London?

STAKEHOLDER 8: There's obviously an extra dimension given the international aspect. And there's also challenges to the lack of familiarity too. You don't know enough about the fan cultures of those we'll be playing against.

JL: Yeah, yeah?

STAKEHOLDER 8: So, when the Croatian fan base comes to London, it's not the same as the Liverpool fan base coming to London for a Premier League match or whatever. Those challenges are around the incoming fans rather than the policing style. The policing style generally I think will be the same in London, regardless of who comes.

This passage shows how fan cultures (in this case Croatian fans) and the emerging fixture lists impact and is a barrier to the policing of football and the extent to which, for example, an interactive approach would be adapted by policing actors. As hinted upon in Chapter 3, international matches and individual supporters are categorized according to 'risk', and UEFA (n.d., Sector 6: 9) required Euro 2020 hosts to adhere to a 'risk-based police deployment strategy'. Yet, this stakeholder was still confident that the 'policing style' generally would 'be the same in London' regardless of the emerging fixtures and incoming fan bases. Still, this illuminates a dynamic domain of football policing. Although there are clearly favoured approaches that are attributed strengths in the eyes of stakeholders, the cited 'lack of familiarity' regarding country-specific fan cultures before Euro 2020 was seen to possibly impact the eventual policing realities.

So, this section maps out how stakeholders, before Euro 2020, expressed their ideas of what constituted favourable or unfavourable approaches towards fans. In a complex European context, it emerged that the stakeholders perceived the overall policing experience to be problematic, but that favourable templates existed and were available. In describing the policing experience across Europe, countries such as England, Denmark, Germany, Ireland and Scotland – wherein the promotion of dialogue was expected by stakeholders – were largely framed as favourable examples. Based on the stakeholders' experiences and historical incidents, other Euro 2020 hosts, like Italy and Spain, were considered less likely to adapt the interactive and dialogue-based approaches advocated by stakeholders.

It may be suggested that the stakeholders' positions on European-wide football policing were influenced, in part, by the extent to which dialogue-based approaches were regularly adapted in the countries referred to. As such, the empirical evidence underlines that football policing remains highly contested. This section has cited issues around 'over-aggressive' policing, stewarding and uncertainty related to incoming fan cultures. Having empirically established this, the next sections examine how the media portrayals could impact the policing and securitization of football fans, and then how the stakeholders reflected on their potential impact on policing- and security-related matters before Euro 2020.

The link between policing and the media

The media plays a central role before and during SMEs with their mediation of threat or potential disorder. Catastrophe-forecasting coverage and the mediation of possible threats may strengthen the organizers' and authorities' arguments for the creation of ring-of-steel security. Moreover, the mainstream mass media can also contribute to stereotypical depictions of football fans (Numerato, 2018). Indeed, some of the stakeholders also commented on how the media narratives had the capacity to inform or influence the eventual policing realities at Euro 2020.

Interestingly, during the period where I conducted some of the interviews, public and media debates around policing and security in English football sparked up following a series of incidents. These occurred in early 2019, just months before the Euro 2020 circus was originally meant to arrive in London. For instance, throughout Euro 2020's qualification rounds, *The Daily Mail* (2019) claimed that there was a 'new breed' of English 'hooligans' – dubbed the 'stag-do brigade' – which followed England in the UEFA Nations League and displayed threatening behaviour whilst being 'drunk and drugged up'. Stakeholder 3 contended that this was a 'fair description', but simultaneously acknowledged that this was 'usual' ahead of big football tournaments (see Crabbe, 2003) and emphasized that only a small minority of supporters were troublemakers: 'one, ten, fifteen idiots, that's not something that should be blown out of proportion' (Stakeholder 3).

The interview accounts also suggested that the media, through their coverage and headlines, plays a role in how fans are policed in international tournaments or can set the tone for the eventual policing realities at events. This is important as alarmist coverage fundamentally may pressure authorities to employ specific measures for fans' safety, although as Stakeholder 3 said, 'the media has a job to try to keep things in perspective'. Interestingly, none of the stakeholders explicitly stated that they, in any form, expected large-scale 'hooliganism' outbreaks in London, apart from isolated incidents of violence or 'anti-social behaviour' from a small minority (see Chapter 6), which could negatively impact the event:

> What will happen, as happened to the [2018] World Cup, there will be people that aren't football fans, but will see this as an opportunity to go out and drink. They're the ones causing troubles. (Stakeholder 1)

However, in spite of the expected isolated incidents caused by a minority, the stakeholders generally expected that those fixtures assigned to London would run smoothly from a policing perspective. As can be seen, some stakeholders did comment on how they expected the media to focus on the prospects of disorder and the subsequent need to police. And, indeed, some of the media discourses did revolve around potential disorder, especially in relation to the Scottish 'Tartan Army's' trip to London for England versus Scotland and the final between England and Italy (discussed in Chapter 6). As can be suggested, the impacts of media and social media coverage on football policing styles represent an interesting avenue for further investigation in domestic and international settings.

Fan networks as agents of knowledge transfer

Consultation and involvement

As integral to this book – and reflected on above and in Chapter 3 – fans occupy a position as important stakeholders before SMEs like Euro 2020. Yet, fan networks like FSE and SD Europe are also vital agents of knowledge transfer during and in-between European Championships, as this section highlights. Those interviewed stakeholders associated with fan networks would commonly account

84 Policing, Policy and Fan Networks

for how fan networks could influence the exchange of best practice and overall policing and safety of fans in Euro 2020's context.

By the virtue of being stakeholders, this enables an opportunity to impact or be impacted by the relevant event. As mentioned, networks such as FSE and SD Europe enjoy access to UEFA's political and governing structures (Cleland et al., 2018; Numerato, 2018). This section suggests that fan networks like FSE and SD Europe possess important roles as actors of transnational knowledge transfer relevant to policing and security matters *before*, *during* and *in-between* European Championships. Such argument leans upon three primary examples: (1) fan networks' presence on pre-event networking and information exchange events and conventions, (2) the running of Fans' Embassies during European Championships, and (3) fan networks' general protection of fans' interests. These empirical findings therefore produce novel insights into some of the *practical* ramifications of fan networks' increased participation, embeddedness and recognition in security and policing consultation processes on fan issues.

The planning stages for SMEs occur over several years. Typically, throughout the 'microspaces of meeting rooms and other sites of persuasion' (McCann, 2011: 117), they involve exchange programs, conferences and workshops aiming to exchange security practices throughout transnational networks of stakeholders encompassing states, organizers and non-governmental organizations (Klauser, 2011; Lauss and Szigetvari, 2010). As mentioned, in Euro 2020's pre-planning, a Council of Europe 'Working Group EURO 2020' was set up, whilst a series of consultative visits were held in different host cities between 2017 and 2019 where Euro 2020 preparations featured on the agenda. For the consultative visit in Bilbao, in February 2019, the key aim was to 'update on the state of preparations' before Euro 2020 and to 'support the national, regional and local authorities on how to better implement the good practices enshrined in the Saint-Denis Convention and the 2015 Recommendation' (Council of Europe, 2019). This visit was attended by, *inter alia*, UEFA, NFIPs, local police forces, SD Europe and FSE (ibid.), whereby the latter two organizations reflected their observer status on the Standing Committee and working group memberships. Reflecting on the roles and remits held by fan networks *before* Euro 2020, one interviewee stated that:

> Really big part [played by fan networks prior to Euro 2020]. Because, it is interesting when you read these booklets and look at these conventions and Councils, there's always these institutions and organizations listed. But, in reality, the people that are going to be affected by hosting a sporting mega-event are locals and football supporters [...] So, it's really important they are involved. But not just involved, but involved in the decision-making [and] observations. (Stakeholder 2)

From this quote, which gives an insight into the wide nature of the 'security field' (Giulianotti and Klauser, 2010), the importance of involvement in the overall event organization comes to the fore. However, from this account, involvement *per se* is not considered sufficient; the stakeholder emphasized the importance of being involved in observations and the decision-making that would impact supporters and local residents. Another interviewee referred to a gradually growing role of FSE before UEFA competitions in both club and international settings:

STAKEHOLDER 9: I suppose there's loads different strands to FSE, loads of different projects [...] We have an out campaign, a fantastic female's campaign, we do the Fans' Embassies, the FSE now [are] getting invited into all the Champions League final pre-visits, representatives from one of the nations who has the chance of getting there. That's also the case at Europa League final, so [the] exposure has grown a lot, especially over the last few years.
JL: [...] Do you feel FSE's role has grown? Is it more significant now than in [Euro] 2016?
STAKEHOLDER 9: Yeah, absolutely, I mean, in 2016 there was one person doing my job.

Here, it is also worth pointing out how the stakeholder refers to a growing exposure over the last few years in the wider field of European football. Meanwhile, speaking on SD Europe's role, another interviewee commented:

> Through the work with the Council of Europe, we are part of the Council of Europe Working Group on Euro 2020. And our remit within that group is to promote the role of SLO at national team level. (Stakeholder 7)

In a way, by connecting the above excerpts to Numerato's (2018) observation concerning a clearer recognition of fan associations in consultation processes by UEFA and the Council of Europe (i.e., through promotion of SLOs or by participating on pre-event visits), then these insights can empirically extend this into the period between Euro 2016 and Euro 2020. As Stakeholder 2 expressed *vis-à-vis* the observer status, this facilitated greater exchanges of information: 'I'd like to say, the observer status, fans and fan organizations being a part of the process, it works. *And it doesn't just work for us. It works for UEFA*' (Stakeholder 2, emphasis added). Emphasized here is a degree of perceived mutual benefit of fan networks' participation in the pre-event consultation processes concerning policing and security.

Fans' embassies

One relevant example of the fan representative stakeholders' work to improve the safety and security of fans in the host cities is the Fans' Embassies service *during* the European Championships. Not to be conflated with *fan zones*, Fans' Embassies are fan-oriented information points set up in host cities that provide visiting fans practical and logistical advice (Kossakowski, 2019) and during Euro 2020, Fans' Embassies representing 18 (of 24) competing teams were activated.

86 Policing, Policy and Fan Networks

Usually, Fans' Embassies are established at World Cups and the 'Euros', and they aim to 'bring together fans of national teams who want to support fellow fans of national teams at international events' (Cleland et al., 2018: 174). Yet importantly, as socio-cultural spaces, Fans' Embassies may also be understood as tools in the 'socio-prevention of incidents of violence' (Marivoet and Silvério, 2019: 722). As Marivoet (2006) highlights, the initial establishment of Fans' Embassies was linked to the clamp down by public authorities and sport governing bodies on violence and xenophobia before SMEs. Fans' Embassies are also strategic tools for supporter empowerment (UEFA, n.d.) and the promotion of a 'positive and peaceful fan culture' (UEFA, 2012b). Indeed, as FSE's (2010: 8) *Fans' Embassies: A Handbook* also acknowledges, the Fans' Embassy service should be 'seen as an element of the overall organisation and security/safety provisions at international tournaments'.

Concerning Fans' Embassies, Stakeholder 4 stated that: 'FSE coordinates Fan Embassy teams at major events. These fan embassy teams are made up by volunteers from participating countries and they are overseen by the FSE'. As focal points providing fans – often visiting a new country – with information and advice, the Fans' Embassies were seen as important initiatives that could improve fans' overall safety. As Güney (2017: 272) writes, Fans' Embassies may provide 'help and assistance in case of emergency (physical violence, theft, etc.) and can be addressed as mediators in conflict situations'. When asked about the Fans' Embassies' impact on fans' overall experiences, one stakeholder stated:

> Really important. Fan embassies have shown to be incredibly effective in the past few international and European tournaments. That's your first point of call [of] contact, if you need any kind of information. Not just about security, but fixtures, what can I take in? What can I do in the city? It's also a great way of fans to meet likeminded people. (Stakeholder 2)

Above, Fans' Embassies' informative and socializing abilities appear as important throughout the host cities. This was echoed by others:

> The biggest thing is obviously the access to the information that the Fan Embassy gets access to through the Embassy. So, if I get any information regarding the transport, regarding fan marches, change of location and so on, things that'll actually cause issue for fans, they can get that straight from us at FSE and we can get it straight to them and it can be put out on any social media stream if need to be [and] text message services which the FSE runs. So, the broadcasting of information is invaluable really to the fans. (Stakeholder 9)

These two quotes advance our understanding of how exactly FSE, which runs the Fans' Embassies, could impact the complex event organization and logistics for tournaments like Euro 2020 *throughout* its month-long duration. Arguably, Fans'

Embassies can serve as informative points of call for fans and provide safe spaces that foster positive social relations between supporters. Yet, the smooth running of Fans' Embassies also depends largely on the complex pre-event work of FSE and their close liaison with other stakeholders and authorities: 'We sometimes meet the police separately, we also try to get whoever is in charge of the mobility plan, transport systems in the city to the stadium, and whatever other form of transport that is needed' (Stakeholder 9). Whilst Fans' Embassies have been subject to limited research, the service may be considered as an extended fan-led and fan-centred security and safety tool.

Fan cultures

Then, considerably more time diffusely and *in-between* international sporting events, the roles of fan networks as pro-active custodians of fans' interest and experts on fan cultures within football's security governance were highlighted. As Stakeholder 4 stated: 'Our main role is to protect the interests of everyone who attends matches and to make sure that UEFA and stakeholders where football fans will attend games understand the mindset those fans'. Further, networks like FSE have the capacity to impact the aforementioned challenges related to distinctive fan cultures, because of the networks' close relationships with and in-depth understanding of fan bases across Europe:

> So, the platform that FSE offers the police is to speak to people who are actually active on the ground and have relationships with their fan base. So, should anything need to go out urgently about something, it can go out via those people who have the communication with the fans. (Stakeholder 9)

This was expanded on in relation to a relevant example:

> The big thing for us is that interaction with each nation's fan group. For example, I'm not an expert on Ukraine. I'm not an expert on how the Ukrainian fans will behave or what they want, but we have [someone] who is, so we can provide a form of dialogue [with] the police, with the security, and give them information as to exactly what they [the fans] want to do and explain how they'll go about and do it and that interaction allow the police to understand. (Stakeholder 9)

In many ways, these accounts underpin this section's main argument. That is, within the 'transnational exchanges in security matters' (Klauser, 2011: 3211), fan networks – constituting stakeholders – are actors of knowledge transfer *before* (in consultation processes, promoting the SLO role), *during* (Fans' Embassies) and *in-between* European Championships and UEFA competitions (as, for example, experts on fan cultures; through site visits; and observers between events). Whereas it is beyond the scope of this book to reconceptualize 'impact' or

88 Policing, Policy and Fan Networks

quantify the exact 'successes' fan networks have in influencing the planning for mega-events like Euro 2020, 'success' might for instance refer to the influence on a short-term decision. Whilst it is noted that fan activists have had limited impact on European security cultures (Numerato, 2018), 'impact' could also be the sheer formal recognition as a dialogue partner. For Garcia and Welford (2015: 523), some groups will 'feel they have achieved success' by being consulted or listened to. Regardless, within the overarching, dynamic and transnational processes of knowledge transfer before and in-between European Championships, this evidence provides a snapshot of the multiple roles of fan networks in the case of Euro 2020.

Situating fans and power relations in the 'troika of security'

In light of the above discussion, it seems prudent to again return to the suggestions made in Chapter 3 concerning fans' multiple roles within a mega-event securitization. The security fields of contemporary mega-event are 'heavily populated with multiplicities of actors, agencies and organizations' (Fussey, 2015: 222). As this book argues, football fans play integral and occasionally contradictory roles within these populated 'security fields'. Often, however, 'the voices of fans are absent from the literature on security and SMEs' (Doidge et al., 2019: 713). In that respect, it is necessary to situate and return to football fans' position within the 'troika of security' given this framework's capacity to explain mega-event security constructions and the roles of football fans.

As already shown, fans at football mega-events play different yet crucial roles within the 'troika of security' and the wider event securitization. First, some groups of fans, their activities or behaviour are occasionally, through legislation and public and media discourses, securitized because they allegedly pose a potential security threat to other fans and general public order (Tsoukala, 2009). By considering the three components of the 'troika' then, *lessons* may, for example, be drawn from previous events in relation to how to police *fans* through dialogue or communication. Or, an agency's *institutional memory* on how to police a particular game may be characterized by previous interactions with specific *fan groups*. Moreover, the precautionary categorization processes will also typically impact how an individual fan or a fan group is approached or policed. Here, one can see how fans, in part, constitute what the processes of the 'troika' attempt to govern and keep under control.

Then, fans concurrently represent the primary consumers and participants of an SME's official spaces, including fan zones or the stadiums. At SMEs where processes of securitization and commodification intersect (Giulianotti, 2011), fans therefore also constitute those referent objects of 'security' that are to be provided with and expect 'safety' in 'secure' environments upon visiting a mega-event, and subsequently protection from other 'internal enemies' like 'hooligans' (Divišová, 2019), or external threats like terrorism, crime or pandemics. Making fans feel secure or safe during mega-events is hence central in relation to maintaining an event's consumer attraction (Eick, 2010) and ensuring that fans objectively remain separated from outlined 'security threats'.

Finally – and most central in context of this chapter – fans, within the 'troika', also possess a distinctive presence in form of organized fan networks. Evidently, when synthesizing this chapter with Chapter 3, fan networks and their representatives actively contribute in the pre-planning of security before events like Euro 2020. Here, fans play an important and recognized security stakeholder role in the wider hierarchy of powerful actors, such as UEFA, local and transnational security forces and the Council of Europe. My argument is that it is crucial to recognize fans as powerful actors within the 'troika of security' as subjects to be 'secured from', event consumers and, lastly, *influencers* in the security-related planning and eventual delivery in Euro 2020's context. In many ways, the case of Euro 2020 empirically documents fans' active and continued roles in the pre-planning of security and their input on police-fan relations. Thus, fans are present in the 'troika', where they possess a threefold role.

Dunning (1999: 126) maintained that 'fans are, individually, the least powerful person in the football figuration'. Recently, Cleland et al. (2018: 26) maintained that such contention would be correct '[i]f supporters operated alone', but that fans can acquire power through their connections, collective actions and mobilizations (see also Hill et al., 2018). In this chapter's context, it is observable that through the collective formations of pan-European networks – that become recognized observers on European policy level – fans can acquire the power to impact wider processes, such as football's contested securitization or policing, which again lends itself partly upon social interactions and relations.[2] In a way, this again demonstrates *why* the 'troika' – despite emanating from an event-specific case study (see Lee Ludvigsen, 2020) – can be extended into novel and securitized football contexts. For instance, now it may be asked how the lessons from Euro 2020 can inform Euro 2024 in Germany, and how transnational fan networks like FSE and SD Europe continue their work towards Euro 2024, or other European club competitions. Whilst this illustrates that the 'troika' can be extended into new event, security and fan contexts, it also underlines the important and *constant* role of fans and fan activities within the 'troika'. Ultimately, as forthcoming mega-events take place, fans are again likely to occupy roles as *users* and *subjects* of, and *contributors* to 'security', impacted by and impacting an event's security providers and hierarchies of power. And here, the 'troika' can assist in unpacking the contested processes that are entangled in a mega-event's security delivery, and how techniques of social and crowd control 'can later be applied to other fields of activity' (Tsoukala, 2009: 118) beyond sport.

Conclusion

This chapter builds substantially on Chapters 2 and 3 but must also be seen as important by itself. In the context of Euro 2020's security pre-planning, this chapter has explored current issues in football-related policing and the roles of fan networks within the consultation processes of policing and security policies. Throughout my interviews, the policing of Euro 2020 and European football repeatedly emerged as one dominant theme that the stakeholders perceived as problematic across Europe. Thus, this chapter sought to examine stakeholders' responses to football policing across Europe, and how fan representatives, through their organizations and participation within the consultation processes, could impact policing- and security-related matters and practices before Euro 2020. Both of these questions remain of high sociological and political worth when situated against the wider convergent moves within European football security and policing responses (Tsoukala, 2009) and the embeddedness of fan networks in the organization of European football competitions in the present-day society (Cleland et al., 2018; Numerato, 2018).

Two empirically informed arguments have been carved out. First, as expected, the policing of football fans across Europe continues to remain problematic from stakeholder perspectives. Some of the mentioned and current issues related to poor stewarding, the approaches to specific fan cultures, and repressive or (over-) aggressive policing. Moreover, the media coverage of *potential* 'hooliganism' or disorder was regarded as problematic and unlikely to provide an accurate picture of the actual extent of the disorder issues. Stakeholders also distinguished between favoured and unfavoured models of football policing. In doing so, and with relevance to practice, country-specific references were commonly made to specific national contexts in which the favoured dialogue-based approaches to football fans could be expected, or not. With this established, this chapter's second key contention is that fan networks, exemplified here by FSE and SD Europe,[3] are now firmly embedded in the consultation process and delivery of policing and security *before*, *during* and *in-between* the European Championships. As discussed, mega-events device fields of transnational exchanges of recommended security know-how, techniques and best practice (Klauser, 2011). And so, within European football's 'security field' (Giulianotti and Klauser, 2010), fan networks must be approached as vital agents of knowledge generation and transfer, just as they are considered as subjects to be secured against, and subjects to be secured in their role as event consumers.

More broadly, this chapter's empirical findings remain extremely important because they extend our understanding of how the networked and fundamentally social world of football (Cleland et al., 2018) is composed of domains wherein specific policies and wider, socio-political projects, struggles and '-ization' processes are challenged or contested. Whereas the earlier literature has captured this (Hill et al., 2018; Millward, 2012; Numerato, 2018; Turner, 2020, 2021; Webber, 2017), this chapter empirically extends knowledge on this trend further into the domain of contemporary 'policing' under the wide and controversial umbrella of *securitization*. Nevertheless, these two contentious processes and the mentioned social world of football were significantly disrupted by the extraordinary and unsettling events that unfolded in the early days of 2020 when a novel coronavirus spread globally. This is explored and reflected on over the next three chapters.

Notes

1 However, Dublin lost its Euro 2020 fixtures in April 2021 (see Chapter 6).
2 For an account of the FSE network's transnational expansion, consult Cleland et al. (2018: 169–174).
3 Though, as crucial to emphasize, networks like FSE and SD Europe do not necessarily speak for *all* fans across Europe, some fan activists may for example feel that 'FSE speak only to a certain subset of engaged fans' (Hodges, 2019: 159).

Bibliography

Bigo, D (2008) EU Police Cooperation: National Sovereignty Framed by European Security? In E. Guild & F. Geyer (eds) *Security Versus Justice? Police and Judicial Cooperation in the European Union.* Aldershot. Ashgate, 91–108.

Brechbühl, A, Schumacher Dimech, A & Seiler, R (2017) Policing Football Fans in Switzerland—A Case Study Involving Fans, Stadium Security Employees, and Police Officers. *Policing* 14(4), 865–882.

Cleland, J, Doidge, M, Millward, P & Widdop, P (2018) *Collective Action and Football Fandom: A Relational Sociological Approach.* New York. Palgrave.

Cottey, A (2007) *Security in the New Europe.* Basingstoke. Palgrave Macmillan.

Council of Europe (2019) Preparations for UEFA EURO 2020. Available from: https://www.coe.int/en/web/sport/-/preparations-for-uefa-euro-20-2 (Accessed 22 August 2021).

Crabbe, T (2003) 'The Public Gets What the Public Wants' England Football Fans, 'Truth' Claims and Mediated Realities. *International Review for the Sociology of Sport* 38(4), 413–425.

Divišová, V (2019) Euro 2016 and Its Security Legacy for Football Supporters: A Conceptual Blurring of Hooligans and Terrorists? *Soccer & Society* 20(5), 757–769.

Doidge, M, Claus, R, Gabler, J & Millward, P (2019) The Impact of International Football Events on Local, National and Transnational Fan Cultures: A Critical Overview. *Soccer & Society* 20(5), 711–720.

Dunning, E (1999) *Sport Matters: Sociological Studies of Sport, Violence and Civilization.* London. Routledge.

Eick, V (2010) A Neoliberal Sports Event? FIFA from the Estadio Nacional to the Fan Mile. *City* 14(3), 278–297.

FSE (2010) *Fans' Embassies: A Handbook.* Hamburg. Available from: https://issuu.com/prosuporters/docs/fse_fans_embassy_handbook-engl.

Fussey, P (2015) Command, Control and Contestation: Negotiating Security at the London 2012 Olympics. *The Geographical Journal* 181(3), 212–223.

Garcia, B & Welford, J (2015) Supporters and Football Governance, from Customers to Stakeholders: A Literature Review and Agenda for Research. *Sport Management Review* 18(4), 517–528.

Giulianotti, R (2011) Sport Mega Events, Urban Football Carnivals and Securitised Commodification: The Case of the English Premier League. *Urban Studies* 48(15), 3293–3310.

Giulianotti, R & Klauser, F (2010) Security Governance and Sport Mega-Events: Toward an Interdisciplinary Research Agenda. *Journal of Sport and Social Issues* 34(1), 48–60.

Giulianotti, R & Klauser, F (2012) Sport Mega-Events and "Terrorism": A Critical Analysis. *International Review for the Sociology of Sport* 47(3), 307–323.

Gorringe, H & Rosie, M (2008) The Polis of Global Protest: Policing Protest at the G8 in Scotland. *Current Sociology* 56(5), 691–710.

Güney, E (2017) Supporter Ownership in Turkish Football. In B. Garcia & J. Zheng (eds) *Football and Supporter Activism in Europe*. London. Palgrave Macmillan, 257–276.

Hill, T, Canniford, R & Millward, P (2018) Against Modern Football: Mobilising Protest Movements in Social Media. *Sociology* 52(4), 688–708.

Hodges, A (2019) *Fan Activism, Protest and Politics: Ultras in Post-Socialist Croatia*. Oxon. Routledge.

Klauser, F (2011) The Exemplification of "Fan Zones": Mediating Mechanisms in the Reproduction of Best Practices for Security and Branding at Euro 2008. *Urban Studies* 48(15), 3202–3219.

Kossakowski, R (2019) Euro 2012, the 'Civilizational Leap' and the 'Supporters United' Programme: A Football Mega-Event and the Evolution of Fan Culture in Poland. *Soccer & Society* 20(5), 729–743.

Lauss, G & Szigetvari, A (2010) Governing by Fun: EURO 2008 and the Appealing Power of Fan Zones. *Soccer & Society* 11(6), 737–747.

Lee Ludvigsen, JA (2020) The 'Troika of Security': Merging Retrospective and Futuristic 'Risk' and 'Security' Assessments before Euro 2020. *Leisure Studies* 39(6), 844–858.

Marivoet, S (2006) UEFA Euro 2004™ Portugal: The Social Construction of a Sports Mega-Event and Spectacle. *The Sociological Review* 54, 127–143.

Marivoet, S & Silvério, J (2019) Football Fan Cultures after the Euro 2004 in Portugal. *Soccer & Society* 20(5), 721–728.

McCann, E (2011) Urban Policy Mobilities and Global Circuits of Knowledge: Toward a Research Agenda. *Annals of the Association of American Geographers* 101(1), 107–130.

Millward, P (2012) Reclaiming the Kop? Analysing Liverpool Supporters' 21st Century Mobilizations. *Sociology* 46(4), 633–648.

Numerato, D (2018) *Football Fans, Activism and Social Change*. London. Routledge.

O'Neill, M (2005) *Policing Football: Social Interaction and Negotiated Disorder*. Basingstoke. Palgrave.

Reicher, S, Stott, C, Cronin, P & Adang, O (2004) An Integrated Approach to Crowd Psychology and Public Order Policing. Policing. *An International Journal of Police Strategies & Management* 27(4), 558–572.

Spaaij, R (2013) Risk, Security and Technology: Governing Football Supporters in the Twenty-First Century. *Sport in Society* 16(2), 167–183.

Stott, C & Reicher, S (1998) How Conflict Escalates: The Inter-Group Dynamics of Collective Football Crowd Violence. *Sociology* 32(2), 353–377.

Stott, C, Hoggett, J & Pearson, G (2012). Keeping the Peace: Social Identity, Procedural Justice and the Policing of Football Crowds. *British Journal of Criminology* 52, 381–399.

Stott, C, Livingstone, A & Hoggett, J (2008) Policing Football Crowds in England and Wales: A Model of Good Practice. *Policing & Society* 18(3), 258–281.

Stott, C, West, O & Radburn, M (2018) Policing Football "Risk"? A Participant Action Research Case Study of a Liaison-Based Approach to 'Public Order'. *Policing and Society* 28(1), 1–16.

Stott, C, Adang, O, Livingstone, A & Schreiber, M (2007) Variability in the Collective Behaviour of England Fans at Euro2004: Policing, Intergroup Relations, Social Identity and Social Change. *European Journal of Social Psychology* 37, 75–100.

Stott, C, Khan, S, Madsen, E & Havelund, J (2020) The Value of Supporter Liaison Officers (SLOs) in Fan Dialogue, Conflict, Governance and Football Crowd Management in Sweden. *Soccer & Society* 21(2), 196–208.

The Daily Mail (2019) Drunk, Drugged up on Cocaine, Under 25 and Clad in Designer Gear, There's a New Breed of Hooligan Following the England team... The Stag-Do Brigade. Available from: https://www.dailymail.co.uk/sport/football/article-6852085/Drunk-drugged-25-theres-new-breed-hooligan-following-England.html (Accessed 28 May 2020).

Tsoukala, A (2007) Security Policies & Human Rights in European Football Stadia. *CEPS CHALLENGE Paper* 5, 1–20.

Tsoukala, A (2009) *Football Hooliganism in Europe: Security and Civil Liberties in the Balance.* Basingstoke. Palgrave.

Tsoukala, A, Pearson, G & Coenen, PT (2016) Conclusions: Social Control at the Expense of Civil Liberties and Human Rights. In A. Tsoukala, G. Pearson & P.T. Coenen (eds) *Legal Responses to Football 'Hooliganism' in Europe.* The Hague. Springer, 169–178.

Turner, M (2020) 'We Are the Vocal Minority': The Safe Standing Movement and Breaking Down the State in English Football. *International Review for the Sociology of Sport*, 1–19.

Turner, M (2021) The Safe Standing Movement: Vectors in the Post-Hillsborough Timescape of English Football. *The Sociological Review* 69(2), 348–364.

UEFA (2011) *UEFA Supporter Liaison Officer Handbook English Version* (2011 Edition). Available from: https://editorial.uefa.com/resources/01ff-0f84280a8aee-e3525baf90b0-1000/uefa_supporter_liaison_officer_handbook_2011_version.pdf.

UEFA (2012a) UEFA/EU Police Training Bears Fruit. Available from: https://www.uefa.com/insideuefa/protecting-the-game/news/0203-0f88225b2d6e-cb94b562accc-1000–uefa-eu-police-training-bears-fruit/?referrer=%2Fuefa%2Ffootballfirst%2Fmatchorganisation%2Fstadiumsecurity%2Fnews%2Fnewsid%3D1889538.

UEFA (2012b) Fan Embassies Prove a Hub for Supporters. Available from: https://www.uefa.com/uefaeuro-2020/news/0254-0d7e1bc9ecbb-4ccc5faa8e02-1000–fan-embassies-prove-a-hub-for-supporters/.

UEFA (n.d.). *UEFA EURO 2020: Tournament Requirements.* Nyon. UEFA. Available from: https://www.uefa.com/MultimediaFiles/Download/EuroExperience/competitions/General/01/95/21/41/1952141_DOWNLOAD.pdf.

Webber, DM (2017) 'Playing on the Break': Karl Polanyi and the Double-Movement 'Against Modern Football'. *International Review for the Sociology of Sport* 52(7), 875–893.

Chapter 5

Pandemic Threats, COVID-19 and Euro 2020's Postponement

Ready, Set, Postponed

Introduction

As Roberts (2020: 617) describes, 'On 1 December 2019 in Wuhan, a city in central China, patient zero was identified infected with an unknown type of coronavirus'. Then, on 31 December 2019, China informed WHO 'that it had identified a new type of coronavirus' (ibid.). Just over three months later, Euro 2020 was postponed by Union of European Football Associations (UEFA) on 17 March 2020. In the context of this unprecedented and significant decision, this chapter will explore the dynamics, discourses and logics surrounding the postponement of Euro 2020 following the COVID-19 pandemic, which unfolded globally in the early months of 2020. More specifically, this chapter sets out to explore how the previously discussed meanings of 'security' were reconfigured in the face of a rapidly expanding pandemic. In a similar vein to Chapter 2, it does so by asking the relevant questions of 'security from what?' and 'security for whom?'.

The sheer rarity of mega-event postponements demonstrates why they hold a special sociopolitical importance. Interestingly, Goldblatt (2019) predicted that Euro 2016 was unlikely to be the last European Championship to ever be staged under a state of emergency. With COVID-19 placing immense pressure on states, societies and their public services around the Europe, Goldblatt's prediction did – for a while – seem to become a reality again for Euro 2020. However, instead of being staged under a 'continent-wide' state of emergency,[1] Euro 2020 never commenced at all in June 2020. Nevertheless, postponements of mega-events require serious academic evaluation (Bar-On, 2017) and critical engagement, whereas analyses of the pandemic's impact in sport can reveal wider trends speaking to the nexus of 'security' and 'health' (Elbe, 2011; Kamradt-Scott and McInnes, 2012; Rushton, 2011).

It is clear that the pandemic has had a monumental impact on mass events globally. Worldwide, sport mega-events (SMEs) and sporting competitions were postponed, cancelled or declared 'null and void' in the early months of 2020 (Parnell et al., 2020). It was also the first time in history that the European Championships in football were postponed. The Olympics, meanwhile, had not been suspended since the Second World War. Tovar (2021: 67) argues that, on a global scale,

DOI: 10.4324/9781003258445-6

'[n]ot even the terrible events of the Second World War were enough to close soccer as the COVID-19 pandemic has'. Abnormal postponements, however, do not occur in vacuums and they raise a host of sociologically unanswered questions. Moreover, the threat of pandemics to SMEs is predominantly mentioned in passing in the pre-COVID mega-event securitization literature. This truly exceptional background provides the backdrop for this chapter, which also aims to account for the key developments related to COVID-19 and Euro 2020 in the dramatic, eventful and unprecedented period between January 2020 and June 2020.

In this period, the media represented the key platform through which stakeholders, key actors and organizations articulated their public responses to COVID-19 in the football world. Hence, this chapter's material is predominantly drawn from an analysis of interview materials within media sources and official statements released by sport governing bodies and stakeholders of the game. Structurally, this chapter starts by situating the nexus between health issues and security. This is then discussed with specific reference to crowded mega-events. The chapter then provides a *tour d'horizon* of the events that led to Euro 2020's postponement before investigating how the coronavirus was framed as a security threat and for whom it was framed as threat to in Euro 2020's case. This remains highly important as it captures what may be considered an epochal shift in mega-event security governance. The apparent shifts of focus and discourse demonstrate a move away from *endemic* and more regular security threats (Chapters 2 and 3) towards an *epidemic* threat, which is temporally characterized by a suddenness and exceptional moment. This chapter illuminates how the meanings of 'security' not only may be subject to change, but how they actually were reconfigured in a mega-event context. And so, Euro 2020's postponement offers a lens through which *some* of the implications of the pandemic's emergence in early-2020 may be understood sociologically.

Health and security: Pandemics as security threats

As I argue, the global health crisis caused by COVID-19 formed another, highly significant part of Euro 2020 securitization. In many ways, the pandemic crisis revealed the key principles of a securitization (Chapter 2) with securitizing actors, receiving audiences, a threat to survival, security referent objects and the implementation of exceptional security measures (Buzan et al., 1998). In several countries, the coronavirus pandemic was framed as a threat to national security whilst 'governments used security measures designed to control by stopping and detaining people in certain places' (Bigo et al., 2021: 5). The linkages between the COVID-19 pandemic and security were thus apparent as the pandemic emerged in early 2020 (see Duarte and Valença, 2021). Moreover, the pandemic was considered by the UN Security Council as threatening to international peace and security (Hassan et al., 2021). Therefore, it is imperative to unpack pandemics and infectious diseases as potential security threats and issues in the twenty-first century.

The relationship between health and security came to fore already in the 1946 WHO Constitution, stating that the 'health of all peoples is fundamental to the attainment of peace and security' (cited in Elbe, 2011). However, throughout the twentieth century, infectious diseases like pandemic influenza were *not* widely recognized as security threats (Kamradt-Scott and McInnes, 2012). Rather, they were considered serious health threats (Davies, 2008). Yet, whilst simultaneously representing global health threats, health issues including infectious diseases, epidemics, pandemics and 'bioterrorism' have increasingly been included on security agendas over the past decades as non-traditional threats to individuals' health and well-being, and to states and their societies (Davies, 2008; Elbe, 2011; Hanrieder and Kreuder-Sonnen, 2014; Kamradt-Scott and McInnes, 2012; Rushton, 2011).

Somewhat paradoxically, in the late 1970s, confidence existed among public health elites that risks from infectious diseases were decreasing (Davies, 2008). Western countries in particular believed that 'technological progress had halted the spread of these diseases', which were assumed to have been replaced by so-called 'diseases of affluence', like diabetes, cancer and heart diseases (Peterson, 2002: 47). Throughout the 1980s and 1990s, such outlook changed drastically as the spread of HIV/AIDS, coinciding with intensified global interconnectedness, amplified anxieties related to worldwide contamination (Hanrieder and Kreuder-Sonnen, 2014). This produced a future-oriented shift, away from already known diseases, towards the 'unlimited potential threats residing in the microbial world' (ibid.: 336). It also meant that emerging and re-emerging infectious diseases have been increasingly framed as both public health and security risks (Kamradt-Scott and McInnes, 2012).

Adding weight to this, the threats posed by SARS and H5N1 ('avian flu') in the 2000s, which received wide media coverage (Wallis and Nerlich, 2005), represented developments that merely intensified arguments maintaining that cyclical infectious diseases should be approached as security threats, given the potential threat posed by infectious diseases to public health, human well-being and political and economic stability (Davies, 2008). Pandemics, therefore, were seen to directly pose threats to states by causing enormous socio-economic disruptions (Kamradt-Scott and McInnes, 2012). Elbe (2011: 850) accords this, highlighting that HIV/AIDS, SARS and H5N1 'played crucial, and also quite distinctive, roles in carving out a medical dimension to the international security agenda'.

In academic spheres, one can observe a growing literature body concerned with pandemics or infectious diseases that conceptually approaches this as 'biosecurity', or that works within the framework of securitization theory (Curley and Herington, 2011; Hanrieder and Kreuder-Sonnen, 2014; Kamradt-Scott and McInnes, 2012). Predominantly, these studies are concerned with the 'processes through which health issues emerge as security problems' that require exceptional responses (Nunes, 2014: 942). However, as demonstrated by Nunes (2014), who works within the security-as-emancipation prism, health issues can be broadened and deepened so to constitute a security problem on an individual and less exceptional level. Nunes argues that health issues can be security problems if they

Pandemic Threats, Covid-19 and Euro 2020's postponement 97

come to 'restrict in a decisive manner the ability of those involved – individuals, families and/or groups – to shape the course of their lives, either by determining their action or by steering their conduct' (p. 952). Others challenge the novelty of the 'health-security' nexus and the validity of securitization theory, arguing that the relationships between health, medicine and security are historically traceable (Howell, 2014). Notwithstanding, the realization of, and responses to, pandemics and infectious diseases as security threats can presently be seen in health and security communities (Rushton, 2011). Significantly, this was also the case throughout the COVID-19 pandemic (see Bigo et al., 2021).

Coordinated responses and security's 'comeback'

Pandemics, when critically and analytically approached as security threats, must be understood as multifaceted. COVID-19, for example, intensified tensions between security, public health and the economy (ibid.). The pandemic consequences are not merely epidemiological on an individual level, but relate to economic, political and social disruption in global societies, since a pandemic's impacts transcend national borders. Hence, it is prudent to speak of a duality of security referent objects. Infectious diseases impede individuals and their health and well-being, yet concurrently, the state is the main provider of public health capacities and services (Curley and Herington, 2011) and states play a key role in responding to pandemic threats (Bigo et al., 2021).

Elbe (2011: 848–849) therefore notes that responses to pandemics may be illuminating for more general understandings of security:

> When the domains of health and security intersect, this does not just shape how particular diseases are governed in the international system; it similarly encourages changes to how security is understood, to how security is provided, and indeed to who practises security in contemporary international relations.

The 'securitization of health', according to Elbe, has another side: it also involves the 'medicalization of insecurity'. Drawing from medical sociological literature, Elbe highlights particularly three changes to security practices that have led to or constitute the 'medicalization of insecurity'. Firstly, as discussed, that is pandemics' solidified position on the security agenda, as national and international security threats requiring security-related responses. Secondly, Elbe captures how medical expertise and medical professionals increasingly have acquired a seat around the 'security table' in political settings. This is important, as it relates to who may practice security. As Elbe argues, 'medical professionals have recently come to play a much more integrated role in security policy' (p. 853). Therefore, adding to an already densely populated 'security field' of actors, individuals with a background in clinical practices, epidemiology and microbiology have increasingly been included in health security programmes and security think tanks whilst

98 Pandemic Threats, Covid-19 and Euro 2020's postponement

enhancing their social influence. Thirdly, Elbe points towards *how* security is provided or ensured. Accordingly, 'expertise in clinical practice, epidemiology and microbiology increasingly form part of the new health security programmes established' (ibid.: 856) over the years. Therefore, security is also provided through more contemporary means such as developing new countermeasures to pandemics and through stockpiling for catastrophic times (see also Elbe et al., 2014). These three transformations feed into the 'medicalization of insecurity'. Notwithstanding, it remains an important observation that past knowledge about previous diseases is not always sufficient to tackle future pandemics, whereas the desire to secure individuals or populations 'through medical countermeasures is not easily translated into practice' (Elbe, 2011: 849). Hence, as in other security contexts, the attempts or desire to secure something do not necessarily nor automatically lead to more or true security in health contexts.

Questions remain regarding the responses to threats stemming from infectious diseases and pandemics. Here, WHO plays a key role in monitoring health risks and coordinating responses on a global scale. Hanrieder and Kreuder-Sonnen (2014) examine WHO's role in the governance of diseases and argue that the supranational organization has emerged as a global emergency governor that has the capacity to define emergencies and crises whilst also provide policy guidelines and guide political responses. They argue that WHO's autonomy in disease surveillance and governance has increased. Meanwhile, Davies (2008) argues that WHO disproportionality prioritizes western, high-income countries and observes how western states and WHO, simultaneously, construct infectious diseases as security threats, but argues that WHO's role is limited. Essentially, the organization still depends on state action, cooperation and state verification of disease outbreaks. Hence, in the security responses to health crises, WHO's autonomy is *delegated* by western states that predominantly are concerned with 'strengthening their domestic borders against the spread of infectious disease epidemics' (ibid.: 313), which can be seen as a security threat to states' socio-economic *status quo*. In a way, this connects with Hassan et al. (2021: 396) reflections one year into the COVID-19 pandemic, as they argue that the WHO 'played a pivotal technical, normative and coordinating role, but has been constrained by its lack of authority over sovereign member states'.

Whilst the literature on the links between security, risk, and COVID-19 still remains under development (see for example Bigo et al., 2021; Domingues, 2020; Duarte and Valença, 2021; Murphy, 2020), Bigo et al. (2021: 4) point towards the 'tendency to consider the virus through the frame of a danger to security'. As they shed a light on, this is problematic because the COVID-19 pandemic has required or become the catalyst for new modes of border protection, surveillance and contact tracing technologies and international collaboration in the field of security. Furthermore, in relation to the nexus between security and COVID-19, Domingues (2020: 7–8, original emphasis) also suggested that:

> In the face of threat, *security has made a comeback*. Although its original meaning certainly remains behind official, closed doors, it is in a new garb

that 'security' has mostly been publicly presented. While cohesion of state and society oriented former assessments, now the 'security frame' seems to have moved, through those war metaphors, towards the defence of society against an *invisible enemy* [...] It is clearly not the state that the coronavirus threatens, but unequally exposed individuals' and populations' survival.

In this sense, this argument suggesting new 'security frames' revolving around an 'invisible enemy' serves as highly important for the subsequent discussion in this chapter, which aims to better understand the changing meanings of 'security' in Euro 2020's context as the COVID-19 pandemic triggered its 12-month postponement.

Infectious diseases and sport mega-events

Throughout this book, the understanding of pandemics as security threats to SMEs is crucial. This book has already argued that security in an SME context must be approached more holistically: it cannot be conflated with 'terrorism' or, to a lesser extent, 'hooliganism' or 'crime' in the mega-event theatres. Limited social scientific research examines the potential threat of pandemics to mega-events and the impacts of postponements. Possibly, such gaps in the literature exist because pandemics seldom lead to SME postponements or cancellations. For instance, the European Championships had never previously been postponed, whereas the 2020 Olympics were the first since the Second World War not to be staged as originally planned.

However, this does not mean that past SMEs have not been threatened or influenced by pandemics or diseases. Before the 2002 World Cup in South Korea/Japan, the SARS outbreak was a cause of concern, leading Toohey et al. (2003) to argue that pandemics must be accounted for when planning for SMEs. More recently, concerns over 'swine flu' existed prior to the 2010 World Cup in South Africa (*The Guardian*, 2010). The 2015 Africa Cup of Nations took place in Equatorial Guinea during the Ebola virus (McCloskey et al., 2020), whereas the Zika virus constituted a public health crisis in Brazil prior to the country's 2016 Olympics (Parnell et al., 2020). Meanwhile, the efforts to prevent sexually transmitted diseases in Olympic Villages are often announced pre-event (*The Telegraph*, 2007). Hence, it is not the case that mega-events have not been threatened by infectious diseases in the past. Rather, SMEs have proceeded in the relative absence of any major disease issues or outbreaks (Parnell et al., 2020).

A pandemic threat to an SME is not necessarily a risk or threat emerging as a result of hosting an event in itself (Jennings, 2012a). In that respect, it poses a different, more 'naturally occurring' (Kamradt-Scott and McInnes, 2012: 95) security threat than for example 'hooliganism'. Further, the pandemic threat is an appropriate illustrator of the argument holding that mega-events can never be detached from their broader contexts. Moreover, SMEs are popular tourist destinations and attract mass crowds. Therefore, in an age of global mobility systems

(Giulianotti et al., 2015), mega-events and their high density of people may work to intensify the spread of infectious diseases within the event city itself or elsewhere, around the world, when attendees return (Dickmann, 2013). Indeed, in the epoch of COVID-19, SMEs have been oft-referred to as potential 'super-spreaders' (Lee Ludvigsen and Parnell, 2021; see Chapter 6).

Essentially, continuous in-and-out flows of spectators and other individuals (staff, volunteers, reporters, athletes) across transnational borders mean increased likelihood of cross-border transmission of infectious diseases (Jennings, 2012b). Furthermore, this security threat *preserves* when those same individuals return to their home cities or countries. Hence, globalizing forces and the geographic spread of SMEs, especially events like Euro 2020 hosted across 11 different countries, mean SMEs may be inherently vulnerable and require a broad approach to prevention, preparedness and response that goes beyond the time and location of the event (Dickmann, 2013).

Preparedness, in terms of national health services and emergency response team (ibid.), is a formal requirement for hosts taking on mega-events (UEFA, n.d.). Moreover, contingency planning comprise elements of states' security apparatuses (Adey and Anderson, 2012). With regard to preventative measures, media coverage, public health organizations and national health authorities commonly work to raise awareness of infectious diseases pre-event. Yet, as Janiec et al. (2012: 2) find, such messages 'went unnoticed by a significant number of fans' attending Euro 2012, underlining the previous limitation of prevention strategies.

As with other security threats that mega-events are subject to, there are degrees of unpredictability and uncertainty (Boyle and Haggerty, 2012) attached to the task of securing against pandemics. Fundamentally, identifying outbreaks is inherently difficult and adds to the list of uncertainties that put restrictions on pre-event planning (Dickmann, 2013; see Chapter 3). In terms of the practical implications of pandemic threats, Dickmann (2013: 85) asks '[w]hat should organisers of major sporting events do when there is a pandemic influenza six months before a scheduled event?'. Interestingly, this worst-case scenario became a reality for two largest SMEs in 2020, namely the Tokyo Olympics and Euro 2020, although COVID-19, of course, is not a pandemic influenza. In her recommendations, Dickmann writes that:

> As the disease is already occurring globally, the risk assessment for major sporting events is based on whether the sporting event comes into conflict with national and international health regulations, recommendations and travel advice. Organisers have to connect and collaborate with the national and international public health authorities in order to make their risk assessment. The basic question is: does this event have a significant negative impact on the society – does this event make the pandemic worse? (p. 85)

Consequently, concerning event organizers' and owners' response to the pandemic security threat, this illuminates important aspects of organizers' responsibility and the melange of interplay between organizers, health organizations, governments and governing bodies in sport (i.e., UEFA, FIFA or IOC) (see Lee Ludvigsen, 2021). This scratches the surface of another central, but under-played question in the literature. That is, whom that ultimately makes the decision to cancel or postpone an event for security purposes; whether this is a decision by the host country, UEFA or FIFA (Bar-On, 2017) – representing two organizations with no territory where they have jurisdiction – or even WHO (Davies, 2008). Whilst, in the case of Euro 2020, UEFA seemingly made this decision, it must also be seen as a decision influenced by governments, WHO guidelines (Lee Ludvigsen, 2021) and pressure from professional leagues.

Moreover, and completely central to this book, the *meanings* of threat in such unprecedented contexts remain unclear, in addition to exactly 'what' or 'whom' that were secured and how pandemics were responded to in as a safety or security threat in sporting contexts. As such, the questions asked by Rushton (2011) – 'security for whom?' and 'security from what?' – *need to* be emulated in sporting contexts. Though, social research examining the relationships between SMEs, security and pandemics remains scant. Perhaps this is related to the sentiment that 'even natural hazards appear less random than they used to' (Beck, 2006: 332) and since SMEs have been staged as planned, despite existing and overhanging threats. As stated, SME cancellations in peacetime are rare occurrences. Yet, COVID-19 significantly altered this when it caused the postponement of international mega-events and led to suspended professional leagues. The pre-existing literature predominantly mentions the apocalyptic scenario of a pandemic merely in passing, but evidently pandemics pose real and perceived security threats to SMEs, in a similar manner to 'terrorism', 'hooliganism' or 'crime'.

A decade since it was published, this section adds another significant SME issue to Giulianotti and Klauser's (2010) research agenda. That is pandemics, which are still yet to be dedicated much critical attention by researchers in a sport context. Similarly, Shipway (2018: 265) argues that there is a need for further research on natural hazards threatening events emanating 'from geological, meteorological, oceanographic, hydrological or biological causes'. This connects with those previously articulated arguments maintaining that a reading of a global health crisis can produce insights into how security is understood, provided or practiced – and how there is both 'space and [a] need for further research on the relationship between securitization and exceptionalism in the crisis politics of international organizations' (Hanrieder and Kreuder-Sonnen, 2014: 343).

More broadly, however, what has been demonstrated thus far are the intersections between 'health' and 'security' that are well established in the political science lexicon. However, in spite of this burgeoning research area, there is validity to what Nunes (2014: 943) submits: 'What lacking is an appreciation of the different meanings that "being secure" can have in the case of health'. This, again, relates to questions of to whom infectious diseases, for example, pose a threat to and to whom they might 'inspire dread' (Curley and Herington, 2011: 144). Following this, the unprecedented COVID-19 catastrophe calls for critically

102 Pandemic Threats, Covid-19 and Euro 2020's postponement

interrogating the shifting meanings of 'health, 'safety' and 'security' in a mega-event setting, whilst simultaneously disaggregating the processes of security that led to Euro 2020's dramatic postponement in the face of a pandemic emergency.

Postponement and the great collapse

The threats posed by or, indeed, the possibility of a pandemic or epidemics were never really touched upon by any of the interviewed stakeholders before February 2020. Nor did I, with an interview-guide informed by the existing literature and documentary data, ask any questions related to this. Although 'tested contingency plans' for epidemics constituted one formal requirement for Euro 2020's hosts (UEFA, n.d., S6: 9), 'epidemics' were only once mentioned in the UEFA's tournament requirements, as Chapter 2 pointed out. Pandemics were never mentioned at all, perhaps underlining the sheer uniqueness of the unfolding situation. However, speculations about a potential postponement of Euro 2020 emerged in late February and in early March 2020. Interestingly, on the day of my interview with Stakeholder 9, some media outlets had reported that Euro 2020 could be cancelled or postponed as the coronavirus spread rapidly across European countries, including Euro 2020 host countries Italy and Spain (*The Independent*, 2020a). Hence, this was the first time that I discussed, with a stakeholder, the emerging and uncertain threat of COVID-19:

JL: So, this is a question I've not been able to ask anyone else because it's so recent [...] in terms of the coronavirus. I'm not sure if you have a medical background, but how is this likely to impact, or is it likely to impact the Euros, do you think? Because I saw some statements the other day that it was being considered?

STAKEHOLDER 9: Yeah, there's been some interesting stuff in the media, hasn't it? [...] Nothing clear around it yet, suppose it'll be impacted nation by nation. There's been moves in Italy already. Inter Milan played behind closed doors yesterday, I believe?

JL: Yeah, they did.

STAKEHOLDER 9: So, there's already concerns, but how far that goes I am not too sure.

JL: Yeah, I don't think anyone knows. Not even the medical experts. So, it's very difficult obviously to speculate.

STAKEHOLDER 9: That's it. I don't know if you know, but the game between Ireland and Italy, in rugby, was postponed. So, that's interesting, that's the case.

Here, it is clear that Stakeholder 9 was aware of the situation, which had caused a postponement of a rugby match in Ireland and forced Italian domestic football to play games behind closed doors. Though, the passage above simultaneously shed a light of a gradually unfolding threat (see Domingues, 2020) and it was, simply put, difficult to know if or how the emerging virus would impact Euro 2020

Pandemic Threats, Covid-19 and Euro 2020's postponement   103

although concerns existed in late February 2020, as the stakeholder acknowledged. However, at the time of the interview, most of the major European football leagues, including the UEFA administered Champions League, were still running.

However, the next few days were characterized by uncertainty and inconsistency in how COVID-19 was responded to within elite sport. At the same time, 'country-after-country went into lockdown' whilst travelling restrictions between regions were increasingly resorted to by governments (Roberts, 2020: 618). On 5 March, *The Daily Mail* (2020a) reported that a postponement or cancellation of Euro 2020 was possible if the coronavirus escalated further. The mentioned inconsistency, meanwhile, was demonstrated by the Champions League fixtures on 10 and 11 March 2020, where some games took place behind closed doors (in Spain and France) and others – such as Liverpool versus Atletico Madrid – was staged in front of a fully crowded Anfield, in the United Kingdom. At this time, WHO also confirmed that COVID-19 was now being treated as a pandemic. As can be seen in Table 5.1, professional sport for the most part entered a lockdown mode in the days between 11 and 13 March.

These developments and WHO's confirmation of the pandemic meant that UEFA were forced to act. This related to both the ongoing Champions League and Europa League but also the upcoming Euro 2020. Thus, UEFA invited representatives and stakeholders to an emergency video-conference meeting, to be held on17 March, in order to discuss how Euro 2020 and European football more widely would respond to the outbreak (UEFA, 2020a). The following day – merely 91 days before Euro 2020's original kick off date – WHO's Director-General, Dr. Tedros Adhanom, declared that Europe had become the 'epicentre' of the pandemic (BBC, 2020).

Table 5.1 Selected competitions/events postponed in February and March 2020

Date (Reported)	Event/competition	Action
24 February	Rugby, six nations (Ireland-Italy)	Postponed
24 February	Serie A (Italy)	Closed doors
9 March	Serie A (Italy)	Suspended
10 March	Valencia-Atalanta (UCL)	Closed Doors
11 March	Manchester City-Arsenal (EPL)	Cancelled
11 March	Liverpool-Atletico Madrid (UCL)	None
11 March	PSG-Dortmund (Champions League)	Closed doors
12 March	National Basketball League (USA)	Suspended
12 March	Major League Soccer (USA)	Suspended
12 March	La Liga (Spain)	Suspended
12 March	Eredivisie (the Netherlands)	Suspended
13 March	Premier League (England)	Suspended
13 March	UEFA Europa League and Champions League	Suspended
17 March	Euro 2020	Postponed to 2021
24 March	Olympic Games 2020	Postponed to 2021

104 Pandemic Threats, Covid-19 and Euro 2020's postponement

In the four days following the news of UEFA calling an extraordinary meeting, media speculations continued apace around Euro 2020's future. A postponement was cited as a likely outcome and, for example, UEFA's Executive Member, Evelina Christellin, said that:

> I do believe it is opportune to leave time for the national leagues to conclude, postponing the Euros by a year [...] We are therefore evaluating whether to postpone Euro 2020 to next year.
>
> (quoted in Bleacher Report, 2020)

Then, on 17 March 2020, which became a defining day in the history of the Euros and in sport, *The Daily Mail* (2020b) ran the headline: 'European football unites for a HISTORIC meeting on Tuesday and the fate of Euro 2020 [...] will be decided'. And, around 12 pm on this day it was first confirmed, somewhat surprisingly, by the Norwegian FA on Twitter that Euro 2020 had been moved to the summer of 2021 (VG, 2020). Then, around 2 pm on 17 March, the marquee announcement from UEFA was published on the organization's official channels where it was confirmed that Euro 2020 had been postponed and rescheduled to the competition's new dates between 11 June and 11 July 2021 (UEFA, 2020b).

In addition to Euro 2020, *Copa America* was also postponed for one year. The importance of these decisions and this day was arguably reflected by the UEFA President's statement maintaining that COVID-19 was the 'the biggest crisis that football faced in history' (quoted in *The Daily Mirror* 2020a). The crisis required a response so extreme that it meant a European Championship was postponed for the first time in history. UEFA's decision also set the scene for the subsequent, but more time diffuse aftermath. Whilst the general public had no access to the virtual conference *per se* it may still be argued that the meeting represented a key, mediatized event under the Euro 2020 umbrella. Further, as argued elsewhere, this simultaneously speak to how COVID-19, in the eyes of sport governing bodies, went from being an abstract risk to becoming a concrete threat in the context of sport (Lee Ludvigsen, 2021) in accordance with the wider society (Domingues, 2020).

For Rosenberg (1989), epidemics are and have historically been social dramaturgic events that occur over three acts. An initial period of denial lasts until the stage where ignoration is no longer an option, and pressure is on the authorities to recognize the problem. The final act is when authorities frame the problem and publicly respond. Interestingly, one may draw distinctive parallels between Rosenberg's acts and the gradually intensifying sporting lockdown captured above, where the pressure to act increases in tact with the pandemic's intensification. Giulianotti (2019) also observes how key events and episodes in the history of football are crucial to the construction of personal and collective understandings of the sport on local, national and transnational levels. Ultimately, it is arguable that the collapse of sport, as a heavily mediatized event and responded to on social media,[2] can be understood as a defining, social drama *within* an even larger dramaturgy (that is, the pandemic on a 'general' level) which, following Roche

(2003), has the potential to work as a time-structuring reference point through its occurrence within the 'mesosocial sphere'.[3]

Hence, if one revisits the pre-event securitization *timeline* of Euro 2020, which begins with the decision to award the hosting rights to 12 countries in 2014, the postponement caused by COVID-19 arguably demonstrated *the* main 'security event' in Euro 2020's context and the sociological making of this very event. Faced with a threat so uncontrollable and generational, the only justifiable option in terms of health and safety was to postpone Euro 2020. Consequently, this multifaceted stage in the event's securitization process raises a number of questions that will be addressed next. This includes what exactly 'threat' meant in this context and the practical implications of COVID-19 as a 'threat' and who ultimately needed protection from COVID-19.

Security and safety from what?

This section calls into question exactly what was diagnostically framed, by sport bodies and key actors, as representing a safety or security threat. It does so in the context of UEFA's 12-month postponement of Euro 2020 following the COVID-19 outbreak, at a time where European football, similarly to many European countries, was in a state of lockdown. The question orienting this section thus is 'security from what?' (see Rushton, 2011). Here, the logical and most obvious answer to such question is COVID-19. However, such an answer provides no deeper nor critical meaning and reveals none of the practical implications of COVID-19 as a so crucial threat to health, safety and security that Euro 2020 could not proceed as envisaged.

As argued, the threat – in the sheer epidemiological meaning of COVID-19 – was a faceless, non-discriminatory and rapidly spreading *virus*, which again caused an *infectious disease*. Whilst this accords the argument that 'the health threats most suitable for securitization are outbreaks of infectious diseases' (Enemark, 2007: 8), the virus and the infectious disease caused by it also resulted in an exceptionally uncertain period of *'crisis'* that, in itself, also emerged as a COVID-19 induced threat, as the 'network of relations' constituting the pandemic (Thacker, 2009). 'Crisis' then refers to 'a serious threat to the basic structures or the fundamental values and norms, which under time pressure and highly uncertain circumstances necessitates making vital decisions' (Rosenthal et al., 1989: 10). I argue that COVID-19, as it was framed, represented a threefold threat in forms of a virus, a disease *and* a crisis. The broader implications of this relate to the anthropomorphic element of such a threat. Since the coronavirus spreads predominantly through human-to-human contact, this effectively means that individuals infected by, or carrying, the virus, or even displaying symptoms, represented potential threats rather than victims or 'objects of compassion' (Wallis and Nerlich, 2005: 2635).

It may be to state the obvious that what threatened Euro 2020 and the wider sporting world in the spring/summer of 2020 – as with the rest of the world – was

106 Pandemic Threats, Covid-19 and Euro 2020's postponement

a pandemic infectious disease. Further, in the period of highest relevance here – between January 2020 and June 2020 – no medicines or vaccines existed yet, which could protect against COVID-19 or offer immunity. As Roberts (2020: 625) writes, '[w]hen, if ever, there would be an effective vaccine and treatment for Covid-19 was unknown'.[4] In the emerging official statements, it was the *virus*, as the infectious, 'faceless' agent that posed the main threat to 'health' and 'safety'. Some statements, however, also illuminated the realities of the social construction of a global crisis as a threat produced by the virus, as the virus threatened not merely individuals' health, but socio-economic elements of sport and wider structures.

Throughout, the threat was commonly referred to as 'exceptional', 'unprecedented', 'unexpected' and as comprising a 'crisis' or 'emergency' where '"business as usual" [would] not suffice and extraordinary measures [were] required' (Kamradt-Scott and McInnes, 2012: 96). For instance, in an interview statement from UEFA President, Aleksander Čeferin, this becomes evident:

> I would say [COVID-19] is the biggest crisis that football faced in history [...] We all know that this terrible virus that is all across Europe made football and all life in Europe quite impossible. We knew we have to stop the competitions.
>
> (quoted in *The Daily Mirror*, 2020a)

Here the 'threat', according to Čeferin, is the 'terrible virus'. The 'terrible virus' caused what is referred to as the 'biggest crisis' in the sport's history, whose unclear impacts had to be secured from as a threat to Euro 2020, European football and, more broadly, 'all life in Europe'. Thus, the 'threatening' elements here refer to both the 'virus' and the related 'crisis' impacting public life. In a different statement on UEFA's official channels, Čeferin again described the situation as a 'crisis' caused by the 'invisible' but rapidly spreading virus (UEFA, 2020b).

Indeed, the rapid spread of viruses is one of those time and space characteristics that have led to a 'clearer recognition of the threats posed by disease in a globalised world' (Rushton, 2011: 779). In a way, this contributed to the severity and urgency and legitimized the implementation of exceptional measures ('stop the competitions') which represented a break away from the normal procedures. These dimensions are significant here, as they underline and connect the transnational scope and speedy nature of the *virus* (SARS-CoV-2) which causes the *infectious disease* (COVID-19) and ultimately the *general crisis* which, in itself, formed a situation with 'limited but unknown duration in which some form of harm or damage is in the midst of emerging' (Adey et al., 2015: 5). Not too dissimilarly, a statement by the then European Club Association (ECA) chairman and UEFA ExCo member, Andrea Agnelli, also reflects this:

> Europe is facing its biggest challenge in a generation, one which is impacting all levels of society including football. The challenge to our game is massive

and as leaders we have a responsibility to do all we can to protect its long-term well-being by mitigating the impact of the virus.

(quoted in ECA, 2020)

Again, one can observe how the virus is diagnosed as the 'threat' causing another larger ('generational') challenge and crisis that is characterized by uncertainty. Hence, the pandemic characterized by an inherent unpredictability gave life to a crisis situation that, similarly, was inherently unpredictable. This threefold and extremely powerful uncertainty – caused by the (i) virus, (ii) the infectious disease and (iii) their unprecedented impacts on 'health', 'safety' and the society, whilst representing 'threats' in themselves, also composed a collectively accumulated 'threat' that made the postponement of Euro 2020 the only 'real' and justifiable option. As Gabriele Gravina, the President of Italy's Football Federation, as one of Euro 2020's hosts, said: 'nobody ever expected to face an emergency like this' (quoted in *The Daily Mirror*, 2020b). Furthermore, Gianni Infantino, President of FIFA, as football's governing body, also spoke of a 'crisis' and an 'exceptional situation' that required exceptional measures (FIFA, 2020a). The framing of the pandemic emergency as the cause of a larger crisis is again evident. UEFA also repeatedly referred to the crisis caused by COVID-19 as a 'global health crisis' and an 'unsettling, challenging and unprecedented situation' (UEFA, 2020b).

The 'virus' was therefore framed as incompatible with basic notions of public safety – which event organizers are obliged to provide (Roche, 2017). Collectively, these discourses provide insights into what threat meant or referred to in the context of European football and Euro 2020 more specifically. The intrinsic meanings of the threats framed throughout spoke to the novel, fast-spreading coronavirus and COVID-19, as a contagious disease in itself. But more broadly, the subsequent and unprecedented crisis *caused by* the virus was also a threat.

There are several implications of this argument. Firstly, the statements capture what Beck (1987: 158) called a 'fully uncomprehended emergency-scientization of everyday life'. As Čeferin said, 'Nobody knows when the pandemic will end' (quoted in *Sky Sports*, 2020a). Thus, the threat's temporal limits and true extent were unknown upon framing the threat. Secondly, it is clear that what comprised a threat in this context 'began' from a virus. An etiological agent that causes human fatalities and new risks to human life, a coronavirus that does not respect the 'established societal divisions' (Beck, 1987: 158). Within a globalization frame, this subsequently meant that a majority of human beings were susceptible to being infected, effectively causing universal vulnerability. This served to amplify the pandemic's disruptive potential.

By importing this into a mega-event setting, events may as mentioned operate both as amplifiers and disseminators of infectious diseases (Dickmann, 2013). Yet, the virus amplifications or disseminations are *not* restricted to the sporting context. Particularly so, when the event would be organized under such extraordinary geographical conditions as Euro 2020 was planned within. This again meant that *if* Euro 2020 – expecting an influx of more than 2.5 million spectators across

12 countries (*The Daily Mail*, 2020a) – was staged as planned, this could have extended the already unprecedented crisis that was so frequently framed by key actors. Further, with mass gatherings posing a basic obstacle to social distancing (Memish et al., 2020), the architectural (i.e., stadium seats immediately next to each other, concealed fan zones) and physical dimensions (mass gatherings, football as a 'contact sport', hugging, celebrating, handshakes) embedded into SMEs, coupled with the geographies of Euro 2020 and the fact that COVID-19 peaked at different times in different countries meant that there is a strong case for holding, as Parnell et al. (2020) write that Euro 2020, if staged as planned, could have intensified the spread of COVID-19 both by amplifying and disseminating COVID-19. Such real concerns also emerged during and following Euro 2020 in 2021 (see Chapter 6).

Naturally, for most SMEs originally scheduled to take place in 2020, this meant a fundamental shift and a reconfiguration of what 'security' could look like. This relates back to the mentioned shift from *endemic threats* addressed pre-event towards the sudden *epidemic threat*. A move away from the 'absence' of the 'usual suspects' of 'terrorists', 'criminals' and 'hooligans', towards a wholly unexpected and unpredictable 'suspect': an infectious disease threat and the associated coronavirus-related global crisis. Therefore, one answer to the 'security from what?'-question is the potential lethal, damaging and disruptive consequences on individuals' health and the socio-economic disruptions that were caused by a rapidly spreading, non-discriminatory infectious disease which crowded events could intensify *if* staged.

Unpacking the 'invisible enemy'

By operationalizing the framing of the COVID-19, there are some important broader implications, perhaps less visible or less signposted in the discourse. Since the virus, in itself, represented an 'invisible enemy' (Domingues, 2020) – as a sub-microscopic infectious agent – this implies that individuals infected by or displaying symptoms of COVID-19 simultaneously could represent a threat that non-infected individuals had to be secured from. Fundamentally, the contagious virus is transmitted through respiratory droplets and *human* contact. In the overarching pandemic context, *people* therefore automatically became a 'threat' to *other people*, as the damage caused by the virus and disease co-depended on human-to-human transmission and proximity. As aforementioned, but extremely important here, SMEs attract enormous groups of *people* to their stadia, fan zones and host cities. By their nature, SMEs are social events (Roche, 2000). In such context, Michel Foucault's (2008 [1977]) writings on the plague may be borrowed and meaningfully applied. For Foucault, the plague induced a carnivalesque festival of transgression:

> A whole literary fiction of the festival grew up around the plague: suspended laws, lifted prohibitions, the frenzy of passing time, *bodies mingling together*

without respect, individuals unmasked, abandoning their statutory identity and the figure under which they had been recognized, allowing a quite different truth to appear. (ibid.: 3, emphasis added)

However, as Foucault warned and reminded us, discipline emerges as the antidote to this celebratory festival, exemplifying his ideas holding that plagues were historically defining moments in which new mechanisms of state power were developed:

> [T]here was also a political dream of the plague, which was exactly its reverse: not the collective festival, but strict division; not laws transgressed, but the penetration of regulation into even the smallest details of everyday life [...] not masks that were put on and taken off, but the assignment to each individual of his "true" name, his "true" place, his "true" body, his "true" disease. (ibid.)

The context of COVID-19 complicates Foucault's account, since this sense of liberation, apparent in his notion of the festival, did not emerge on a general level nor blend in with the carnivalesque festivities of a mega-event until Euro 2020's commencement one year later (see Chapter 6). The 'absence' of a festival in June 2020 relates to the argument of *people* as threats to other *people*. The nature of the new coronavirus blurred the *virus free/virus carrier* dichotomy to a degree where the immediate epidemic legacy was no collective festival of mingling, but rather new forms of power, extreme regulation and new meanings of 'security'.

What occurs here is that infected individuals become 'carriers' or 'cases' – and subsequently 'a danger' to others, rather than victims of an infectious disease requiring concern and affection, which they – of course – concurrently are (Wallis and Nerlich, 2005). As Thacker (2009: 143) highlights, '[t]he strange form of life that is the epidemic is at once the life that must be secured, and the life that must be secured against'. Following Foucault (2008 [1977]), the risk is thus that the regulatory mechanisms through which COVID-19 was responded to give rise to disciplinary projects and the development of new exclusionary forms of biopower acquired through the surveillance of individuals' health and bodies. Consequently, this may demonstrate the problem of 'correlation between the technique of security and the population as at once object and subject of these security mechanisms' (Foucault, 2004: 13). Indeed, such biopolitical element connects with one of the warned pitfalls and counterproductive risks related to the securitization of pandemics. Potentially this may 'create a space where individuals are seen as the enemy rather than the pathogens that affect them' (O'Manique and Fourie, 2009: 250) and where '[a]nything and everything is "sick" or can actually or potentially make one "sick" – quite independently of how a person actually feels' (Beck, 1992: 205).

Consequently, the meanings of desired 'undisrupted' or 'clean' environments change too. Instead of referring to environments free for non-official brands, rival products or 'undesirable' behaviours (Eisenhauer et al., 2014), 'clean environments' instead became – between January and June 2020 – synonymous with events and stadia without *people*. As Lars-Christer Olsson, the President of European Leagues and active in UEFA's emergency working group said, in regard to the resumption of European football, this resumption could take place in a 'clean environment' without spectators (quoted in *The Times*, 2020).

Still, however, what *remained* present within these cleansed and hermetically sealed off spaces – such as 'behind closed doors' games – was the visibility of official brands and partners, whose presence is rather unaffected. If anything, these spaces, 'themed with the brand decor of the event', (Eisenhauer, 2013: 35) are increasingly centralized and broadcasted globally in the absence of people or 'disruptive' elements. The pandemic threat thus reconfigured the meanings of 'safety' and 'security' in the SME context – and potentially in sport in a post-pandemic world – and 'virus carriers', whilst serving as a warning of the failures or limitations of securitization, further provided a human face to the 'faceless' virus and thereby 'threatened' other, non-infected individuals and populations.

The repeatedly framed virus almost becomes anthropomorphized as it infects (or is *believed* to infect) a 'human host' (Thacker, 2009), and this results in numerous security risks being signified through humans, which again results in draconian and regulatory measures and the wider securitization of freedom of movement through, for example, travel bans, quarantines or curfews. Ultimately, it also resulted in mega-event postponement to minimize the pathogen spread. This is significant and adds another layer to this book's earlier arguments. Namely, that mega-event threats are fluid, contextual and subject to change according to spatial conditions. Whilst they still are, COVID-19 notwithstanding demonstrated that individuals' medical conditions and symptoms also influence this and to what extent one is a threat *to* 'security' or in need *for* 'security'. As such, to restrict the damage of COVID-19, event postponement mitigated the threat of infected individuals transmitting the virus onto individuals lacking immunity in the stadia, fan zones and when returning to their home communities. Hence, it simultaneously served to limit the threefold framed threats of the virus, the disease and the crisis.

Whilst every mega-event is faced with a novel set of 'knowns' and 'unknowns' (cf. Horne, 2007), what was *known* was that sport would not be exempt from the wider disease-related crisis. Importantly, since the rapidly spreading virus constituted an 'invisible enemy' (Domingues, 2020), this meant that the 'visible' or human element of this threat – in form of individuals that were infected or carrying symptoms – was 'secured against' as a 'threat'. In fact, it actually also came to encompass 'those who were not unwell but were suspected nevertheless of having been in contact with the "virus carrier" and having not yet developed symptoms' (Bigo et al., 2021: 5). Hence, in answering the overarching questions in this section of 'whom that composed a threat?' or 'security from what?', this was the virus, infectious disease and crisis, which collectively comprised the COVID-19 threat.

Pandemic Threats, Covid-19 and Euro 2020's postponement 111

In praxis, however, this meant that people *with or without* the virus constituted a threat so exceptional that it induced a historical event postponement.

Security and safety for whom?

Having engaged in a critical discussion of the meanings of threat in the face of the global COVID-19 outbreak, I will now meaningfully address what emerges as a natural follow-up question. That is to 'whom' or 'what' COVID-19 – as a virus, disease and global crisis – posed a threat to in Euro 2020's context, as referent objects of security and safety. This is particularly important to address because any '[a]ttempts to securitise global health discourses involve the securitisation of multiple and possibly competing referent objects' (Curley and Herington, 2011: 162). The advanced argument here is twofold, but must be understood in the context of COVID-19's global nature and how 'health' reinforces or intersects with 'safety' and 'security' (Elbe, 2011; Rushton, 2011). 'Health' and 'security' do not equate. Yet, neither are they mutually isolated. As mentioned, for some critical security scholars, health can be fundamental to the objective and subjective conditions of security and therefore paramount to include in security thinking (Booth, 2007; Nunes, 2014).

As argued here, Euro 2020's postponement was predominantly framed in the name of 'health', 'safety' and 'security' for a loosely defined 'football community' and, more broadly, for the 'general public', both of whom had to be protected from COVID-19. Notwithstanding, the evidence also allows for arguing that states' services, stability and infrastructures required levels of protection. Indeed, one of the reasons behind Euro 2020's postponement was, partly, to avoid any unnecessary or extra pressure on national public services (UEFA, 2020b).

With an inward facing extremity threat, 'health' and 'safety' were articulated primarily with reference to the welfare of *individuals* and to a lesser degree *state objects*. Furthermore, the framing of 'safety' would often be accompanied by a precautionary-action lauding 'safety first' sentiment that repeatedly came to fore. The 'safety first' frame endorses pre-emptive emergency responses which prioritize 'health' and 'safety', whilst simultaneously downplaying the importance of sport when juxtaposed to supposedly 'larger' global issues (Lee Ludvigsen and Millward, 2020).

The individual 'safety first' framing was demonstrated by UEFA's coined term, 'purpose over profit', which was the organization's 'guiding principle in taking [the] decision [to postpone] for the good of European football as a whole' (UEFA, 2020b). This implies that 'purpose' – as the protection and priority given to fans, players and staff (Parnell and Widdop, 2020) – outscored 'profit', which would have been synonymous with allowing sporting competitions to proceed as planned, considering the financial losses associated with postponement. As Čeferin acknowledged, moving Euro 2020 to 2021 came at 'a huge cost' for UEFA (2020b), and accordingly the postponement came at an estimated financial cost of €300 million (Parnell et al., 2021: 21).

Prior to this, a postponement was publicly called for. Gabriele Gravina called for 'an act of responsibility and a contribution to all Federations to a path that aims for the safeguard of the health of all athletes, fans and citizens of the world' (quoted in *Sky Sports*, 2020b). In the wider football world, FIFA President Gianni Infantino stated that: 'People's health is much more important than any game' (quoted in *The Daily Mail*, 2020c). Already here, one may spot the references to a vaguely defined 'football community' ('athletes' and 'fans') and the 'general public' ('citizens of the world'). Moreover, FIFA (2020a) urged for the avoidance of 'unnecessary health risks' to players and the general public.

Similarly, when the much-anticipated decision concerning Euro 2020's future was announced, the postponement statement from UEFA (2020b) emphasized the protection of health and national public services amidst the COVID-19 catastrophe. As Čeferin said, 'The health of fans, staff and players has to be our number one priority' (quoted UEFA, 2020b). At face value, the statements reveal two distinctive referent objects central to this section. First, and predominantly, that is individuals (i.e., 'fans, staff and players') whose health had to be – and was made – the 'number one priority'. Thus, on an individual level, COVID-19 was framed as a threat that individuals had to be secured or protected from. Second, it can be seen that the state, as a broad referent object, is not completely absent above. As highlighted, the states' services ('national public services') that, if subjected to the pressure of a mega-event, could seemingly impact the states' stability, economy and infrastructures (Davies, 2008). Although the latter framing was less frequent, it still remained extremely important, because this was one of the outlined reasons in UEFA's postponement announcement.

National public services in Euro 2020 countries were therefore also outlined as in need for protection. This must be viewed in context of the timing of the postponement. At the time, numerous national public services already faced large challenges related to hospital admissions caused by COVID-19 (Memish et al., 2020; Parnell et al., 2020). Additionally, even in non-pandemic times, mega-events place significant burdens on host countries' public services. Hence, the rapidly spreading coronavirus, transcending transnational borders, posed a threat to the welfare of individuals and state services. These frames will be further unpacked, but this demonstrates the *duality* of pandemics threats. Whilst primarily affecting 'communities of individuals with little reference to the political borders which contain them' (Curley and Herington, 2011: 141), the state still remains the chief provider of public health capacities and is the 'most significant actor within the political arena of global public health protection' (ibid.: 142).

In several of the responses to UEFA's decision to postpone Euro 2020, the need to ensure 'healthy' and 'safe' solutions for fans, athletes and staff, *and* the general public is documented. For example, the Interim CEO of the Irish FA, Gary Owens, declared that 'UEFA has made the right decision today in the interests of the health and well-being of football players, fans and staff alike' (quoted in *The Independent*, 2020b). Similarly, the CEO of the English FA, Mark Bullingham, stated that: 'People's health and well-being has to be the primary concern for

Pandemic Threats, Covid-19 and Euro 2020's postponement   113

us all, so we fully support UEFA's decision to postpone Euro 2020' (quoted in *The Independent*, 2020c). Meanwhile, SD Europe (2020) announced that: 'We agree that football is quite simply not a priority over the health of fans, players and other professionals working in the European game, nor the population as a whole'. UEFA also announced a resolution related to the coordinated response to the impact of COVID-19 on competitions, signed by UEFA, the European Club Association, European Leagues and FIFPRO Europe. Here, the four organizations emphasized their 'fundamental commitment to protecting the health, safety, and well-being of players, clubs, supporters, officials, staff and the broader football community' (UEFA, 2020c).

Evidently, these statements were composed of the repeated and uniform framing of individuals' 'health' and 'safety' as the main orientation point in the decision-making when faced by the pandemic. Interestingly, this refers to the 'health' and 'safety' of individuals within what may be characterized as a loosely defined 'football community'. The exact members of this constructed 'community' seemed – at least tentatively – to be players, staff and others connected to the sport in a professional capacity. However, these are also members of the frequently framed 'general public', which also needed protection. Yet, whilst the 'football community' fits under the umbrella of the 'general public', not all individuals in the 'general public' would consider themselves or be considered a part of the discursively framed 'football community'. What can be extracted from the above discourses is the *externalization of threat* (Curley and Herington, 2011). Seemingly, the emphasis is not merely on the 'safety' required for the 'football community' or sporting context, but extended beyond this, to encompass and refer to the 'general public'.

Despite this, the overlap of the two remains central here, because the nature of the pathogen threat ultimately did not distinguish and could spread between the 'football community' and the 'general public'. Hence, sport governing bodies' decisions to postpone events were not solely made in the name of the safety for fans and competing athletes. This relates back to mega-events as amplifiers and disseminators of diseases For example, if attendees (or other members of the 'football community') travelled back to their home communities and hypothetically spread the pathogen to the general public there (Dickmann, 2013). Hence, amidst the attempts to distinguish between sports-based and *non*-sports-based populations, these distinctions are in fact weakened when faced with a global pandemic, as the groups essentially were composed of many of the same individuals sharing a mutual need for security and safety from the same threat. The sport governing bodies' articulated need to protect both sporting communities *and* the externalized general public, through discursive exercises, should therefore be understood as related to the fundamental intersection between individuals in sport – comprising the socially constructed football world (see Parnell et al., 2021) – and the wider society. In practical terms, disconnecting the two is unworkable.

Furthermore, one important dimension that is evident in the framed statements above is how the statements visibly provide assessments of the decision to postpone Euro 2020. Such assessments are seemingly oriented by a prioritization process:

individuals' health/safety *versus* allowing the event to be staged. One implication of this is the aforementioned 'safety first' frame that became apparent in statements. This frame was initially developed in an earlier study that examined how fans responded to emerging security threats (Lee Ludvigsen and Millward, 2020). Notwithstanding, the remarkable dimension enriching the 'safety first' frame here is that such sentiment was articulated by stakeholders in the mentioned football world and by key actors situated within sports' governing bodies.

The 'safety first' logic is characterized by a sentimental attitude maintaining that priority *has to be* given to resolving supposedly 'larger' issue at stake in the society (i.e., a pandemic), than what sports represent (ibid.). Interestingly, such sentiment touches the surface of the ideological criticisms of sport by Umberto Eco (1986) and Noam Chomsky (1983, 2004). Broadly, their critiques of sports' position in society maintain that sport work as a sociopolitical distraction that absorbs attention that could have been dedicated to more pressing issues.[5] In part, the 'safety first' frame underscores this: sport must, unquestionably, evade for 'real' issues that 'really' matter. In a crisis, sacrificing a sporting competition (i.e., by postponing it) thus becomes a matter of course and a minor price to pay when concretely or hypothetically juxtaposed to notions of individuals' 'health' and 'safety'. This comes to fore again in the below statements:

> In this dramatic moment, the most important thing is people's health and getting out of this crisis.
>
> (Čeferin quoted in *The Telegraph*, 2020)

> In light of the current Covid-19 outbreak, UEFA have now taken the decision to postpone the Men's EURO tournament to 2021. While this will come as disappointing news to many, the health of fans, players, officials and the general public must be the priority [...] The safety of the public will always come first.
>
> (The Mayor of London, 2020)

Again, these statements collectively demonstrate a series of sociologically relevant aspects. Firstly, they again underline how the football world and its wider societal context became increasingly inseparable when faced by a threat that, as already discussed, did not distinguish between sports and *non-sports* settings. Repeatedly, in the responses to COVID-19, 'health' and 'safety' are framed both in sporting terms and in terms of the 'general public'. Secondly, the above statements reinforce how a precautionary decision justified in terms of 'health' and 'safety', exemplified by the decision to *postpone*, was uniformly agreed-upon and endorsed by key actors and sports bodies reacting to UEFA's decision. Simultaneously, this reveals how a *cancellation* of the event – or making the 'Euros' 'null and void' – in the name of 'safety' – was not called for; it is the postponement that is commended.

This, again, suggests that even in spite of a pandemic, Euro 2020 as a mega-event was not merely an insignificant distraction that easily could be erased (cf. Eco, 1986;

Chomsky, 2004) without complications. Instead, conditions for a flexible rescheduling process permitting secure conditions were facilitated. Furthermore, in the context of sports' neoliberal hyper-commodification (Giulianotti, 2002), a full-scale cancellation could have translated into additional financial losses from lost sponsorship, broadcasting and match-day revenues. In that sense, the idea of 'safety first' does not equate with a full-scale abandonment of original intensions or sports-related interests. Whereas this extends and presents an important revision to the 'safety first' argument – that key stakeholders, seemingly, preferred a postponement over cancellation – the section has demonstrated how health and safety for individuals were not merely repeatedly referred to, but discursively framed as the only justifiable and logical option to prioritize, in an uncertain period and in line with medical practitioners' recommendations (Corsini et al., 2020; Memish et al., 2020).

Finally, having engaged with the key question, 'security for whom?', it is possible to draw some comparisons with Chapter 2, which asked a similar question based on a critical analysis of pre-event policy documents. There are, however, certain limitations to such comparisons, since COVID-19 was completely unexpected and unprecedented. Whereas those in need for protection from security and safety threats did not change significantly and, as such, represent a degree of correspondence – despite the completely unexpected pandemic threat – it can be seen that the 'football community's' and the public's *health* primarily was what required protection. Faced with the pandemic threat, 'health' served as a more prominent contributing condition to notions of 'safety' and 'security', than in pre-planning documents. Thacker (2009: 138–139) argues that epidemics are always 'against the people' and something 'held in common'. This can be seen in light of COVID-19, as the 'general public' – or the 'citizens of the world' (Gravina quoted in *Sky Sports*, 2020b) – were framed as in need for 'safety' more regularly on a global level, rather than solely the individuals expected to be present in Euro 2020's host cities. This also connects with the aforementioned global nature of the COVID-19 crisis and that the pandemic, seemingly, was approached by sport governing bodies as a matter of global public health and not merely a sporting-specific or event-specific threat restricted to the football world.

Securitization processes are contextual. Security-related discourses therefore reveal referent objects that are unique to the context they are articulated in and the audiences they are articulated to (Curley and Herington, 2011). Consequently, it is argued that that when faced with an unprecedented and rapidly intensifying threat, key stakeholders and sports' governing bodies framed 'health', 'safety' and 'security' predominantly in reference to individuals' welfare. That is not to say that the security of nation states was completely eschewed from the discourses, because over-stretched national services, and thus potential state instability, were outlined as in need for protection in the event owner's justification to move the competition. In the realm of sport, the 'health' and 'safety' of a loosely defined 'football community' and an externalized referent in form of the general public ultimately had to be prioritized – or *come first*.

Conclusion: From endemic to epidemic threats

In the context of the rapidly spreading and infectious coronavirus that sent shockwaves through the world in the early days of 2020, this chapter argues that this marked a profound shift from endemic threats towards an epidemic security and safety threat in the world of SMEs. And further, that this exact shift as situated in the domain of mega-events simultaneously is illustrative of the wider global impacts of COVID-19 in many areas of social life and security contexts. In March 2020, Euro 2020 was postponed by UEFA over health and safety concerns as the COVID-19 public health crisis 'brought about unprecedented changes' and unsettled 'multiple facets of our existence' (Matthewman and Huppatz, 2020: 676). The decision to postpone, the build-up leading to this decision and its aftermath consequently marked highly significant and dramatic moments. Not merely in the over 60-year long history of the European Championships in football, but more generally in the universe of global sport. As contended, Euro 2020 offers a lens through which we may understand the unfolding threat of COVID-19 in the early stages of the pandemic. Furthermore, just like Euro 2020, other mega-events including the Tokyo 2020 Olympics and the 2020 *Copa América* were also forced into postponement in March 2020, as the world of sport mirrored the rest of the world and entered modes of lockdown (Tovar, 2021).

In the context of the catastrophic COVID-19 pandemic, this chapter has discussed the powerful nexus between 'health' and 'security'. In modern societies, I argue, pandemics and infectious diseases may be approached as threats to the safety and security of states and individuals. When brought together with Chapters 1–4, what can be extracted from this chapter is a shift in the meanings, logics and basic management of mega-event security. For example, Chapters 3 and 4 spoke primarily to the activities, policies and processes assisting the pre-planning for what/whom – for the purpose of this discussion – may be called endemic threats. Whilst potentially damaging, these threats, such as 'terrorism' or 'hooliganism', are more regular and *endemic* within and across the mega-event landscapes, where they possess historical relations through previous incidents (Cleland, 2019; Stott, 2003). Indeed, they are defined by certain tempo-spatial limits and whilst unpredictable, *some* lessons and knowledge on how to secure against these exist. Synthesized with the previous chapters, this chapter therefore captures the shift from *endemic* threats towards an *epidemic* threat – that is COVID-19 – characterized by an exceptional moment as it transpired. However, this epidemic threat is more faceless, invisible, marked by a temporal suddenness, spatial diffuseness and completely novel. Ultimately, COVID-19 transpired as a 'truly seismic shock' (Mazey and Richardson, 2020: 561). It also revealed new, overlapping security threats and referent objects and required new extraordinary responses and saw the securitization of public health thoroughly embedded into mega-event-related discourses. This is important because it accurately demonstrates how the meanings of 'security' at football mega-events are not merely subject to change (Chapter 2). Indeed, this chapter evidences exactly how the meanings of security change in relation to external, catastrophic events like a pandemic. This will naturally be elaborated upon further in the next chapter, which locates new trends and COVID-19-related security processes that emerged as Euro 2020's new dates approaches and, eventually, was delivered in front of fans in 11 European countries, whilst the pandemic was still ongoing and had entered new phases, despite the WHO's grave concerns (Reuters, 2021).

Finally, another dimension to this chapter's arguments, enhancing its social scientific value, is its potential to act as a preliminary base and provide some foundations for future interdisciplinary conversations between the sociology of sport and critical security studies. Over a decade ago, Booth (2007: 458) argued that 'global health is one of today's battlegrounds, and one of tomorrow's subject areas in security studies'. Such argument can now be replicated in many sociological and political fields in what will represent the 'post-pandemic' epoch. It can confidently be exported into the study of mega-events, and it seems likely that COVID-19's impact on sport and societies will formulate a key area of research enquiry the next decade. Such responsiveness is highly necessary however. Before COVID-19, limited research existed on the threats of infectious diseases to mega-events. This is related to the fact that generational crises like COVID-19, fortunately, are extremely rare occurrences. Notwithstanding, mega-events have been disrupted by infectious diseases even 'pre-COVID'. This adds substantial weight to the importance of responsively, responsibly and critically analyzing such catastrophic and shocking events when they do occur. Indeed, no one knows for certain exactly when a pandemic will next disrupt all human and social life. However, the consensus seems to be that this is a question of 'when?' rather than 'what if?' and that the football world will not be exempt.

Notes

1 For example, Euro 2020 host, Spain, declared a 15-day state of emergency in March 2020. Meanwhile, Switzerland – where UEFA and FIFA have their headquarters – declared a state of emergency on 16 March.
2 For example, to collate the enormous masses of reactions to COVID-19's impact on sports, certain media outlets had dedicated 'live blogs' that were updated continuously with the latest coronavirus news in sports.
3 This refers to 'the intermediary sphere through which the life world, and its "microsocial" processes, is connected with "macrosocial" systems' (Roche, 2003: 100).
4 In March 2020, it was believed that vaccines could be between 12 and 18 months away from availability.
5 For example, Eco (1986: 186) linked football 'with the absence of purpose and the vanity of all things'. Chomsky (2004: 100) meanwhile observes how sport divert the masses – or sport fans – away 'from things that really matter'.

Bibliography

Adey, P & Anderson, B (2012) Anticipating Emergencies: Technologies of Preparedness and the Matter of Security. *Security Dialogue* 43(2), 99–117.

Adey, P, Anderson, B & Graham, S (2015) Introduction: Governing Emergencies: Beyond Exceptionality. *Theory, Culture & Society* 32(2), 3–17.

Bar-On, T (2017) *Beyond Soccer: International Relations and Politics as Seen through the Beautiful Game.* Maryland. Rowman & Littlefield.

BBC (2020) Coronavirus: Europe Now Epicentre of the Pandemic, Says WHO. Available from: https://www.bbc.co.uk/news/world-europe-51876784 (Accessed 2 April 2020).

Beck, U (1987) The Anthropological Shock: Chernobyl and the Contours of Risk Society. *Berkeley Journal of Sociology* 32, 153–165.

Beck, U (1992) *Risk Society: Towards a New Modernity.* London. Sage.

Beck, U (2006) Living in the World Risk Society: A Hobhouse Memorial Public Lecture Given on Wednesday 15 February 2006 at the London School of Economics. *Economy and Society* 35(3), 329–345.

Bigo, D, Guild, E & Kuskonmaz, EM (2021) Obedience in Times of COVID-19 Pandemics: A Renewed Governmentality of Unease? *Global Discourse* 11(1–2), 1–2.

Bleacher Report (2020) UEFA "Evaluating" Whether to Postpone Euro 2020 because of the Coronavirus. Available from: https://bleacherreport.com/articles/2880916-uefa-evaluating-whether-to-postpone-euro-2020-because-of-coronavirus (Accessed 3 April 2020).

Booth, K (2007) *Theory of World Security.* New York. Cambridge University Press.

Boyle, P & Haggerty, KD (2012) Planning for the Worst: Risk, Uncertainty and the Olympic Games. *British Journal of Sociology* 63(2), 241–259.

Buzan, B, Wæver, O & de Wilde, J (1998) *Security: A New Framework for Analysis.* London. Lynne Rienner Publishers.

Chomsky, N (1983) What the World Is Really Like: Who Knows It – and Why. In P. Mitchell & J. Schoeffel (eds) *The Chomsky Reader.* London. Vintage.

Chomsky, N (2004) Spectator Sports. In P. Mitchell & J. Schoeffel (eds) *The Indispensable Chomsky.* London. Vintage.

Cleland, J (2019) Sports Fandom in the Risk Society: Analyzing Perceptions an Experiences of Risk, Security and Terrorism at Elite Sports Events. *Sociology of Sport Journal* 36(2), 144–151.

Corsini, A, Bisciotti, GN & Eirale, C, et al. (2020) Football Cannot Restart Soon During the COVID-19 Emergency! A Critical Perspective from the Italian Experience and a Call for Action. *British Journal of Sports Medicine* 54(20), 1083–1187.

Curley, M & Herington, J (2011) The Securitisation of Avian Influenza: International Discourses and Domestic Politics in Asia. *Review of International Studies* 37(1), 141–166.

Davies, S (2008) Securitizing Infectious Disease. *International Affairs* 84(2), 295–313.

Dickmann, P (2013) Mitigating the Impact of Infectious Diseases at Sporting Events. *ICSS Journal* 1(1), 81–87.

Domingues, JM (2020) From Global Risk to Global Threat: State Capabilities and Modernity in Times of Coronavirus. *Current Sociology*, 1–18.

Duarte, D & Valença, M (2021) Securitising Covid-19? The Politics of Global Health and the Limits of the Copenhagen School. *Contexto Internacional* 43(2), 235–257.

ECA (2020) ECA Executive Board Supports Decision to Postpone UEFA EURO 2020. Available from: https://www.ecaeurope.com/news/eca-executive-board-supports-decision-to-postpone-uefa-euro-2020/ (Accessed 27 May 2020).

Eco, U (1986) *Faith in Fakes: Travels in Hyperreality.* London. Random House.

Eisenhauer, S (2013) *Managing Event Places and Viewer Spaces: Security, Surveillance and Stakeholder Interests at the 2010 FIFA World Cup in South Africa.* PhD thesis. University of Technology Sydney.

Eisenhauer, S, Adair, D & Taylor, T (2014) FIFA-isation: Spatial Security, Sponsor Protection and Media Management at the 2010 World Cup. *Surveillance & Society* 11(4), 377–391.

Elbe, S (2011) Pandemics on the Radar Screen: Health Security, Infectious Disease and the Medicalisation of Insecurity'. *Political Studies* 59(4), 848–866.

Elbe, S, Roemer-Mahler, A & Long, C (2014) Securing Circulation Pharmaceutically: Antiviral Stockpiling and Pandemic Preparedness in the European Union. *Security Dialogue* 45(5), 440–457.

Enemark, C (2007) *Disease and Security: Natural Plagues and Biological Weapons in East Asia.* London. Routledge.

FIFA (2020a) FIFA Statement 13 Mar 2020. Available from: https://www.fifa.com/who-we-are/news/fifa-statement-x8681 (Accessed 27 March 2020).

Foucault, M (2004) *Sécurité, Territoire, Population – Cours au Collège de France, 1977–1978,* M. Senellart (eds.). Paris. Seuil/Gallimard.

Foucault, M (2008 [1977]) "Panopticism" from "Discipline & Punish: The Birth of the Prison". *Race/Ethnicity: Multidisciplinary Global Contexts* 2(1), 1–12.

Giulianotti, R (2002) Supporters, Followers, Fans, and Flaneurs: A Taxonomy of Spectator Identities in Football. *Journal of Sport and Social Issues* 26(1), 25–46.

Giulianotti, R (2019) Football Events, Memories and Globalization. *Soccer & Society* 20(7–8), 903–911.

Giulianotti, R & Klauser, F (2010) Security Governance and Sport Mega-Events: Toward an Interdisciplinary Research Agenda. *Journal of Sport and Social Issues* 34(1), 48–60.

Giulianotti, R, Armstrong, G, Hales, G & Hobbs, D (2015) Global Sport Mega-Events and the Politics of Mobility: The Case of the London 2012 Olympics. *The British Journal of Sociology* 66(4), 118–140.

Goldblatt, D (2019) *The Age of Football: The Global Game in the Twenty-First Century.* London. Macmillan.

Hanrieder, T & Kreuder-Sonnen, C (2014) WHO Decides on the Exception? Securitization and Emergency Governance in Global Health. *Security Dialogue* 45(4), 331–348.

Hassan, I, Mukaigawara, M, King, L, Fernandes, G & Sridhar, D (2021) Hindsight Is 2020? Lessons in Global Health Governance One Year into the Pandemic. *Nature Medicine* 27(3), 396–400.

Horne, J (2007) The Four "Knowns" of Sports Mega-Events. *Leisure Studies* 26(1), 81–96.

Howell, A (2014) The Global Politics of Medicine: Beyond Global Health, Against Securitisation Theory. *Review of International Studies* 40(5), 961–987.

Janiec, J, Zielicka-Hardy, A, Polkowska, A, Rogalska, J & Sadkowska-Todys, M (2012) Did Public Health Travel Advice Reach EURO 2012 Football Fans? A Social Network Survey. *Eurosurveillance* 17(31), 1–3.

Jennings, W (2012a) *Olympic Risks.* Basingstoke. Palgrave Macmillan.

Jennings, W (2012b) *Mega-Events and Risk Colonization: Risk Management and The Olympics.* Discussion Paper 71. London. London School of Economics and Political Science, 1–27.

Kamradt-Scott, A & McInnes, C (2012) The Securitisation of Pandemic Influenza: Framing, Security and Public Policy. *Global Public Health* 7(2), 95–110.

Lee Ludvigsen, JA (2021) When 'The Show' Cannot Go on: An Investigation into Sports Mega-Events and Responses during the Pandemic Crisis. *International Review for the Sociology of Sport,* 1–18.

Lee Ludvigsen, JA & Millward, P (2020) A Security Theater of Dreams: Supporters' Responses to "Safety" and "Security" Following the Old Trafford "Fake Bomb" Evacuation. *Journal of Sport and Social Issues* 44(1), 3–21.

Lee Ludvigsen, JA & Parnell, D (2021) Redesigning the Games? The 2020 Olympic Games, Playbooks and New Sports Event Risk Management Tools. *Managing Sport and Leisure,* 1–13.

Matthewman, S & Huppatz, K (2020) A Sociology of Covid-19. *Journal of Sociology* 56(4), 675–683.

Mayor of London (2020) EURO 2020 Postponed. Available from: https://www.london.gov.uk/coronavirus/coronavirus-events-updates (Accessed 26 May 2020).

Mazey, S & Richardson, J (2020) Lesson-Drawing from New Zealand and Covid-19: The Need for Anticipatory Policy Making. *The Political Quarterly* 91(3), 561–570.

McCloskey, B, Zumla, A, Ippolito, G, Blumberg, L, Arbon, P, Cicero, A, Endericks, T, Lim, PL & Borodina, M (2020) Mass Gathering Events and Reducing Further Global Spread of COVID-19: A Political and Public Health Dilemma. *The Lancet* 395(10230), 1096–1099.

Memish, ZA, Ahmed, QA, Schlagenhauf, P, Doumbia, S & Khan, A (2020) No Time for Dilemma: Mass Gatherings Must Be Suspended. *The Lancet* 395, 1191–1192.

Murphy, MP (2020) COVID-19 and Emergency eLearning: Consequences of the Securitization of Higher Education for Post-Pandemic Pedagogy. *Contemporary Security Policy* 41(3), 492–505.

Nunes, J (2014) Questioning Health Security: Insecurity and Domination in World Politics. *Review of International Studies* 40, 939–960.

O'Manique, C & Fourie, P (2009) Security and Health in the 21st Century. In M.D. Cavelty & V. Mauer (eds) *Routledge Handbook of Security Studies*. London. Routledge, 243–254.

Parnell, D, Bond, AJ, Widdop, P & Cockayne, D (2021) Football Worlds: Business and Networks during COVID-19. *Soccer & Society* 22(1–2), 19–26.

Parnell, D & Widdop, P (2020) Unprecedented, Uncharted and Unrealistic: UEFA Postpones EURO 2020 by 12 Months. *Football Collective*. Available from: https://footballcollective.org.uk/2020/03/18/unprecedented-unchartered-and-unrealistic-uefa-postpones-euro-2020-by-12-months/ (Accessed 26 March 2020).

Parnell, D, Widdop, P, Bond, A & Wilson, R (2020) COVID-19, Networks and Sport. *Managing Sport and Leisure*, 1–7.

Peterson, S (2002) Epidemic Disease and National Security. *Security Studies* 12(2), 43–81.

Reuters (2021) Euro 2020 Crowds Driving Rise in COVID-19 Infections, Says WHO. *Reuters*. Available from: https://www.reuters.com/world/europe/who-warns-third-coronavirus-wave-europe-2021-07-01/ (Accessed 23 August 2021).

Roberts, K (2020) Locked Down Leisure in Britain. *Leisure Studies* 39(5), 617–628.

Roche, M (2000) *Mega-Events and Modernity: Olympics and Expos in the Growth of Global Culture*. London. Routledge.

Roche, M (2003) Mega-Events, Time and Modernity: On Time Structures in Global Societies. *Time & Society* 12(1), 99–126.

Roche, M (2017) *Mega-Events and Social Change: Spectacle, Legacy and Public Culture*. Manchester. Manchester University Press.

Rosenberg, C (1989) What Is an Epidemic? AIDS in Historical Perspective. *Daedalus* 118(2), 1–17.

Rosenthal, U, Charles, MT & 't Hart, P (eds) (1989) *Coping with Crisis: The Management of Disasters, Riots and Terrorism*. Springfield. Charles C. Thomas.

Rushton, S (2011) Global Health Security: Security for Whom? Security from What? *Political Studies* 59(4), 779–796.

SD Europe (2020) SD Europe Statement: UEFA EURO 2020. Available from: https://www.sdeurope.eu/sd-europe-statement-uefa-euro-2020/ (Accessed 12 April 2020).

Shipway, R (2018) Building Resilience and Managing Crises and Disasters in Sport Tourism. *Journal of Sport & Tourism* 22(3), 265–270.

Sky Sports (2020a) Coronavirus: UEFA President Aleksander Ceferin Says Season Risks Being Lost. Available from: https://www.skysports.com/football/news/11945/11965081/coronavirus-uefa-president-aleksander-ceferin-says-season-risks-being-lost (Accessed 3 April 2020).

Sky Sports (2020b) Coronavirus in Sport: Latest Updates from across the World. Available from: https://www.skysports.com/more-sports/live-blog/32461/11945306/coronavirus-latest-how-outbreak-is-affecting-sport (Accessed 5 April 2020).

Stott, C (2003) Police Expectations and the Control of English Soccer Fans at 'Euro 2000'. *Policing* 26(4), 640–655.

Thacker, E (2009) The Shadows of Atheology: Epidemics, Power and Life after Foucault. *Theory, Culture & Society* 26(6), 134–152.

The Daily Mail (2020a) EURO 2020 Coronavirus Q&A. *The Daily Mail*. Available from: https://www.dailymail.co.uk/sport/sportsnews/article-8062033/EURO-2020-CORONAVIRUS-Q-tournament-postponed-scrapped.html (Accessed 12 March 2020).

The Daily Mail (2020b) European Football Unites for a HISTORIC Meeting on Tuesday and the Fate of Euro 2020, the Champions League and More Will Be Decided... Here's Everything on the Table on What Will Be a Defining Day for the Sport. Available from: https://www.dailymail.co.uk/sport/football/article-8117033/All-key-questions-European-football-comes-decide-games-fate.html (Accessed 19 March 2020).

The Daily Mail (2020c) "The Health of People Is Much More Important" FIFA President Gianni Infantino Insists International Matches Will Be Postponed if Deadly Coronavirus Continues to Spread. Available from: https://www.dailymail.co.uk/sport/sportsnews/article-8057247/FIFA-president-Gianni-Infantino-insists-matches-postponed-deadly-coronavirus-spreads.html (Accessed 19 March 2020).

The Daily Mirror (2020a) Coronavirus: UEFA and FIFA Put Rivalry Aside in Bid to Solve Football's "Biggest Crisis". Available from: https://www.mirror.co.uk/sport/football/news/coronavirus-uefa-fifa-put-rivalry-21709696 (Accessed 17 April 2020).

The Daily Mirror (2020b) Coronavirus Latest across Europe as Italian FA Chief Prepares Euro 2020 Proposal. Available from: https://www.mirror.co.uk/sport/football/news/coronavirus-latest-across-europe-italian-21697027 (Accessed: 17 April 2020).

The Guardian (2010) South Africa Worried by Possibility of World Cup Swine Flu Outbreak. *The Guardian*. Available from: https://www.theguardian.com/football/2010/feb/15/world-cup-swine-flu#:~:text=South%20Africa%20faces%20a%20health,Aaron%20Motsoaledi%20told%20parliament%20today.&text=Motsoaledi%20said%20the%20department%20of,from%20the%20World%20Health%20Organisation. (Accessed 17 April 2020).

The Independent (2020a) Coronavirus Forcing UEFA into Crisis Talks as Euro 2020 Fears Mount. *The Independent*. Available from: https://www.independent.co.uk/sport/football/international/euro-2020-coronavirus-news-postponed-uefa-latest-a9365166.html (Accessed 27 May 2020).

The Independent (2020b) Coronavirus: FA Chief Expects "Things to Get Complicated" if 2019/20 Club Season Forced into July. Available from: https://www.independent.co.uk/sport/football/premier-league/coronavirus-premier-league-july-schedule-euro-2020-fa-a9408581.html (Accessed 27 May 2020).

The Independent (2020c) When is the Euros, Why Is It Delayed and Who Will Play in the Tournament? Available from: https://www.independent.co.uk/sport/football/international/euro-2020-coronavirus-postponed-uefa-delay-cancelled-new-date-a9407281.html (Accessed 23 March 2020).

The Telegraph (2007) Olympic Love "Could Fuel an Epidemic". *The Telegraph.* Available from: https://www.telegraph.co.uk/news/uknews/1555510/Olympic-love-could-fuel-an-epidemic.html (Accessed 12 April 2020).

The Telegraph (2020) 'Season Is Lost' if Coronavirus Crisis Prevents Resumption before End of June, Says UEFA President. Available from: https://www.telegraph.co.uk/football/2020/03/28/season-lost-coronavirus-crisis-prevents-resumption-end-june/ (Accessed 27 May 2020).

The Times (2020) Plan to Use Wembley for Season Finish. Available from: https://www.thetimes.co.uk/article/plan-to-use-wembley-for-season-finish-nlpw6xlnj (Accessed 27 May 2020).

Toohey, K, Taylor, T & Lee, C (2003) The FIFA World Cup 2002: The Effects of Terrorism on Sports Tourists. *Journal of Sport & Tourism* 8(3), 186–196.

Tovar, J (2021) Soccer, World War II and Coronavirus: A Comparative Analysis of How the Sport Shut Down. *Soccer & Society* 22(1–2), 66–74.

UEFA (2020a) UEFA Calls Meeting of European Football Stakeholders. Available from https://www.uefa.com/insideuefa/mediaservices/mediareleases/newsid=2640887.html (Accessed 27 May 2020).

UEFA (2020b) UEFA Postpones EURO 2020 by 12 Months. Available from: https://www.uefa.com/insideuefa/about-uefa/news/newsid=2641071.html (Accessed 27 May 2020).

UEFA (2020c) Resolution of the European Football Family on a Coordinated Response to the Impact of the COVID-19 on Competitions. Available from: https://www.uefa.com/insideuefa/about-uefa/news/newsid=2641077.html (Accessed 27 May 2020).

UEFA (n.d.) *UEFA EURO 2020: Tournament Requirements.* Nyon. UEFA. Available from: https://www.uefa.com/MultimediaFiles/Download/EuroExperience/competitions/General/01/95/21/41/1952141_DOWNLOAD.pdf.

VG (2020) Fotball-EM utsatt til 2021 – Derfor Avslørte Norge Nyheten. Available from: https://www.vg.no/sport/fotball/i/vQKKp5/fotball-em-utsatt-til-2021-derfor-avsloerte-norge-nyheten (Accessed 19 March 2020).

Wallis, P & Nerlich, B (2005) Disease Metaphors in New Epidemics: The UK Media Framing of the 2003 SARS Epidemic. *Social Science & Medicine* 60(11), 2629–2639.

Chapter 6

Redesigning, Re-Imagining and Delivering Euro 2020 in a Pandemic

Introduction

11 July 2021 marked the completion of Euro 2020. However, the month-long tournament, won by Italy, still differed from the one imagined in the early bidding and planning stages and in documentary form (Chapters 2–4). This chapter argues that Euro 2020, in the light of COVID-19 – and especially immediately before and during the competition – became a 'testing ground' for new (COVID-oriented) security and safety policies, practices and knowledge generation related to, or potentially assisting the wider reopening of mass gatherings events and societies more broadly following the coronavirus-induced lockdowns, rules and restrictions. Specifically, the chapter identifies processes of security-related redesign and the event-specific re-imagination between June 2020 (the event's original starting month) and June and July 2021 when Euro 2020 eventually commenced and was completed in 11 rather than 12 European cities. Within this year-long time period, however, numerous critical developments must be briefly revisited. First, and integrally, vaccines providing increased immunity to COVID-19 were cleared for use towards the end of 2020. Across Europe, this became the starting point for vaccination programs that were rolled out in the early months of 2021. Second, one year into the pandemic, key lessons on how to respond to the pandemic globally and nationally were more advanced than at its early stages (Hassan et al., 2021). Still, 'second waves' of COVID-19 occurred in several countries worldwide. Third, in the worlds of sport and football, numerous events and leagues did return from mid-May 2020 and onwards with reduced or no crowds inside the stadiums, depending on local or national transmission levels and guidelines.

However, despite the arrival of vaccines and some fans across Europe being able to return to the stadiums, the new coronavirus variants detected in late-December 2020 led to several renewed 'hard lockdowns' in several Euro 2020 countries. It also impacted transnational competitions like the Champions League and the 2022 World Cup qualifiers, whereby travelling restrictions, in some cases, prevented players and teams from competing in specific countries due to national travelling restrictions or quarantine policies. Within this highly complex context,

DOI: 10.4324/9781003258445-7

the resumptions of postponed mega-events like Euro 2020 and the 2020 Olympics were severely disrupted and packed with uncertainty. Concerning Euro 2020, this naturally led to questions being asked around the possibility of staging a 12-country Euro 2020 with spectators under such unpredictable circumstances (Sky Sports, 2021a). As hinted upon, 12 countries were indeed reduced to 11 when Ireland, in April 2021, lost their Euro 2020 fixtures. All this comprise the contextual background for this chapter, which sheds a light on how Euro 2020 was *redesigned*, *re-imagined* and *delivered* during a global pandemic.

This chapter, drawing mainly from media sources, press releases and documentary data, first explores one key question characterizing Euro 2020's build-up: whether fans would be allowed in the stadiums or not. Then, central developments related to security, safety and health are unpacked as the chapter explores how test events, emerging lessons and safety measures moulded the redesigned and re-imagined Euro 2020. Meanwhile, the launch and delivery of Euro 2020 is captured here with regard to its policing, security and notable incidents during the competition. This included the dramatic scenes at Wembley for Euro 2020's final characterized by social disorder, where ticketless fans forced their way through the stadium gates and past stewards before the game. Particularly two key arguments emerge from the chapter. First, the discourses and decision-making surrounding fans' (non-)presence reinforce the notion of fans as integral for a mega-event's potential as a sporting spectacle. Second, and more integral to this book's main argument, the final security and safety preparations and the execution of Euro 2020 exemplify and update the idea that sporting spaces constitute 'laboratories' or 'testing grounds' for *new* technological innovations (Yang and Cole, 2020) and security and safety practices (Clavel, 2013; Numerato, 2018; Tsoukala, 2009). Yet, because the pandemic symbolizes a historical moment – both outside and inside football – the 'testing ground'-conception obtained a new set of meanings and arrived with novel implications.

Fans, no fans, some fans?

The presence of fans and visitors is commonly considered to be integral for the making of football and mega-events' carnivalesque atmospheres and the live football spectacle (Turner, 2013). Notwithstanding, following the temporary COVID-19-related suspension of live sport (Chapter 5) and the resumption of sporting events and competitions behind 'closed doors' or reduced crowds, it was always expected that the return of fans to the Euro 2020's stadiums would emerge as a pressing question before the tournament. Indeed, similar questions emerged before the 2020 Olympics which, in March 2021, banned all international spectators from attending the event in Tokyo.

In Euro 2020's case, the prospects of and planning for fans' return were additionally complicated due to the tournament's networked and 'pan-European' format (Parnell et al., 2020). Indeed, fan travels across the Euro-zone were, originally, situated within the Euro 2020 format's very core. Yet, given the impacts of COVID-19 on the event's build-up, the format of fixtures requiring teams, fans, media and officials to travel between European cities was particularly incompatible with the existing travelling restrictions and guidelines to contain COVID-19's spread. The discussions dominating Euro 2020's build-up may therefore be summarized as a question of allowing fans (with *no* restrictions), no fans (closed doors) or some fans (limited crowds). As argued, from the perspective of the event owners and its partners, the prospect of *no* fans could be viewed as possibly impeding Euro 2020's potential as a 'global spectacle', partly explaining the push towards the presence of fans or, at least, *some* fans.

However, upon proceeding, additional context is necessary. From October 2020 and onwards, Union of European Football Associations (UEFA) allowed for European stadiums to open up for a small number of fans. However, this was on strict conditions and included 30% of the relevant stadium capacity and required the approval of the relevant local authorities (UEFA, 2020a). UEFA (2020b) also published an 8-page long handbook titled the *UEFA Minimum Health & Hygiene Requirements for the Return of Spectators*, containing the minimum requirements that organizers and associations would have to implement when resuming UEFA competition matches with fans in the stadiums. Important to note, this document was merely intended as a *supplement* to the 'rules established by national/local authorities' (ibid.), illustrating that the fans' return to European stadiums was largely dictated by and subject to local and national authorities' guidelines and/or restrictions.

Expectedly, this added to the uncertainties regarding the presence of domestic and international fans before Euro 2020, simply because the host countries, between June 2020 and June 2021, dealt with very different and rapidly changing COVID-19 transmission rates and responded differently to COVID-19. Therefore, there were periods, between September and December 2020, where fans, at limited numbers, were allowed inside the stadiums in some of the largest leagues in Europe, including the German Bundesliga, the English Premier League and the Champions League. Predominantly, however, the emergence of new virus variants, travelling restrictions and bans led to a general return to 'closed doors' throughout European football from December 2020 and throughout the next four and five months. The rapidly changing and extremely unpredictable situations in several of the Euro 2020 host countries, including but not limited to England, Scotland, Ireland, Denmark and Germany, posed as a main obstacle for the prospect of fans at Euro 2020, since guarantees on the presence of fans at Euro 2020 could not be provided between March 2020 (the postponement) and April 2021.

As reported, this resulted in discussions around the possibility of 'downsizing' Euro 2020 and potentially staging the mega-event in 11, 10 or 9 countries instead. This came to fore in the below statement from the UEFA president, which cites a pre-emptive 'backup option' in the case of persisting issues:

> Vaccination has started and I think we will be able to have full stands in the summer [...] For now, the plan is to play in all 12 countries. Of course, there are backup options in case a country has a problem.
>
> (quoted in Reuters, 2021a)

However, this statement also paints a picture how the vaccination roll-out generated some optimism for UEFA regarding the possibility of a Euro 2020 with 'full stands'. Notwithstanding, concerning fans' (non-)presence, certain reports suggested that each Euro 2020 host could choose between four different options that had to be confirmed to UEFA by early-April 2021. These included full stadiums, 50% of stadium capacity, 33% of stadium capacity or empty stadiums (ESPN, 2021). The presence of fans was also discussed on 27 January 2021, when UEFA met with representatives from the 12 host cities to discuss the operational matters ahead of Euro 2020. Subsequently, UEFA (2021a) stated:

> As a result of that [different circumstances in each host city] and the fast-changing nature of the situation around the pandemic, the deadline for the submission of plans to accommodate fans inside the stadiums has been moved to early April.

In a different interview, Ceferin again commented on the fans, stating that: 'We have several scenarios, but the one guarantee we can make is that the option of playing any Euro 2020 match in an empty stadium is off the table' (quoted in Sky Sports, 2021b). Ceferin also noted that the deadline for host cities to confirm their decisions was moved to 20 April and remained adamant that Euro's hosting style would preserve, at least, some of its 'pan-European' shape and that staging Euro 2020 in 10 or 11 countries was possible if the 'ideal scenario' of 12 stadiums could not be achieved (ibid.).

The articulated position of UEFA and the above statements on the host cities and fans remain important here, since they speak to the framed importance of fans for the making of football mega-event spectacles. As can be suggested, it seems that host cities that could not guarantee a presence of fans inside their stadiums – and seemingly would be unable to provide the same spectacle as host cities that *did* allow fans – could risk not hosting Euro 2020 at all. Hence, media speculations surfaced on whether Dublin and Glasgow could be cut from Euro 2020 and whether England could end up as the single host of Euro 2020. The latter speculation was, however, outright rejected by then UK Health Secretary, Matt Hancock, who responded to these claims saying: 'I haven't seen anything on that, I understand that that's not right' (quoted in *The Independent*, 2021a).

When 12 become 11: Dublin, Bilbao and guaranteed fan presence

One significant date on Euro 2020's timeline was 9 April 2021. Just over two months before Euro 2020 launched in Rome, eight host cities confirmed to UEFA that they *would* allow fans to attend fixtures throughout the tournament. In UEFA's (2021b) statement, the vaccination roll-outs, measures for reopening national economies, the warmer summer season and improved health factors were framed as factors enhancing the prospects of a safe return of fans for Euro 2020. However, the number of fans that would be allowed back for Euro 2020's stadiums varied. St. Petersburg and Baku would both allow 50% of their stadium capacities; Budapest allowed for a full stadium, whereas Amsterdam, Bucharest, Copenhagen and Glasgow guaranteed for between 25 and 33%. Meanwhile, Wembley initially allowed for 25% of its capacity, although the caps on spectators were subject to change.

On 14 April, it was also confirmed that Rome would allow up to 25% of their stadium's capacity to be filled (Reuters, 2021b). Further, three cities – Baku, Budapest and Saint Petersburg – planned to activate exemptions from COVID entry restrictions and requirements for travelling ticket holders, subject to negative COVID-19 tests (UEFA, 2021b). Finally, the decisions on the last three host cities – Munich, Bilbao and Dublin – were made on 23 April 2021. Crucially, this led to important changes to Euro 2020's format and a reduction in the number of host countries. Unable to guarantee the presence of fans, Dublin lost their hosting rights and fixtures (to St. Petersburg and London), whereas Bilbao's four games were moved to Seville's *Estadio La Cartuja* (30% of stadium capacity). Munich, meanwhile, provided guarantees for a minimum of 14,500 spectators. Whilst this meant that all Euro 2020 stadiums would have a presence of fans, this also meant, as Table 6.1 shows, a reduction from 12 to 11 host countries. In Ireland's case, the prospects of hosting Euro 2020 with fans were framed as incompatible with principles of public health. For example, the Irish Minister for Tourism, Culture, Arts, Gaeltacht, Sports and Media, Catherine Martin, said, 'despite our commitment to hosting the games, the public health situation has meant we were not able to give UEFA the assurances they required' in relation to the minimum number of present fans (quoted in Sky Sports, 2021c).

The discourses, decisions and logics surrounding the return of fans for Euro 2020 touch the surface of some wider sport mega-event (SME)-related trends and dynamics. First, the drive towards a maximization of spectator numbers under the

Table 6.1 Euro 2020 host cities' stadium capacities and capacity limit upon Euro 2020's commencement

Host city	Stadium capacity	Capacity limit
Amsterdam	48,000	33%
Baku	62,000	50%
Budapest	61,000	100%
Bucharest	52,000	25%
Copenhagen	35,000	45%
Glasgow	48,000	25%
London	90,000	25%
Munich	66,000	22%
Rome	64,000	25%
Seville	60,000	30%
St. Petersburg	61,000	50%

Source: Sky News (2021a).

pandemic circumstances and restrictions could be seen in context of the economic aspirations of owners, sponsors and licensees. Especially so, in the light of the financially disruptive postponement which, reportedly, came to about €300 million (Parnell et al., 2021). Hence, on a basic level, the guaranteed fan presence at Euro 2020's stadiums – as opposed to closed-door games – would activate some consumption circles through ticket sales and other match-day revenue streams.

However, it is also important that the conscious push towards a fan presence is seen in context of the wider aspiration of all SME owners and organizers to make their event franchises into memorable spectacles on the global scene (Marivoet, 2006) and enhance the mega-events' global brands. Hence, the desire to generate a spectacle and financial returns is inter-linked. To achieve this, sport governing bodies typically 'set the rules of the game in accordance with their own interests' (Włoch, 2012: 307). Moreover, as Włoch (2012) argues, on the international scene, sports' governing bodies may be interpreted as global governors that are entitled to implement authoritative and arbitrary conditions on their selected host countries. In this vein, and as applied to the extraordinary context of the safe return of fans for Euro 2020, it seems that host countries, partly, were expected to meet or try to accommodate UEFA's interests concerning the fans' stadium presence. It seems prudent to suggest that the prospect of a Euro 2020 largely staged behind closed doors was viewed as possibly impeding the tournament franchise's global brand and consumption circles. And so, the hosting format was flexibly adapted so that it encompassed one less country, but a larger number of attending fans.

Overall, the version of Euro 2020's final build-up, which can be extracted from media reports, concerning the presence of fans also reveals a set of trends in the universe of SMEs speaking to speaking to intra-relations between states and sports' governing bodies. Here, the event owners' policies and partnerships set the parameters and push strict conditions upon host countries (Włoch, 2012). Host countries seeking to acquire the prestigious hosting rights for, for example, a variety of purposes, including 'soft power', generation of national identity or tourism (Roche, 2000), must then adapt, guarantee and follow the strict conditions (Zirin, 2016). By analyzing the developments concerning fans, some fans or no fans in the final months before Euro 2020, one may observe a somewhat similar logic emerge in a new context, whereby host countries had to guarantee the presence of fans as an enabler for and necessary ingredient to the desired European-wide 'spectacle'.

Pilot events, webinars and medical expertise: A new epoch of sporting events as 'testing grounds'

Numerous sporting events and competitions were postponed or cancelled throughout the early months of 2020. Naturally, as postponed events' rescheduled dates approached, this required a new set of safety and security practices, techniques and risk management strategies. In part, the pandemic created a situation in which event organizers and stakeholders would *learn-by-doing* (Lee Ludvigsen and Parnell, 2021). As Parent and Ruetsch (2021: 309) write:

> The COVID-19 pandemic [...] will certainly push organisations to readjust risk and readiness approaches, programmes, and plans – far beyond the obvious health and sanitary themes. With staff confined for several weeks, the pandemic is proving to be a "live test" for organisations to accelerate their transition to a more resilient, sustainable, and reactive (or even proactive?) model.

The idea of an organizational 'live test' remains central here and can be applied to the activities of the diverse stakeholders before the rescheduled Euro 2020. In that sense, this section explores the emerging practices and lessons in the fields of security and safety as Euro 2020 had to be redesigned and re-imagined before its start on 11 June 2021. Simultaneously, this gives us a glimpse of exactly what this book argues represented a new epoch of SMEs as 'testing grounds' for security-related practices and methods, that essentially were merged with principles of public health.

One key strategy in the epoch of 'COVID-secure' SMEs has been the employment of designated test or pilot events. Importantly though, the executions of test events before the 'main event' are not exclusive to the times of COVID-19. Yet, it may still be argued that test events acquired new sets of objectives and social meanings during and after the period in which live spectator sport was largely suspended or took place behind closed doors in the relative absence of knowledge on how to stage events safely during a pandemic (Lee Ludvigsen and Parnell, 2021). Ultimately, in the *post-2020* epoch, pilot events have primarily revolved around the testing of COVID-19-related security measures, communication, social distancing, stadium entry/exit regulation, disinfection and scientifically understanding the relationship between mass gatherings and transmission.

Event owners, organizers and managers hence faced a first key challenge, which was to ensure that sporting events returned behind closed doors. The second challenge, however, was to ensure that fans returned in a gradual and safe manner. In Euro 2020's context, one of the events likely to have generated some key lessons was the UEFA 2020 Super Cup final at *Puskas Arena*, Budapest (between the Champions League and Europa League winners, on 24 September 2020). Ahead of this, the UEFA Champions League 2019/2020 season had been completed inside a bio-secure 'bubble' in Lisbon, Portugal, which was closed off for the public.

For the Super Cup final, between Bayern Munich and Sevilla, UEFA's Executive Committee decided to employ this one-off match as a pilot event, and this allowed for a reduced number of fans into the stadium (UEFA, 2020c). Overall, 30% of the stadium capacity was allowed into the 60,000-seater stadium and some of the safety and security measures at this match included face masks, 1.5-metre social distancing, queuing lanes and thermal cameras for the measurement of body temperatures. Stewards were also employed to ensure that fans complied with the social distancing measures at the event which worked as an important step for the return of fans to European football grounds (UEFA, 2020d).

The Super Cup was utilized by relevant organizations, authorities and stakeholders to learn more about the impacts of fans' gradual return. Football Supporters Europe (FSE), for example, conducted a study at the event and consequently published a report titled *UEFA Super Cup Budapest: FSE Review* (2020). This report was based on FSE representatives' liaison with UEFA before, during and after the final. FSE also attended the match, spoke with the organizing committee and Hungarian police, met fan representatives from Sevilla and Bayern Munich and devised an online survey for attending fans. The report, published online, found that fans generally felt safe when attending, that the event was well organized, but that certain areas of communication could be improved:

> Communication around many aspects of the 2020 UEFA Super Cup in Budapest lacked clarity and this needs to be addressed ahead of further games. Fans need to receive clear and precise information on a range of subjects related to the public health situation in the host city. Messaging on the entry process was vague, meaning fans were uncertain what evidence they needed to provide at the Hungarian border to prove a negative test result. The same applies to the wearing of masks inside the stadium, the temperature check process, and whether standing is permitted. FSE recommends clear, precise communication on important public health and safety matters to ensure that fans are as safe as possible when attending games. (p. 16)

Further, FSE recommended that:

> [M]eeting points should be suspended for all UEFA finals and tournaments so long as the pandemic is ongoing—this recommendation is made on the related grounds of public health and limited demand. FSE further hopes that under the current circumstances such facilities operate in line with national health and safety measures. (ibid.)

These recommendations give an insight into the processes of learning that occurred during and after the Super Cup pilot event, as the communication of key information was assessed as being in need of improvement. Further, this also extends my earlier argument (Chapter 4) on fan networks and their representatives as important actors of knowledge transfer in European football and before European Championships. Evidently, this extended into the activities related to fans' return to stadia before Euro 2020.

Furthermore, another networking event – in form of a webinar, hosted by the Sport Convention team of the Council of Europe – took place in November 2020. The webinar event was titled the 'Impact of COVID-19 pandemic on national and international Safety, Security and Service policies and practices at football and other sports events'. This webinar aimed to facilitate the 'exchange of views between public authorities and sports organisations on the impact of the COVID-19 pandemic in the organisation of sports events with a focus on policies and practices to guarantee safety, security and service at sport events' (COE, 2020). It was attended by representatives from UEFA, FIFA, FSE and national policing forces and worked as a (digital) platform for relevant stakeholders to meet, discuss and share recent experiences of hosting football matches and sporting events during the pandemic.

In the policy-transfer literature, it is noted that processes of 'lesson-drawing' or 'policy transfer' take place in globalized microspaces, wherein 'best practices' are discussed, trust is generated and lessons are shared (Larner and Le Heron, 2002). In this context, McCann (2011: 120) writes that conferences, meetings and visits are 'key relational sites' and integral to the 'social process of teaching and learning about policy and, thus, to the contingent, cumulative, and emergent knowledge production processes that coconstitute urban policy mobilities'. As applied to the context of SME policy mobilities, the webinar represented a continuation of Chapter 3's mentioned networking events. However, in an online space and with new COVID-19-related issues on its agenda. In the safe and secure return of football mega-events, fan representatives maintained their role as agents of knowledge transfer, as emphasized in a statement from the Council of Europe T-RV Committee and T-S4 committee:

> Supporters and supporter organisations should be further involved in all the stages of the decision-making process of public health and security authorities and football bodies, namely as regards the restrictions put in place to preserve health and security during the crisis and on the return to 'new normal'. The engagement of supporters in all stages of the organisation of a sporting event increases the legitimacy of the restrictive measures and their understanding, therefore reinforcing the confidence of supporters and their consented compliance of rules.
>
> (quoted by FSE, 2021)

Furthermore, when Euro 2020 rapidly started to approach, from March 2020 and onwards, it also became clear that other domestic football games would be employed as test events in certain Euro 2020 host cities. In London, the League Cup and the Football Association (FA) Cup finals – both staged at Wembley – were used as test events. This, however, should not merely be seen in context of London's status as Euro 2020 host, but in light of the roadmap of the United Kingdom out of the country's third lockdown, which aimed to lift most restrictions on 21 June 2021. Ultimately, this involved a series of pilot events under the government and science-led 'event research programme', which sought to examine the risks from indoor and outdoor crowded events like sporting events, concerts and nightclubs. As a part of this programme, the FA Cup final – played less than a month before the Euro 2020 circus arrived in London – was played in front of 21,000 fans that had to provide a negative lateral flow COVID-19 test upon entrance. For this test event, too, FSE were present to ensure that fans' voices were consulted in the overarching return to stadia protocols. Crucially, London's Euro 2020 fixtures would also form a joint in the events research programme, which formed a strategy for the reopening of the British society.[1] In the Netherlands, the Dutch FA also reported that a new study by Fieldlab Events would be carried out at the Netherlands' match versus Latvia (27 March 2021) at Euro 2020 stadium, *Johan Cruyff Arena*, with 5,000 spectators. As the Dutch FA announced, this study would focus on rapid testing and the use of a smartphone app through which negative test results could be registered and form a key part in the return of spectators before Euro 2020 (KNVB, 2021).

Collectively, this demonstrates the centrality of designated test events and networking events focused on COVID-19-related knowledge generation and transfer before and during Euro 2020. Seemingly, these began in September 2020 and were staged in the final build-up of and even throughout Euro 2020. Importantly, all this feeds into the central argument that football spaces and stadiums may be used as testing grounds or institutional laboratories for the introduction of new technologies, partnerships, security practices and modes of social control (Clavel, 2013; Tsoukala, 2009; Yang and Cole, 2020). However, in the context of COVID-19, two important revisions (or expansions) to this argument must be made. First, the 'testing ground' analogy becomes evident in a very *literal sense* with the announcement of designated test or pilot events. Second, in the new epoch, the objectives and rationales for the test events were primarily revolving around public health and the coronavirus, as generated practices and lessons could serve to inform Euro 2020 as the 'main event'.

Within UEFA (2021c), another key development in Euro 2020's redesign was the confirmed appointment of a medical advisor, Dr. Daniel Koch, an expert on global pandemics. For Bigo et al. (2021: 6), the pandemic meant that 'doctors entered into the field of the traditional professionals of security'. Hence, the redesign of Euro 2020 sheds a light on a set of new trends speaking to SME security including test events, networking events and the acquaintance of relevant expertise. To an extent, it also reveals the roll-out of new technological advancements that were introduced for the purpose of health and safety, including the heavily discussed COVID vaccine passport. A vaccine passport is, in brief, an attest that confirms an individual's immunity to a specific disease (e.g., COVID-19). Reportedly, at Wembley, vaccinated fans would have to show evidence of this through a smartphone application (*The Independent*, 2021b) or through Scottish or Welsh vaccination record services (Sky News, 2021b). Whilst such measure was highly criticized for being discriminatory, it also represented the very first time that a COVID passport had been required to attend a UK sporting event (*The Guardian*, 2021a). In a way, the COVID passport encapsulates what, for now, is the 'new normal' of sporting event attendance.

Considering the time of writing, it is beyond this book's scope to provide an empirical investigation of the exact practices, lessons and technologies that were tested and applied across Euro 2020's countries. However, it remains important to grant some critical attention to these new trends. Especially those surrounding the implementation of new strategies and technologies to ensure the return of spectators. Hutchins and Andrejevcic (2021) discuss this in relation to the 2020 Olympics in Tokyo but some of their arguments may be transplanted into Euro 2020's context. They warn against a 'new normal' wherein surveillance measures for COVID-19 safety purposes are incorporated into the markedization of mega-events and accelerate processes of social sorting. Similarly, Yang and Cole (2020: 12) compare the sporting stadium with a 'laboratory of innovation' and emphasize that 'the instalment of the post-pandemic "new normalcy"' will impact the future stadium experience. The danger is, ultimately, that technologies implemented at SMEs can erode civil liberties and perpetuate inequalities (Hutchins and Andrejevcic, 2021) through the presupposition of access to applications, smartphones or internet access.

Finally, concerning the implemented safety measures at Euro 2020 stadiums, UEFA (2021d) published a 'code of conduct' for spectators, whereas Wembley's COVID-19 guidelines provided a stark reminder for fans that 'this won't be your usual stadium visit' (UEFA, n.d.). Ultimately, some of the measures included wearing a mask, avoiding physical contacts, specific time slots for arrival, restrictions on movements inside the stadium and the availability of sanitizers inside the stadium (ibid.). Despite this, the extent to which these were rigorously adapted by local event organizers throughout Euro 2020 may be questioned. For example, as one supporter commented, the 'Covid-test requirement was a nonsense, it wasn't checked properly for any of the England games I came to. You could have shown them anything on your phone' (quoted in Reddy, 2021). Whilst the practical implementation of COVID measures and their effectiveness clearly pose as subjects for future research, the developments above feed into this chapter's argument concerning Euro 2020's redesign and how mega-event security, at least for now, have come to revolve around ongoing learning and minimizing social contact in face of the pandemic (Hutchins and Andrejevcic, 2021).

Let the games begin: Local and transnational modes of security and policing

On Friday 11 June 2021, Euro 2020 commenced in Rome as Italy beat Turkey 3-0 in the competition's opening fixture. So, this section examines the policing and security throughout the month-long competition which, upon its launch, was the largest sporting event to be hosted during the pandemic. A few days before the tournament's opener, some reports emerged from host countries around the security-related and organizational readiness. In Russia, the local organizers were reportedly confident in the COVID-19 security measures put in place in Saint Petersburg (Yahoo, 2021). Contrarily, the updates from Scotland indicated that the safety measures in place for Glasgow's fan zone were still 'under construction' just a week before the tournament arrived in the city (*Glasgow Times*, 2021). The city's COVID safety regime, requiring no tests or vaccine passports of fans, was also described as the 'most lenient in Europe' (Sky News, 2021c). In a way, these examples accurately capture some of the very distinctive challenges when securing and managing multinational SMEs. In the build-up, nations' level of preparedness, both organizationally and in terms of security and safety, is likely to differ, even in the final days before event commencement. Though, despite this, and compared to the other SME staged in 2021's summer months, Tokyo 2020, the final days before Euro 2020 commencements were still not *dominated* by uncertainty nor media reports of extraordinary organizational setbacks causing concerns.[2]

In terms of the actual policing and security operations during the event, this did as expected, and despite COVID-19, still encompass a number of spaces beyond the stadiums, such as the official fan zones and public squares. As Stakeholder 8 pointed out before the event: 'I think my understanding is [that] it's a requirement of UEFA for hosting cities to organize fan zones for visiting fans'. However, like most of the Euro 2020 stadiums, the assembled host city fan zones also featured strict restrictions in terms of allowed spectators depending on national COVID-19 restrictions. Meanwhile, some planned fan zones were cancelled or reduced in their format. In London, for example, the Trafalgar Square fan zone initially allowed up to 750 people (BBC, 2021a) with fans at socially distanced seated tables, whilst the Potters Field Park Football Village could allow up to 2,500 people. In other host cities, such as Glasgow and Budapest, the number of fans allowed into fan zones were higher (at 6,000 and 11,000, respectively).[3] Ultimately, what this suggests is that fan zones and fan villages, as central to modern-day SMEs, again worked as central focal points in the wider SME organization. Yet, simultaneously, the fan zones – for which the gathering of crowds is central – were also redesigned in light of the public health crisis.

Concerning the football policing operations, Euro 2020 revealed a number of new operational trends, whilst also reinforcing existing trends within football policing (Chapter 4) and policing more broadly. In London, for example, a full-time, dedicated 'Euros Policing Team' consisting of one sergeant and six constables was set up. Accordingly, the establishment of a dedicated Euros team represented a new approach compared to those at previous SMEs in the city (*Kilburn Times*, 2021). Furthermore, in statement from the London Metropolitan Police (quoted by NextDoor, 2021), the police organization's readiness for the policing of a safe and secure Euro 2020 in London was commented upon. Whilst Euro 2020's unique 'policing needs' were highlighted, it was also stated that the expertise within 'the Met' would be utilized and drawn upon, in addition to an alert and visible presence (ibid.). Moreover, the enormous scale of the Euro 2020 policing operation in London comes to the fore in the below statement:

> There will also be a full range of officers from Public Order, the Central Football Unit, Territorial Support Group and Project Servator, Mounted Branch, Dog Unit, Firearms Unit, Air Support, and the Marine Unit to respond to any crime or critical incidents which may occur. Plain clothed spotters within the crowds will be in place to identify any troublesome fans. (ibid.)

Redesigning, Re-Imagining and Delivering Euro 2020 in a Pandemic   135

Other publicly announced security measures and policing strategies for Euro 2020 in London included specially trained officers, hostile vehicle mitigation, counter-drone technology and the deployment of specialist counter-reconnaissance officers (Counter Terrorism Policing, 2021). Although the mega-events differed both in scale and nature, what is clear here is that the security assemblage for Euro 2020 in London bore some resemblance to that of the 2012 Olympics which similarly consisted of multiple policing agencies, state-of-art technologies and a highly visible and dense police presence (Fussey, 2015; Zirin, 2016). This is unsurprising – as Fussey and Coaffee (2012: 279) remind us, despite the varying levels of threat between SMEs, there are 'similarities in the trajectories, form and application of sporting mega-event security strategies'.

Throughout the tournament, and in its wider European context, the security and policing of Euro 2020 received occasional media attention. Particularly, *The Independent*'s (2021c) report into the European-wide security operation and its coordination presented an insight into the highly sophisticated and transnational security operation enacted by Euro 2020. As reported, the EU and Europol established an operational 'nerve centre' with around 40 police liaison officers from 22 nations specifically for Euro 2020. Located in Hague, in the Netherlands, this hub was set up for the purpose of intelligence-sharing on any emerging threats, and it was also assisted by a 'network of about 500 "spotters"' (ibid.). Commenting on the challenges of securing Euro 2020, Europol's Executive Director, Catherine De Bolle, said:

> It is the first ever championship organized by 10 different countries instead of only one or two, as we had seen in past editions […] It is also the first large-scale event organized during the COVID-19 pandemic related to sports. And all this, of course, presents important security challenges.
>
> (quoted in *The Independent*, 2021c)

As Sheptycki (2020) argues, COVID-19 may be widely understood as a 'massive global field experiment' in the operationalization of policing in varying different sociopolitical contexts. Evidently, such argument may also be situated in the world of football, where Euro 2020, as the first SME organized during the pandemic, raised a new set of challenges. This also included the *in-and-out* flows of people between countries, although this was somewhat complicated by the pandemic, and impacts prospects of 'hooliganism'. As a cooperation centre chief stated, 'Because of COVID, I think the number of hooligans will be limited. But it's still difficult for us because most of them will travel by car, and there will be a lot more movement because we play in several countries' (quoted in Reuters, 2021c). Furthermore, the wide array of security threats that Euro 2020 potentially could be exposed to, and had to be 'secured from', was touched upon. Essentially, it was reported as a specific task force was established in order to 'tackle threats including cybercrime, terrorism, match-fixing, trafficking counterfeit goods including fake COVID-19 certificates, and other intellectual property crimes' (*The Independent*, 2021c). Perhaps

136   Redesigning, Re-Imagining and Delivering Euro 2020 in a Pandemic

particularly noteworthy here, is the relatively novel security issue of 'fake COVID-19 certificates' which naturally emerges in light of the pandemic.

Moreover, the emphasis on information-sharing between countries – and its value as proved by a past track record – was also clear in a press release from Europol (2021) on the securing of Euro 2020 and the practices that were established to ensure safety and security. Here, it was reported on the set-up of an International Police Cooperation Centre (IPCC) of the National Football Contact Points that was coordinated by the Dutch police. The aim of this 'special operational set-up' was to facilitate for 'swift cooperation and provide the necessary operational support for a safe and secure championship' (ibid.). As reported, the IPCC UEFA EURO 2020 participants included 17 EU member states, 7 non-EU states (either represented in the competition as host countries or participating teams) and 2 organizations, INTERPOL and UEFA (ibid.).

Besides this, private security agencies were also entangled in the wider Euro 2020 'security field' (cf. Giulianotti and Klauser, 2010). Indeed, the English national team sacked their private security team as their players and officials had felt unsafe in the team hotel. Resultantly, 'England officials [told] UEFA they no longer had trust in the tournament-appointed security operation' and brought in their own security firm that had overseen the security at England's training ground, St George's Park (Sky Sports, 2021d). Arguably, the inherently transnational Euro 2020 security assemblage thus revealed the 'public-private partnerships' that are embedded in modern-day mega-event security governance (Roche, 2017).

It was also remarkable that within this trans-European process, it was the first 'post-Brexit' SME of the United Kingdom, where London hosted the highest number of matches. In isolation, Brexit allegedly had little impact on the overall security operation and its required European-wide information- and intelligence-sharing. As assistant director of the United Kingdom Football Policing Unit (UKFPU), Adrian Roberts, said:

> Brexit no has no effect whatsoever on the really important business that we do … with all other countries […] I think the risk is larger because of the COVID situation […] because all of the intelligence that maybe we might have had at an earlier stage by now, it's all in the unknown.
>
> (quoted in *The Independent*, 2021c)

As the comment on the heightened risks due to the 'COVID situation' suggests, and as this chapter argues, the pandemic created a completely unprecedented context for the security operation to be operationalized and executed within. Whilst ensuring 'safety' and 'security' remained the overarching aims, the settings in which to achieve this were significantly altered by the pandemic. The new challenges were also commented upon by UEFA's Events SA CEO, Martin Kallen, who said:

> In 2012, with Ukraine and Poland, there was a whole new infrastructure to be built in two countries, and, in 2016 in France, the main issue was security

and terrorism, and they did an excellent job in creating a safe and secure environment for fans [...] In 2020, it was already unique with so many different countries, but the pandemic meant nothing was certain anymore and has brought new issues every day – how we clean and disinfect stadiums, how we deal with testing, how we can bring spectators back.

(quoted in UEFA, 2021e)

In a way, the quote points towards Euro 2020's novelties as alluded to in the introductory sketch of this book: the new format and the pandemic. Moreover, and more generally, the above descriptions and accounts of the Euro 2020 security and policing operations serve to reinforce a number of this book's pre-event suggestions and those findings of the existing literature.

First, the level of cooperation and information-sharing between European countries and involvement of the EU, Interpol and Europol for Euro 2020's security operation can be viewed in light of convergent developments within the networked fields of European policing and security (Bigo, 2008; Cottey, 2007). The pursuit of 'security' is central to the European political agenda and presently 'European security [...] is deeply institutionalized; states co-operate with each other in a range of different institutions and across the spectrum of different security issues' (Cottey, 2007: 17). This, again, has contributed to the establishment of cooperative networks seeking to combat crimes and increase security (Bigo, 2008). The involvement of Europol in the realm of football policing is, as Tsoukala (2009: 120–121) notes, also indicative of the 'determination to standardize the policing of football hooliganism as much as possible'.

Hence, whilst transnational information-sharing and collaboration for international SMEs are not by themselves representative of new processes (Tsoukala, 2009), this serves to illustrate how Euro 2020's security, throughout its duration, was influenced by 'international processes and stipulations' and located within a 'complex field of agencies' (Klauser, 2011: 132). Although it is complicated at this stage to evidence the forthcoming suggestion, the linkages of public/private, local and international security actors for Euro 2020 may potentially reinforce Klauser's (2011: 126) argument that 'sport mega-events can be catalysts for more enduring international security collaborations'. Similarly, Spaaij (2013: 178) highlights that international cooperation in football policing 'serve as an example of, or precursor to, other forms of police cooperation within Europe', including the policing of protests or transnational social movements. Whereas further empirical research is needed on the inner workings and dynamics of security actors for Euro 2020, this simultaneously touches the surface of one of the possible 'security legacies' imbued in Euro 2020.

Secondly, the above breakdown demonstrates that despite the arrival of new, 'COVID-19 induced' threats or issues such as social contact, travelling, fake COVID-19 certificates, testing and disinfected stadiums, this did not mean other, non-COVID threats were absent from the planning, as will be discussed in the next section. Although COVID-19 undeniably represented the security issue that was most discussed and referred to, it was confirmed by the Counter Terrorism Policing (2021) of the United Kingdom in their statement on Euro 2020 that whilst COVID-19 had suppressed the threat of terrorism, this did not mean terrorism risks were completely absent. Hence, whilst the mediatization and anticipation of 'terrorism threats' appeared less intense than ahead of previous, post-9/11 mega-events and Euro 2016, it may still be argued that real and perceived threats of international terrorism remain present and a cause for concern for relevant authorities at politically significant and spectacular SMEs in the age of the pandemic.

Finally, as discussed earlier, Boyle and Haggerty (2012) observe how authorities and security officials will display that they are preparing for worst-case scenarios and 'planning for the worst' despite the impossibility of this. This may be exhibited through so-called 'fantasy documents' issued to ease public anxieties or to meet the set requirements by event owners. Commonly, the fantasy documents will also specify how security will be achieved in the context of SMEs. In a way, the statements from the Metropolitan Police (quoted by NextDoor, 2021) and Europol (2021) – outlining specific information-sharing arrangements and other security measures – feed into Boyle and Haggerty's (2012) influential idea and may be applied to the security delivery of Euro 2020. Albeit such press releases might not provide a full picture of the security details and technicalities, they still provide *a* picture and illustrate accurately the argument maintaining that mega-event security should not merely be done: it 'must be *seen* to be done' (ibid.: 254, original emphasis) and signs of preparedness must be exhibited for the public.

Mediation, activism and the Tartan Army in London

In terms of specific games, the group stage fixture between England and Scotland at Wembley was subject to much media attention focused on potential risks in its build-up. This fixture serves as a useful case to understand how potential football-related disorder, as one security issue, was discursively presented in the media, but also how the pandemic added new layers to this. Whilst 'hooligan' or 'potential troublemaker' behaviours are commonly presented as a threat to *public order* (see Chapter 4) the timing of Euro 2020 meant that masses of fans were also seen as a potential threat to the securitized domain of *public health* (see Boon-Kuo et al., 2021).

A body of literature on the mediation of football fans, 'hooliganism' and disorder exists in the cases previous football mega-events (Crabbe, 2003; Poulton, 2005). Whilst such portrayals are found to not always provide accurate pictures of the actual incidents (Millward, 2009; Weed, 2001), this book has previously noted how the mediation of, and social construction of, threats can impact the overall securitization of an event. Media discourses may also impact the security or policing-related responses. Further, Tsoukala (2009: 128) asserts that even in the absence of incidents, 'the press fuels insecurity by means of self-fulfilling prophecies' that may aid the sustainment of, or amplify, threat.

Redesigning, Re-Imagining and Delivering Euro 2020 in a Pandemic   139

The discourses related to control and order were particularly evident on the match-day of England versus Scotland (18 June 2021) and its immediate build-up. Though, some context is necessary here first. First, there is a long-standing football rivalry between England and Scotland. Because this match was staged at Wembley, this meant relatively easy access to London for Scottish fans, with and without tickets, via cars or trains. Second, the Scottish fans – the 'Tartan Army' – have historically been considered to behave in a peaceful and friendly manner (Giulianotti, 1995) yet do not define themselves with ideas of 'Britishness' nor 'Englishness' (Millward, 2009). For example, Giulianotti (1995) observed 'anti-English' sentiments to be growing in his ethnography of the Tartan Army at the 1992 Euros.

In the final days before England-Scotland, it was reported that London Mayor Sadiq Khan 'pleaded for the Tartan Army to stay at home' unless they possessed match tickets, due to the COVID-19 restrictions (*The Daily Mail*, 2021a). During the pandemic, directions to avoid gathering in groups have, indeed, 'formed a key plank in COVID laws and policing' (Boon-Kuo et al., 2021: 81) and fans without match-tickets were also warned over COVID rules and 'excessive drinking' as the Metro (2021) stated that 'plain-clothed officers' would be present to 'look for trouble-makers' in order to 'crackdown on excessive drinking'. Then, *The Daily Mail* (2021b) announced that 'Hundreds of police officers will form a ring of steel at Wembley' in order to prevent 'ticketless fans' and the fear of a 'mass invasion by the Tartan Army'. Thus, the prospect of ticketless fans travelling to London was presented as a potential disorder problem, but unlike previous events it also composed a potential public health problem with potential masses of crowds gathering across London's streets.

On the day of the match, it was reported that the Metropolitan Police had issued a central London dispersal zone, until 3:00 pm the next day, which provided the police with 'extra powers to break up groups of two or more people, where they believe[d] their behaviour is causing a nuisance, harassment or distress' (Sky Sports, 2021e). Reportedly, around 20,000 Scottish fans descended to London, which also highlights mega-events' impact on public spaces and everyday life in host cities.

Although reports from London suggested that the policing of the English and Scottish fans had been resolved 'efficiently', with *The Daily Mirror* Chief Reporter Andy Lines noting that the '[p]olice have been great all day. When there have been problems - they moved in quickly and efficiently' (quoted in *The Daily Mirror*, 2021), short clips published by *The Scotsman* (2021) also showed 'hundreds of police' with batons 'storming' Leicester Square. The aftermath of the match – ending with a goalless draw – was characterized by large crowds and partying in London's Leicester Square. As reported, 30 arrests were made for offences including public disorder, drunk and disorderly behaviour and assault (*The Guardian*, 2021c). Whilst *The Daily Mail* (2021c) ran the headline 'Tartan Army 1 - 0 Met Cops' and claimed that Scottish fans causing carnage had trashed Leicester Square, *The Times* (2021) under the headline 'Scotland fans rapped after ignoring plea not to go to London', focused on how Scottish fans had failed to follow the pre-match advice. Here, Scotland's tourism minister, Ivan McKee was quoted saying that: 'There are Covid restrictions in place for very good reasons and everybody should follow those restrictions [...] Football fans are no exception' (quoted in *The Times*, 2021a).

Significantly, the build-up and aftermath of England versus Scotland demonstrates how even the media and public discourses were reconfigured in distinctive way compared to previous SMEs. During Euro 2020, staged amidst a pandemic, media coverage focused on the *double risk* of fans. First, as football fans were presented as a potential threat to public order, requiring 'ring of steel' policing. Second, fans – as members of public – and their prospective physical proximity were framed as incompatible with restrictions and social distancing measures implemented to ensure public health in the face of COVID-19. Hence, the media coverage of this specific match illuminates the intersections between public disorder and public health in the pandemic. Whilst other key questions emerge, such as why the Scottish fans were not offered a separate fan zone or public viewing area, this episode can actually help us understand the securitization of public health and how public gatherings – in the age of a pandemic – were not merely represented as potential sites of public disorder, but the spread of an infectious disease and a threat to public health.

The aftermath of England-Scotland also reaffirms this: a surge in Scottish COVID-19 cases was linked to Euro 2020. Two weeks after the game, data from Public Health Scotland showed that over 1,900 people who had tested positive had attended one or more Euro 2020 events, whilst 1,300 of these had tested positive after travelling to London.[4] In light of this, international concerns about Euro 2020's crowds were expressed at EU level (*The Guardian*, 2021b) and by the WHO, whereby the latter organization claimed that the tournament's crowds and associated travelling had been the catalyst behind the rise of COVID-19 transmissions in Europe in early July (Reuters, 2021d). Whilst it remains important to acknowledge that the knowledge base remains under development, even at the time of writing, one pre-print study jointly run by Public Health England and the Culture department linked over 9,000 COVID cases to Euro 2020 fixtures in London. The study concluded that Euro 2020 'generated a significant risk to public health across the UK even when England played overseas' (Smith et al., 2021: 7). In a way, this demonstrates not merely how Euro 2020 was specifically employed to extend scientific knowledge on infection rates, but how mega-events as forecasted may act as super-spreaders amid pandemics.

In terms of 'non-COVID-19' threats, Euro 2020 predominantly proceeded without any major disruptions. Though, there were a couple of security-related incidents or 'disruptions' that took place. Possibly, as with earlier SMEs, there may also have been incidents or 'crimes that carried political baggage and were never made public' (Armstrong et al., 2017: 136) or reported upon. However, on 15 June, during Germany-France in Munich, a Greenpeace activist, with a protest message against Euro 2020 sponsor *Wolkswagen*, who parachuted into the Allianz Arena was caught by the TV cameras. The parachute activist, who lost control over the parachute, crashed with the stadium's overhead camera wires before nearly crashing into the crowds of spectators and eventually landing on the pitch.[5] In all, two people were injured and security forces intervened quickly. Whilst Greenpeace apologized for the incident, it was reported in the aftermath that the situation could have ended differently, as it posed a breach of the enforced no-fly zone around the stadium. Bavaria's Interior Minister for the State, Joachim Herrmann said, 'Due to the Greenpeace banner the marksmen did not intervene', however, 'if the police had come to a different conclusion that they might have been dealing with a terrorist attack, the aviator may well have paid with his life' (quoted in *The Guardian*, 2021d).

On Wednesday 23 June, Munich was in focus again, when a 'pitch invader' ran onto the pitch with a rainbow flag, during Germany-Hungary, to protest against UEFA's decision to not allow for the Allianz Arena to illuminate in rainbow colours as a response to anti-gay laws in Hungary.[6] Whilst the pitch invader was quickly caught by security guards, the episodes in Munich underline the linkages between protest, activism and security policies at SMEs, where governing bodies occasionally will minimize flags, banners or messages 'in the name of remaining politically neutral' (Millward, n.d.: 22).

Moreover, on 16 June, the same day as Italy's group stage match against Switzerland, a suspected car bomb was found in a parked-up car close to *Stadio Olimpico*. The package, spotted by a fan, was eliminated in a controlled explosion by Italian security forces, and it was not believed to be linked specifically to the tournament (*The Independent*, 2021d). Yet, given the proximity to the stadium and many fans venturing the stadium, this episode highlights how contemporary mega-events are impacted by wider security threats within their cities and the areas around the stadiums. In that sense, the five weeks of Euro 2020 were no exception.

A carnival of chaos: The Wembley security breach

Most noteworthy, however, were the incidents occurring during the day and night of Euro 2020's closure (11 July). These incidents were characterized by the outbreaks of football-related social disorder in relation to the final between Italy and England in London. Whilst the final itself did not kick off until 20:00 GMT, large crowds of fans had gathered across the English capital including Wembley throughout the day to socialize and party. This led to, *inter alia*, the evacuation of King's Cross station due to pyrotechnics and merely hours before kick-off, real-time reports on social media emerged over Wembley going into 'lockdown' after separate incidents where 'hordes of ticketless fans had breached sections of the stadium and stormed the concourse' (Reddy, 2021).

As *The Independent*'s Melissa Reddy (2021) described it, '[f]ences were torn down and thrown aside, with multiple eyewitnesses suggesting thousands had pushed in, including through a disabled entrance'. This again led to violent clashes, 'with videos capturing an adult punching a kid in the head inside the stadium, while a group of men kicked an Asian male while he was on the floor' (ibid.). Shortly after, it was confirmed that there had been a breach of security at Wembley resulting in a number of people managing to enter the stadium without tickets. Subsequently, the English FA's Chief Executive Mark Bullingham confirmed that a review would be conducted into the incident and said that, 'There were a large number of drunken yobs trying to force their way in, we run a stadium not a fortress' (quoted in BBC, 2021b). The aftermath of the match also saw confrontations and clashes between fans and the police continue as 86 arrests were made and 19 police officers were injured across London (Reuters, 2021e). Following the final at Wembley, UEFA's ethics and disciplinary committee opened a disciplinary proceeding against the FA. From the FA's perspective, the public disorder was described as 'unprecedented' and 'nothing like we've ever seen at Wembley before any other event' (*The Times*, 2021b). Whilst the FA claimed that the majority of issues appeared in areas that were the police's responsibility, the Metropolitan Police, in another statement, claimed that police intervention saved the final from being abandoned, that stewards were 'overwhelmed' when fans began to push through security checks and that the policing operation itself had not failed (BBC, 2021c).

Naturally, all this raises some very important question concerning the organizational lessons that must be drawn from the Euro 2020 final. Considering Wembley's central position in domestic and international football calendars, for cultural events, and its likely importance in future English mega-event bids, these lessons can therefore inform forthcoming mega-events. At the time of writing, it is also not unlikely that there will be a UK-wide bid for the hosting rights of the 2030 World Cup. Hence, such questions speak for example to the division of responsibility, communication and coordination between private security firms at event venues and the police and the wider stadium infrastructure and ring. They also relate to the availability of regulated public viewing events for non-ticket holders and the relatively late kick-off time (20:00 GMT). Following violent clashes between Glasgow Rangers fans and the Manchester police during the 2008 UEFA Cup final, Millward (2009: 395) maintained that outbreaks of football-related social disorder and the associated human failures and organizational errors or shortcomings require critical reflection; otherwise, the 'future costs may be far greater'. In a way, it seems timely and appropriate to replicate such argument in the context of Euro 2020's final, so that reflection and learning can serve to avoid similar episodes at future one-off football matches or mega-events.

Conclusion: Towards a 'new normal'

[S]ome fans have noted that the football stadium served as a 'gym', as a 'laboratory' to pilot strategies and technologies of control before implementing them in a broader public space.

(Numerato, 2018: 15)

Matching arguments to the quote above have also been expressed by other researchers in the context of football's or sport's technological or security-related developments (Clavel, 2013; Tsoukala, 2009; Yang and Cole, 2020). It is established that SMEs represent 'privileged sites and moments for the testing of advanced high-tech surveillance systems' (Klauser, 2013: 291) and the development of new security collaborations. In a way, this chapter supports the relevance of such perspective. Yet, this chapter updates such perspective's meanings in the pandemic context. It is argued that the final preparations before Euro 2020's commencement, and its delivery, underpin the idea that sporting spaces may be approached analytically and practically as social and spatial 'testing grounds' or *de facto* gymnasiums for new security and safety measures. Nonetheless, particularly one key difference is crucial to underline.

Sporting spaces have socio-historically been employed to pilot new crowd management techniques and surveillance technologies to combat disorder and 'hooliganism' (Armstrong and Giulianotti, 1998; Hodges, 2019). Then, the post-9/11 'war on terror' landscape, which according to Roche (2017: 129), symbolized a 'new era' of mega-event security, added to this. Subsequently, SMEs became 'testing grounds' for new technological solutions and security practices that supplemented or laminated pre-existing security infrastructures to protect crowded spaces from terror (Coaffee et al., 2011; Giulianotti, 2013). What Euro 2020's final build-up and delivery collectively exemplify is *another* new moment – or era – whereby SMEs were employed as testing grounds or opportunities for the implementation of new COVID-19 induced or related security and safety measures (COVID-pilot events, apps/QR-codes, vaccine passports, social distancing, tracing technologies, etc.). These were piloted through designated 'test events', guided by security and health experts and spread through networking events and information exchanges. As Euro 2020 commenced, COVID-19-related security and safety practices were integrated into Euro 2020's local and international networks of security actors that addressed COVID-19 and other layers of threats including those that have been most prominent at previous SMEs, like 'terrorism', 'crime', and 'hooliganism'. This epitomizes Euro 2020's redesign. Yet, the broader implications of such argument are that this revises and extends our understanding of SMEs as increasingly significant institutional laboratories for the pursuit of 'security' and the means employed to achieve it. Euro 2020 ultimately served as a live test event for the *reopening of societies* during and post-pandemic.

This largely descriptive chapter also discussed the discourses and decisions related to the presence of fans in Euro 2020's build-up in relation to SMEs as commercially attractive spectacles. It also shed a light on the security-related operations and incidents *throughout* the month-long competition, including the scenes of disorder throughout London for the final between England and Italy. And so, whereas Euro 2020 came to a dramatic conclusion at Wembley on 11 July 2021 – following a year-long delay – this chapter argues that this competition's delivery was shaped by its security-related redesign and overall re-imagination. It must be repeated, though, that whilst a mega-event lasts for a very intense and all-consuming five-week period, their aftermaths can influence cities for many years. To end this chapter, an interesting discussion point is therefore whether Euro 2020's 'security legacies' now may extend into new SME contexts, such as the upcoming Euro 2024 in Germany or other public settings. However, as researchers warn us in the context of COVID-19, such legacies may also induce new modes of governance and sorting come to 'characterize our new "normal"' (Hutchins and Andrejevcic, 2021: 376–377). It therefore represents an important task for future post-event research to carefully and critically explore how security methods and (so-called) best practices from Euro 2020 – as the first gigantic SME hosted during the pandemic – come to shape the 'new normal' of SME security governance. Whilst 9/11, for two decades, has been regularly viewed as *the* turning point within the academic study of 'security' and mega-event securitization (Giulianotti and Klauser, 2010; Roche, 2017), which paved way for a 'new normal' defined by exceptionality and state-of-art security, the COVID-19 crisis has come to represent another external moment initiating an epoch with transformative potential. This historical moment and indeed metamorphic passage will likely influence the dynamics, logics and formations of mega-event security for years to come.

Notes

1 See: https://www.gov.uk/government/publications/information-for-ticket-holders-attending-the-euro-2020-events-research-programme-matches/euro-2020-events-research-programme-matches-ticket-holder-qa (accessed 2 July 2021).
2 Reportedly, 10,000 volunteers for the 2020 Olympics quit over COVID-safety fears just over a month prior to the Olympics (see CNN, 2021).
3 See: https://www.skysports.com/football/news/11095/12322831/euro-2020-scotland-fans-without-tickets-for-england-group-game-urged-not-to-travel-to-london.
4 See: https://www.theguardian.com/world/2021/jun/30/surge-in-scottish-covid-cases-raises-euro-2020-safety-concerns.
5 See: https://www.youtube.com/watch?v=KDVWclRNjys, YouTube video (accessed 28 June 2021).
6 See: https://theathletic.com/news/germany-vs-hungary-rainbow-fan-uefa/l5pesyVe GAsy.

Bibliography

Armstrong, G & Giulianotti, R (1998) From Another Angle: Police Surveillance and Football Supporters. In C. Norris & J. Moran (eds) *Surveillance, Closed Circuit Television and Social Control*. Aldershot. Ashgate, 113–135.

Armstrong, G, Giulianotti, R & Hobbs, D (2017) *Policing the 2012 London Olympics: Legacy and Social Exclusion*. London. Routledge.

BBC (2021a) Euro 2020: Thousands of Scotland fans gather in central London. *BBC*. Available from: https://www.bbc.co.uk/news/uk-scotland-57516928 (Accessed 20 June 2021).

BBC (2021b) FA Review after Fans Break into Wembley for Final. *BBC*. Available from: https://www.bbc.co.uk/news/uk-57803366 (Accessed 15 July 2021).

BBC (2021c) Euro 2020: Met Denies Wembley Police Operation Failed. *BBC*. Available from: https://www.bbc.co.uk/news/uk-england-london-57841689 (Accessed 15 July 2021).

Bigo, D (2008) EU Police Cooperation: National Sovereignty Framed by European Security? In E. Guild & F. Geyer (eds) *Security Versus Justice? Police and Judicial Cooperation in the European Union*. Aldershot. Ashgate, 91–108.

Bigo, D, Guild, E & Kuskonmaz, EM (2021) Obedience in Times of COVID-19 Pandemics: A Renewed Governmentality of Unease? *Global Discourse* 11(1–2), 1–2.

Boon-Kuo, L, Brodie, A, Keene-McCann, J, Sentas, V & Weber, L (2021) Policing Biosecurity: Police Enforcement of Special Measures in New South Wales and Victoria during the COVID-19 Pandemic. *Current Issues in Criminal Justice* 33(1), 76–88.

Boyle, P & Haggerty, KD (2012) Planning for the Worst: Risk, Uncertainty and the Olympic Games. *British Journal of Sociology* 63(2), 241–259.

Clavel, A (2013) Armed Forces and Sports Mega Events: An Accepted Involvement in a Globalized World. *Sport in Society* 16(2), 205–222.

CNN (2021) About 10,000 Tokyo Olympic Volunteers Have Quit with Games Closing in. *CNN*. Available from: https://edition.cnn.com/2021/06/03/sport/tokyo-olympics-volunteers-covid-intl-hnk/index.html (Accessed 11 June 2021).

Coaffee, J, Fussey, P & Moore, C (2011) Laminated Security for London 2012: Enhancing Security Infrastructures to Defend Mega Sporting Events. *Urban Studies* 48(15), 3311–3327.

COE (2020) Impact of Covid-19 on S4 Policies and Practices – Webinar. Available from: https://www.coe.int/en/web/sport/violence-convention/-/asset_publisher/y26bgYl86FcF/content/impact-of-covid-19-on-s4-policies-and-practices-webinar?_101_INSTANCE_y26bgYl86FcF_viewMode=view/ (Accessed 22 August 2021).

Cottey, A (2007) *Security in the New Europe*. Basingstoke. Palgrave Macmillan.

Counter Terrorism Policing (2021) Counter Terrorism Policing Call on British Public to 'Know the Game Plan' for Security while Enjoying Euro 2020. Available from: https://www.counterterrorism.police.uk/counter-terrorism-policing-call-on-british-public-to-know-the-game-plan-for-security-while-enjoying-euro-2020/ (Accessed 12 July 2021).

Crabbe, T (2003) The Public Gets What the Public Wants' England Football Fans, 'Truth' Claims and Mediated Realities. *International Review for the Sociology of Sport* 38(4), 413–425.

ESPN (2021) 'No Point' Hosting Euro 2020 Across 12 Countries with No Fans – FIFPro Secretary. *ESPN*. Available from: https://www.espn.co.uk/football/uefa-european-championship/story/4305074/no-point-hosting-euro-2020-across-12-countries-with-no-fans-fifpro-secretary (Accessed 4 March 2021).

Europol (2021) Keeping the UEFA Euro 2020 Championship Safe – 10 June 2021 Press Release. Available from: https://www.europol.europa.eu/newsroom/news/keeping-uefa-euro-2020-championship-safe (Accessed 22 August 2021).

FSE (2020) UEFA Super Cup Budapest: FSE Review. FSE. Available from: https://documentcloud.adobe.com/link/track?uri=urn:aaid:scds:US:ba981c51-4d47-4e47-913a-cb9e1c607158 (Accessed 20 July 2021).

FSE (2021) FSE Calls for Fan Involvement in Return to Stadia Discussions. Available from: https://www.fanseurope.org/en/news/news-3/2467-fse-calls-for-fan-involvement-in-return-to-stadia-discussions-2.html (Accessed 22 August 2021).

Fussey, P (2015) Command, Control and Contestation: Negotiating Security at the London 2012 Olympics. *The Geographical Journal* 181(3), 212–223.

Fussey, P & Coaffee, J (2012) Balancing Local and Global Security Leitmotifs: Counter-Terrorism and the Spectacle of Sporting Mega-Events. *International Review for the Sociology of Sport* 47(3), 268–285.

Giulianotti, R (1995) Football and the Politics of Carnival: An Ethnographic Study of Scottish Fans in Sweden. *International Review for the Sociology of Sport* 30(2), 191–220.

Giulianotti, R (2013) Six Security Legacies of Major Sporting Events. *ICSS Journal* 1(1), 95–101.

Giulianotti, R & Klauser, F (2010) Security Governance and Sport Mega-Events: Toward an Interdisciplinary Research Agenda. *Journal of Sport and Social Issues* 34(1), 48–60.

Glasgow Times (2021) Covid Measures for Glasgow Euro 2020 Fan Zone still 'Under Consideration'. *Glasgow Times*. Available from: https://www.glasgowtimes.co.uk/news/19348773.covid-measures-glasgow-euro-2020-fan-zone-still-under-consideration/ (Accessed 23 June 2021).

Hassan, I, Mukaigawara, M, King, L, Fernandes, G & Sridhar, D (2021) Hindsight Is 2020? Lessons in Global Health Governance One Year into the Pandemic. *Nature Medicine* 27(3), 396–400.

Hodges, A (2019) *Fan Activism, Protest and Politics: Ultras in Post-Socialist Croatia.* Oxon. Routledge.

Hutchins, B & Andrejevcic, M (2021) Olympian Surveillance: Sports Stadiums and the Normalization of Biometric Monitoring. *International Journal of Communication* 15, 363–382.

Kilburn Times (2021) A Full-time Dedicated Euros Policing Team will Police Wembley Stadium. *Kilburn Times*. Available from: https://www.kilburntimes.co.uk/news/keeping-wembley-safe-during-euro2020-7960250 (Accessed 27 May 2021).

Klauser, F (2011) Commonalities and Specificities in Mega-Event Securitisation: The Example of Euro 2008 in Austria and Switzerland. In C.J. Bennett and K.D. Haggerty (eds) *Security Games, Surveillance and Control at Mega-Events.* London. Routledge, 120–136.

Klauser, F (2013) Spatialities of Security and Surveillance: Managing Spaces, Separations and Circulations at Sport Mega Events. *Geoforum* 49, 289–298.

KNVB (2021) Study by Fieldlab Events during Netherlands v Latvia in Johan Cruijff Arena. Available from: https://www.knvb.com/news/extra/oranje/1171/study-fieldlab-events-during-netherlands-v-latvia-johan-cruijff-arena (Accessed 22 August 2021).

Larner, W & Le Heron, R (2002) The Spaces and Subjects of a Globalising Economy: A Situated Exploration of Method. *Environment and Planning D: Society and Space* 20(6), 753–774.

Lee Ludvigsen, JA & Parnell, D (2021) Redesigning the Games? The 2020 Olympic Games, Playbooks and New Sports Event Risk Management Tools. *Managing Sport and Leisure*, 1–13.

Marivoet, S (2006) UEFA Euro 2004™ Portugal: The Social Construction of a Sports Mega-Event and Spectacle. *The Sociological Review* 54, 127–143.

McCann, E (2011) Urban Policy Mobilities and Global Circuits of Knowledge: Toward a Research Agenda. *Annals of the Association of American Geographers* 101(1), 107–130.

Metro (2021) Fans Warned over Covid Rules and Excessive Drinking as Euros Set to Begin. Available from: https://metro.co.uk/2021/06/09/euro-2020-london-fans-warned-over-covid-rules-and-excessive-drinking-14744898/.

Millward, P (2009) Glasgow Rangers Supporters in the City of Manchester: The Degeneration of a 'Fan Party' into a 'Hooligan Riot'. *International Review for the Sociology of Sport* 44(4), 381–398.

Millward, P (n.d.) End of Project Report: Queering Football–Tackling Homophobia and Promoting Anti-Discrimination around Major Sports Events [unpublished]. Liverpool John Moores University, 1–33.

NextDoor (2021) The Met Polices Euro 2020. Available from: https://nextdoor.co.uk/agency-post/england/wandsworth/wandsworth-police/the-met-polices-euros-2020-17592200911025/

Numerato, D (2018) *Football Fans, Activism and Social Change*. London. Routledge.

Parent, MM & Ruetsch, A (2021) *Managing Major Sports Events*. London/New York. Routledge.

Parnell, D, Bond, AJ, Widdop, P & Cockayne, D (2021) Football Worlds: Business and Networks During COVID-19. *Soccer & Society* 22(1–2), 19–26.

Parnell, D, Widdop, P, Bond, A & Wilson, R (2020) COVID-19, Networks and Sport. *Managing Sport and Leisure*, 1–7.

Poulton, E (2005) English Media Representation of Football-Related Disorder: 'Brutal, Short-Hand and Simplifying'? *Sport in Society* 8(1), 27–47.

Reddy, M (2021) Fan Violence the Only Thing That Disgraces England in Euro 2020 Final Defeat. *The Independent*. Available from: https://www.independent.co.uk/sport/football/england-fans-euro-2020-final-b1882271.html

Reuters (2021a) Fate of Euro 2020 Tournament Hangs on Vaccine Efforts. *Reuters*. Available from: https://www.reuters.com/article/uk-soccer-uefa-euros/fate-of-euro-2020-tournament-hangs-on-vaccine-efforts-idUKKBN29G280

Reuters (2021b) UEFA Confirm Rome as EURO 2020 Host City after Crowd Guarantees. *Reuters*. Available from: https://www.reuters.com/article/uk-soccer-italy-idUKKBN2C124Y

Reuters (2021c) Soccer-Europol Ready for 'Important Security Challenges' of Scattered Euros. *Reuters*. Available from: https://www.reuters.com/article/uk-soccer-euro-security-idUKKCN2DM1SC

Reuters (2021d) Euro 2020 Crowds Driving Rise in COVID-19 Infections, Says WHO. *Reuters*. Available from: https://www.reuters.com/world/europe/who-warns-third-coronavirus-wave-europe-2021-07-01/

Reuters (2021e) London Police Say 86 Arrested around Euro 2020 Soccer Final. *Reuters*. Available from: https://www.reuters.com/world/uk/london-police-say-86-arrested-around-euro-2020-soccer-final-2021-07-12/

Roche, M (2000) *Mega-Events and Modernity: Olympics and Expos in the Growth of Global Culture*. London. Routledge.

Roche, M (2017) *Mega-Events and Social Change: Spectacle, Legacy and Public Culture*. Manchester. Manchester University Press.

Sheptycki, J (2020) The Politics of Policing a Pandemic Panic. *Australian & New Zealand Journal of Criminology* 53(2), 157–173.

Sky News (2021a) COVID-19: How Bad Is Coronavirus in the Cities Hosting Euro 2020? Available from: https://news.sky.com/story/covid-19-how-bad-is-coronavirus-in-the-cities-hosting-euro-2020-12328662 (Accessed 01 July 2021).

Sky News (2021b) COVID-19: Vaccine Passports or Proof of Negative Test to Be Used at Wembley for Euro 2020 Matches. Available from: https://news.sky.com/story/covid-vaccine-passports-to-be-used-at-wembley-for-euro-2020-matches-12328009.

Sky News (2021c) COVID-19: Scotland's Euro 2020 COVID Safety Regime Criticised as 'The Most Lenient in Europe'. Available from: https://news.sky.com/story/covid-19-scotlands-euro-2020-covid-safety-regime-criticised-as-the-most-lenient-in-europe-12328458?dcmp=snt-sf-twitter.

Sky Sports (2021a) Euro 2020: Will There Be International Fans in Stadiums at This Summer's Tournament? Available from: https://www.skysports.com/football/news/19692/12255548/euro-2020-will-there-be-international-fans-in-stadiums-at-this-summers-tournament.

Sky Sports (2021b) Euro 2020: Host Cities Must Allow Fans into Grounds or Risk Being Dropped, Says UEFA president. Available from: https://www.skysports.com/football/news/11095/12247490/euro-2020-host-cities-must-allow-fans-into-grounds-or-risk-being-dropped-says-uefa-president.

Sky Sports (2021c) Euro 2020: Wembley to Stage Extra Knockout Game in Tournament after Dublin Dropped as Host City by UEFA. Available from: https://www.skysports.com/football/news/19692/12284455/euro-2020-wembley-to-stage-extra-knockout-game-in-tournament-after-dublin-dropped-as-host-city-by-uefa.

Sky Sports (2021d) England Sack Part of Euro 2020 Security Team Following Safety Concerns. Available from: https://www.skysports.com/football/news/12016/12337858/england-sack-part-of-euro-2020-security-team-following-safety-concerns.

Sky Sports (2021e) England vs Scotland: Met Police Make Arrests amid Central London Dispersal Order during Euro 2020 Clash. Available from: https://www.skysports.com/football/news/12040/12336014/england-vs-scotland-met-police-issue-central-london-dispersal-order-ahead-of-euro-2020-clash.

Smith, AE, Hopkins, S, Turner, C, Dack, K, Trelfa, A, Peh, J & Monk, P (2021) Preprint Version: Public Health Impact of Mass Sporting and Cultural Events in a Rising COVID-19 Prevalence in England. Available from: https://khub.net/documents/135939561/338928724/Public+health+impact+of+mass+sporting+and+cultural+events+in+a+rising+COVID-19+prevalence+in+England.pdf/05204895-1576-1ee7-b41e-880d5d6b4f17 (Accessed 22 August 2021).

Spaaij, R (2013) Risk, Security and Technology: Governing Football Supporters in the Twenty-First Century. *Sport in Society* 16(2), 167–183.

The Daily Mail (2021a) 'Up to 20,000 Scotland Fans Are Heading for Hyde Park' as Sadiq Khan Warns Ticketless Supporters Not to Gather in London for Euro 2020 Clash with England amid Fears over Spike in Covid Cases. *Daily Mail.* Available from: https://www.dailymail.co.uk/news/article-9692151/Sadiq-Khan-warns-ticketless-Scotland-fans-not-gather-London-Euro-2020-clash.html

The Daily Mail (2021b) Hundreds of Police Officers Will Form a Ring of Steel at Wembley for England's Euro 2020 Clash with Scotland to Prevent Ticketless Fans Accessing the Stadium amid Fears of a Mass Invasion by the Tartan Army. *Daily Mail.* Available from: https://www.dailymail.co.uk/sport/football/article-9694631/Hundreds-police-form-ring-steel-Wembley-Tartan-Army-march-London.html.

The Daily Mail (2021c) Tartan Army 1 – 0 Met Cops. *Daily Mail.* Available from: https://www.dailymail.co.uk/news/article-9700213/Tartan-Armys-night-carnage-Scotland-fans-trash-Leicester-Square.html.

The Daily Mirror (2021) England and Scotland Fans Scuffle in Ugly Scenes Outside Wembley after Euro 2020 Draw. *Daily Mirror.* Available from: https://www.mirror.co.uk/sport/football/news/breaking-ugly-scenes-outside-wembley-24353263.

The Guardian (2021a) Covid Passports Will Be Discriminatory and Must Be Scrapped, Say MPs. *The Guardian.* Available from: https://www.theguardian.com/politics/2021/jun/12/covid-passports-will-be-discriminatory-and-must-be-scrapped-say-mps.

The Guardian (2021b) Covid: Euro 2020 Crowds 'A Recipe for Disaster', Warns EU Committee. *The Guardian.* Available from: https://www.theguardian.com/world/2021/jul/01/covid-euro-2020-crowds-a-recipe-for-disaster-warns-german-minister.

The Guardian (2021c) Police Arrest 30 in London after England v Scotland Euro 2020 Match. Available from: https://www.theguardian.com/uk-news/2021/jun/19/police-arrests-london-after-england-scotland-euro-2020-match.

The Guardian (2021d) Greenpeace Euro 2020 Parachutist Lucky Not to Be Shot Down, Says Politician. *The Guardian*. Available from: https://www.theguardian.com/environment/2021/jun/16/police-hold-greenpeace-activist-after-euro-2020-parachute-stunt-goes-awry.

The Independent (2021a) Matt Hancock Claims UK Won't Offer to Host Euro 2020. *The Independent*. Available from: https://www.independent.co.uk/sport/football/matt-hancock-euro-2020-england-wembley-b1805271.html (Accessed 2 April 2021).

The Independent (2021b) Euro 2021: COVID Vaccine Passports to Be Used for Wembley Matches. The Independent. Available from: https://www.independent.co.uk/sport/football/euro-2020-vaccine-passports-wembley-b1861877.html

The Independent (2021c) Police at Nerve Center in The Hague Share Euro 2020 Intel. *The Independent*. Available from: https://www.independent.co.uk/news/police-at-nerve-center-in-the-hague-share-euro-2020-intel-europol-police-the-hague-the-hague-netherlands-b1863607.html (Accessed 19 June 2021).

The Independent (2021d) Suspected Car Bomb Found Near Rome's Stadio Olimpico Ahead of Italy's Euro 2020 Game. *The Independent*. Available from: https://www.independent.co.uk/sport/football/euro-2021-car-bomb-rome-b1867528.html (Accessed 19 June 2021).

The Scotsman (2021) Hundreds of Police Seen 'Storming' London's Leicester Square as Fans Clash during Scotland v England Match. *Scotsman*. Available from: https://www.scotsman.com/news/uk-news/euro-2020-hundreds-of-police-seen-storming-londons-leicester-square-as-fans-clash-during-scotland-v-england-match-3279208 (Accessed 20 June 2021).

The Times (2021a) Euro 2020: Scotland Fans Rapped after Ignoring Plea Not to Go to London. *The Times*. Available from: https://www.thetimes.co.uk/article/euro-2020-scotland-fans-rapped-after-ignoring-plea-not-to-go-to-london-fwzqkxd8c (Accessed 10 July 2021).

The Times (2021b) 'Wembley Under Siege: How England Fans Stormed the Euro 2020 Final. *The Times*. Available from: https://www.thetimes.co.uk/article/wembley-under-siege-how-england-fans-stormed-the-euro-2020-final-wl6gv9rd5 (Accessed 22 August 2021).

Tsoukala, A (2009) *Football Hooliganism in Europe: Security and Civil Liberties in the Balance*. Basingstoke. Palgrave.

Turner, M (2013) Modern 'Live' Football: Moving from the Panoptican Gaze to the Performative, Virtual and Carnivalesque. *Sport in Society* 16(1), 85–93.

UEFA (2020a) UEFA Allows Return of Fans at Maximum 30% of Capacity Pending Approval of Local Authorities. Available from: https://www.uefa.com/insideuefa/mediaservices/mediareleases/news/0262-1081de31d4dc-eb42ed3fe9e8-1000–return-of-fans-at-maximum-30-of-capacity-pending-local-approval/ (Accessed 30 June 2021).

UEFA (2020b) UEFA Minimum Health & Hygiene Requirements for the Return of Spectators. UEFA. Available from: https://editorial.uefa.com/resources/0262-1081a4df2c6d-98022dcc8f82-1000/uefa_minimum_health_hygiene_requirements_for_the_return_of_spectators_.pdf (Accessed 30 July 2021).

UEFA (2020c) UEFA Meets General Secretaries of Member Associations. Available from: https://www.uefa.com/insideuefa/mediaservices/mediareleases/news/0260-102b2c2ace44-637fb4a08f89-1000–uefa-meets-general-secretaries/ (Accessed 13 July 2021).

UEFA (2020d) UEFA Super Cup: Fans Must Comply with Special Measures to Protect Health. Available from: https://www.uefa.com/insideuefa/about-uefa/news/0261-10735 cb08dbd-62041a47bb3c-1000–safety-message-for-super-cup-fans/?iv=true (Accessed 13 July 2021).

UEFA (2021a) UEFA Meets EURO 2020 Hosts. Available from: https://www.uefa.com/insideuefa/about-uefa/news/0265-116f42eb4c69-6bafcc7bae90-1000/ (Accessed 13 July 2021).

UEFA (2021b) Eight EURO 2020 Hosts Confirm Matches with Spectators. Available from: https://www.uefa.com/insideuefa/mediaservices/mediareleases/news/0268-11fff5dff16f-4cf8e9e33935-1000–eight-euro-2020-hosts-confirm-matches-with-spectators/ (Accessed 13 July 2021).

UEFA (2021c) Top Swiss Expert on Global Pandemic Appointed as UEFA EURO 2020 Medical Advisor. Available from: https://www.uefa.com/insideuefa/mediaservices/mediareleases/news/0265-117149c1460d-36a763f715e6-1000/ (Accessed 13 July 2021).

UEFA (2021d) UEFA EURO 2020 Code of Conduct for Spectators: March 2021. Available from: https://editorial.uefa.com/resources/0268-11fe38356536-8f3c3625933e-1000/20210408_uefa_euro_2020_code_of_conduct_-_spectators_final.pdf (Accessed 30 July 2021).

UEFA (2021e) EURO 2020, a Tournament Like No Other: Q&A with Martin Kallen. Available from: https://www.uefa.com/insideuefa/about-uefa/news/026a-1278357a67a8-93258700287b-1000–euro-2020-q-a-with-martin-kallen/ (Accessed 12 July 2021).

UEFA (n.d.) COVID-19 Guidance for Your EURO 2020 Match. Available from: https://www.uefa.com/uefaeuro-2020/event-guide/london/stadium/covid-19-guidance/ (Accessed 12 July 2021).

Weed, M (2001) ING-GER-LAND AT EURO 2000: How Handbags at 20 Paces' Was Portrayed as a Full-Scale Riot. *International Review for the Sociology of Sport* 36(4), 407–424.

Włoch, R (2012) UEFA as a New Agent of Global Governance: A Case Study of Relations between UEFA and the Polish Government against the Background of the UEFA EURO 2012. *Journal of Sport and Social Issues* 37(3), 297–311.

Yahoo (2021) Russian Euro 2020 Organisers 'Not Afraid' of Coronavirus. *Yahoo.* Available from: https://sports.yahoo.com/russian-euro-2020-organisers-not-130004380.html (Accessed 10 July 2021).

Yang, C & Cole, CL (2020) Smart Stadium as a Laboratory of Innovation: Technology, Sport, and Datafied Normalization of the Fans. *Communication & Sport*, 1–16.

Zirin, D (2016) *Brazil's Dance with the Devil: The World Cup, the Olympics and the Fight for Democracy.* Chicago. Haymarket Books.

Chapter 7

Conclusions

Uncertainty, Legacy and New Threats

This book argues that sport mega-events (SMEs) serve as end products and expressions of wider developments in the fields of security. Through its argument and empirical material, this book contributes not solely to the sociology of sport, but to wider debates situated in the sociological and critical study of 'security'. The book's key contention remains important because, as Chapter 1 alluded to, in what is oft-characterized as an uncertain post-9/11 world, scholars have argued that the security efforts made before and during contemporary SMEs give us a 'glimpse into the most painstaking security planning outside of warfare' (Boyle et al., 2015: 112). Others assert that the 'sport mega-event field [is] ideal for investigating how, today, people and objects on the move are monitored, filtered and protected in highly differential and flexible ways' (Klauser, 2017: 8–9). Importantly, such significant claims were made well before the COVID-19 pandemic, which, in distinctive ways, elevated the focus on safety and security at SMEs even further. Furthermore, mega-events, on a general level, provide social scientists with windows to analyze wider changes, social issues and modes of social control (Boykoff, 2020, 2017; Roche, 2000). Hence, aiming to make better sense of the social realities surrounding mega-event securitizations, whilst upholding the tradition of investigating mainstream sociological or political issues through the lens of global sport, this book has set out to examine the processes, activities, logics and policies that oriented the constructions and meanings of 'security' in the valuable case of Euro 2020.

Throughout its chapters, the book has explored the socio-historical roots of mega-event securitizations (Chapter 1), the meanings and constructions of mega-event security (Chapters 2 and 3) and the relationships between fan networks, policing and changing policies (Chapter 4). Then, in context of the COVID-19 pandemic's impact on Euro 2020 and the wider society, the book explores the dramatic postponement of Euro 2020 (Chapter 5) and how this mega-event, reflexively, was redesigned, re-imagined and eventually delivered whilst the pandemic was still ongoing across Europe and the globe (Chapter 6). The book's key arguments must be seen in light of the contentions and acceptances that the modern, globalized world is increasingly preoccupied with the concepts and management of security (Zedner, 2009), risk (Beck, 1992) and threats to our personal safety

DOI: 10.4324/9781003258445-8

152   Conclusions

(Bauman, 2000). This has elevated the need to secure places, objects and people in the present day.

In such context, the book argues that Euro 2020's security-related developments, pre-planning, constructions and delivery – assembled to secure the geographically extraordinary event – prove as an exemplary site for especially two distinct practices of security governance in the present-day world. Consequently, such argument is extremely important and possesses implication beyond the football world because it confirms mega-event security's position as *end products* and *expressions* of wider security dynamics, practices, developments and outlooks.

First, this relates to the mobilities and (re)circulations of (in)formal security-related policies, knowledge and practices on a transnational scale. Yet, this must also be seen within the wider frames of policy transfer (Klauser, 2012), the roles of fan networks in the consultation processes (Numerato, 2018) and the turn towards cooperation networks and European-wide knowledge-sharing in a transnationalized epoch of security (Bigo, 2000; Tsoukala, 2009). Second, Euro 2020 manifested the exercise of precaution and future-oriented security outlooks and policies. These outlooks too are shaped by wider security trends in a post-9/11 world (Mythen and Walklate, 2008). Whilst these driving forces have appeared in existing research on SMEs (Boyle and Haggerty, 2009; Klauser, 2011a), the reality is that every SME possesses unique local characteristics and contexts which they are planned and delivered within. This claim comes especially true in relation to Euro 2020 which, for the very first time, took up a 'pan-European' shape. In addition to ensuring safe or secure events that accounted for the changing dynamics in the international system, the book also shows how these underpinning processes can tie firmly into commercial and sanitizing processes that are brought together under the umbrella of 'security'.

With reference to this book's aims, tied up to exploring security constructions and meanings, the *construction* of 'security' hence sheds a light on what 'security' *means*. Ultimately, this means that 'security' does not solely serve purposes related to basic public safety. It concurrently relates to a range of private interests and business-related aspirations surrounding neoliberal mega-events. As security complexes at SMEs intensify and the need to secure becomes increasingly apparent, these may be concealed or shielded. Referring back to the two major processes, the recirculation of security policies or practices may then facilitate for commercially fruitful spheres. Meanwhile, precautionary principles may work to justify those policies that are reproduced in new contexts or assist the implementation of new extraordinary security measures.

However, this book also argues that the meanings of 'security' in the mega-event context were significantly reconfigured in light of COVID-19. Ultimately, Chapters 5 and 6 collectively capture a monumental security management shift: away from endemic security threats towards the pandemic threat characterized by its inherent suddenness, its seismic and exceptional moment and geographic diffuseness. Because the nature of the securitized 'invisible' coronavirus meant that most people represented both a 'security threat' *and* the subject to be 'secured',

Conclusions   153

the meanings of cleansed and secure spaces also changed temporarily and spatially and referred to spaces with no or restricted crowds.

This book has provided an original insight to and re-mobilized a framework for understanding the multiple mechanisms through which 'security' is constructed in the pre-planning of an SME. I explain this through the extended 'troika of security' (Chapter 3) which captures the processes, policies and activities that enable lesson-drawing, precautionary logics and the employment of institutional memory. The processes, assessments, activities and policies that assisted the construction of 'security' at SMEs are largely shaped by broader processes that aim to establish 'security' in the present-day world. As such, by building on existing insights from past mega-events (Armstrong et al., 2017; Boyle and Haggerty, 2009; Klauser, 2010, 2011a, 2011b, 2012, 2017), this book has relocated retrospective and future-oriented processes and assessments that collectively encapsulate the securitization of Euro 2020 and, essentially, contribute to notions and aims of security.

Therefore, this work contributes with original knowledge and with an extension of a conceptual framework that assists the sensemaking of exactly how the recirculation of existing models and templates occurs beside the contemplation of worst-case scenarios in the interrogation of the case of Euro 2020. Thereby, this book also answers the call for production of new case studies of event-specific security strategies and governance for a more comparative study of SMEs (see Giulianotti and Klauser, 2010). Moreover, and crucially, within this, the book has located and empirically accounted for the presence of fan networks, which I argue constitute agents of knowledge generation and transfer. In itself this is important, because despite mobilizations and the increased recognition in security matters, the voices of fans and fan networks have, largely, been missing from the earlier literature on mega-event security (Doidge et al., 2019). Hence, the multiple – and sometimes blurry – roles of football fans within a mega-event's security governance are captured empirically and conceptually in this book.

Overall, the book offers a comprehensive and original contribution to the field with its robust analysis and extended framework, which identify and extend key processes in SME securitizations. This originates from the Euro 2020 case study, as a highly extraordinary yet underappreciated SME. Accepting the potential limitations to the case study approach, Euro 2020 was, in a nutshell, the first European Championship in football to be staged across 11 countries, to be postponed and eventually staged during a pandemic. Through a critical engagement with publicly accessible policy documents, guidelines, media sources and interviewed stakeholders, this book has provided an original breakdown of the processes of learning, knowledge exchange, policing, the realities of uncertainty and the requirements that collectively informed the security assemblage of Euro 2020. With its theoretical purchase, empirical findings and mobilized framework, the book – by employing an SME as a site of analysis – contributes to wider debates in sociology and critical security studies with an understanding of the mechanisms through which 'security' is pursued, constructed or managed in post-9/11 societies and securitized contexts. These drivers for security governance are based on recirculation and precaution and encapsulate wider social processes at play in the modern society.

Furthermore, it is clear that SMEs have become increasingly securitized. Scholars also argue that SMEs are likely to become increasingly securitized as new threats emerge (Cleland and Cashmore, 2018). In spite of public and academic discourses around mega-event security, considerably less research considers the deeper meanings of 'security'. Hence, this book has been committed to a critical analysis of what the contested concepts of 'security' and 'safety' mean (or *can* mean) in an SME context. Here, this book borrowed insights and lenses located within critical security studies that are yet to be made full use of in the study of SME securitization or the social study of sport. Beyond merely showing that these insights are applicable and ready for further deployment in the study of SME securitizations, this book has provided an empirical but theoretically underpinned understanding of the meanings of 'security' in an SME context. The book therefore contributes to existing knowledge on the social meanings and roles of 'security' in the twenty-first century. This is done, not by *redefining* what is considered an essentially contested concept, but rather critically rethinking what 'security' means at SMEs.

Ultimately, what constitutes a security threat or referent object in an SME context is highly contested and flexible. Whilst often impacted by developments occurring in a domain external to sport (i.e., a pandemic or a terrorist attack), the threat and referent object are assigned specific meanings in the SME realm. The meanings of 'security' and 'threat' are contextual, fluid and, as demonstrated by COVID-19, subject to drastic change. This book showed how 'security' refers not solely to the subjective or objective perceptions of event spectators or athletes, nor the relative absence of 'hooligans' or 'terrorists'. Instead, 'security' has dual meanings and spatial dimensions that relate directly to the efforts to guarantee 'clean' or 'sanitized' spaces in which security-policies ultimately ensure high commercial activity that is compatible with the profitable aspirations of event owners, sponsors and hosts.

At one stage in the pre-planning, 'security' therefore referred to the absence of pre-defined threats, problems and brands which could not be allowed to disrupt the event's people, atmospheres nor consumption circuits. Yet, the meanings of 'security' do not end there. I argue that the meanings of 'security' were substantially reconfigured following COVID-19. However, the 'invisible' nature of this sub-microscopic and contagious threat meant that infected people (or people *with* or *without* symptoms) became immediate 'threats' to other people. Indeed, as Bigo et al. (2021: 7) assert, the 'lived experience of being potentially infected and a danger to others is crucial for the unease created by the pandemic'. Given the anthropomorphic facet of COVID-19, this threat therefore blurred the already indefinite lines between whom (or what) that were 'secured', and whom or what that were 'secured against'. By capturing this shift *as it occurred*, this book has distinctively offered a critical and empirical account of what 'security' could mean at Euro 2020 and further, how the meanings of 'security' are not merely subject to change, but how they actually change in light of the COVID-19 mega-crisis,

Conclusions 155

which has forced us to 'rethink our social worlds' and to conduct a 'reimagination of the social' (Matthewman and Huppatz, 2020: 680).

A final note that can be made for now is that the security complexes that have been (re)generated since Munich 1972, 9/11, and the 2015 *Stade de France* attack continue to be upheld in modern societies. However, the pandemic has had a re-configurational effect on these complexes. In that sense, this book's case study, Euro 2020, became a *key moment* on the socio-historical timeline of mega-events as 'testing grounds' for new security- and safety-related knowledge and measures in modern societies.

The evolving research agenda

This book will end by discussing avenues for future research. At the time of writing, it is over a decade since Giulianotti and Klauser's (2010) interdisciplinary research agenda was published, consisting of what was emerging issues at the time. Hence, this section complements this with an emerging research agenda for this field for the 2020s and onwards. To be sure, there are still gaps in the literature. In a way, this was confirmed by Tian and Wise's (2020) recent knowledge domain assessment and survey of 870 academic articles published (between 2008 and 2018) in three international journals dedicated to the social study of sport.[1] Whilst acknowledging that research on mega-event security occasionally is published in more mainstream outlets or as monographs, it is still noticeable that 'security', 'securitization', 'policing' or 'surveillance' fail to emerge from this survey as any of the most covered areas or key words in the sociology of sport from 2008 to date. In itself, this implies the pressing need for continued development in the field.

The areas for future investigation could, however, be approached by academics from various fields and are not confined to the sociology of football or sport. Indeed, one of the key strengths of the existing literature is its interdisciplinary nature, featuring important and sometimes collaborative contributions from sociologists, security scholars, criminologists, urban geographers, legal scholars and political scientists, to name a few of the represented subject areas. When advancing in a constructive fashion, it remains crucial that this field preserves its interdisciplinary nature. Not merely in terms of active scholars, but also in terms of the conceptual and theoretical approaches to security. In that respect, there is more scope in future research for looking, to an even larger degree, towards the field of International Relations, and particularly those lenses offered by critical security studies. Like this book, this could be by considering or working within the key premises of, or even acknowledging, the theoretical frameworks offered from critical security studies projects (Chapter 2).

It seems as natural as it is necessary to point towards the impacts of COVID-19 on mega-events as one broad area that should be approached by researchers. Yet, it is vital to acknowledge that at the time of writing, it remains complicated to reach firm conclusions concerning the pandemic's medium to long-term impacts. Parnell et al. (2020: 6) assert that 'certainly, when the next pandemic comes (which it will), we are better prepared in sport and society'. This implies that COVID-19 has generated a set of valuable lessons and further consideration points for organizers and stakeholders of future events. Two questions that remain are 'how?' or 'which exact lessons?'. Researchers are therefore encouraged to examine stakeholders' perspectives of the challenges and emerging lessons related to the delivery of mega-events during COVID-19. In the context of Euro 2020, this relates to how this particular event served to produce lessons for domestic or European football more generally in the immediate aftermath of the tournament. Yet, it also relates to how Euro 2020 may have informed the wider societal reopening of indoor and outdoor events with mass crowds in the 11 host countries. Such research would thus have the potential to extend our understanding of mega-events as time-specific moments of policy learning that may shape 'COVID societies' (Lupton, 2020) or the new, post-pandemic normalcy.

It also remains important to study the individual responses to security in sport. In this area, there is substantial scope for building on existing work (Cleland, 2019; Cleland and Cashmore, 2018) and to consider how COVID-19 has impacted the ways in which individuals consider their own security, safety or health when attending events throughout and following the pandemic. Simultaneously, it remains crucial to not neglect the residents of the neighbourhoods and local communities that mega-events are staged within, around or upon. Residents will typically experience the build-up and peak times of a mega-event's security and policing operations (Boykoff, 2020). But when the curtains close, the floodlights fade and 'when "the show" appears to be over' (Roche, 2000: xi) residents may find their everyday lives impacted in some way by distinctive post-event 'security legacies'. In that respect, there is leeway for combining the commitment to the empirically study of mega-events' legacies whilst subscribing to the aforementioned critical approaches to security in case studies of past and future events.

The existing research also finds that local residents not uncommonly feel excluded from the extraordinary mega-event spaces and spectacles (Armstrong et al., 2017; Boykoff, 2016; Kennelly and Watt, 2011). In mega-events' build-ups, it has become common to either forcibly remove 'undesirable' individuals, communities or local businesses, and displacing them through intersecting neoliberal market or security policies (Kennelly and Watt, 2011). Against this, it is encouraged here to gather individuals' own experiences of heightened policing, enhanced surveillance and generally, the mega-event circus which can be longitudinal undertaking when accounting for the diffuse time period from when a city decides to bid for hosting rights to long after the event's days are over. Whilst this undeniably would supplement and expand the academic horizons of mega-events and security scholarship, the findings emanating from such research could also have the capacity to speak to broader neoliberal, urban and gentrifying processes impacting local communities in global and contemporary cities. Hence, this section – resting upon this book's findings and recent developments – argues that the study of SME securitization is continually evolving and still promises an intriguing array of pathways for interdisciplinary research in a 'post-pandemic' world.

Conclusions 157

Epilogue

So while Euro 2016 will be the first European football championship to be held during a state of emergency, *it is unlikely to be the last*. Declared in the aftermath of the Paris attacks of November 2015, which included an attempted suicide bombing of the France-Germany match at Stade de France, *the state of emergency has recently been extended to cover the football [...]* Consequently, nearly 80,000 state security personnel will be supplemented by 15,000 private security guards and a 10,000-strong military reserve, trained to deal with catastrophic bomb attacks on the fanzones and chemical warfare in the stadiums. *It is interesting to note that while the official and commercial zones for outdoor viewing will be going ahead*, secured with tens of millions of euros of additional funding, no one else will be allowed to hold their own unofficial outdoor events or screenings. Such is the fate of public space in an era of asymmetrical warfare.

(Goldblatt, 2016, emphasis added)

The above extract from David Goldblatt marks this book' closure. His sharp account reflects the sociopolitical realities and exceptionalities of SME security in the modern world. It is now prudent to ask whether the norm defines the exception – or if the exception, in fact, determines the norm in mega-event security. Instead of Euro 2020 going ahead in a state of emergency, as Goldblatt may have hinted towards, the tournament was not staged at all in June and July 2020. Instead, it was postponed, so that it could take place later, between 11 June and 11 July 2021. It is far from unlikely, though, that the future imagined above becomes the normalized reality, in which notions of festivity and spectacle 'goes ahead' despite background noises triggered by exceptionalism, enhanced state powers, social injustice and alertness.[2] Indeed, the 2020 Olympics took place whilst host city Tokyo was under a COVID-19-related state of emergency.

Since the nineteenth century, mega-events' social significance has merely intensified (Roche, 2000). Following 9/11 and COVID-19, the exact same may be observed regarding the securing of mega-events and security more generally (Bigo et al., 2021; Zedner, 2009). Cleland and Cashmore (2018) recently argued that in line with new, emerging threats, security and surveillance measures at SMEs are likely to develop even further. Undoubtedly, a pandemic now represents one of these 'new threats', but this may also relate to cyber-attacks or ecological issues. Cleland and Cashmore's suggestion connects with my closing argument. What this book's chapters reaffirm – when brought together – is the appropriateness of arguing that mega-events work as a 'mirror' and 'motor' (cf. Giulianotti and Robertson, 2007) of securitization processes. SMEs provide specular reflections of wider security dynamics and may be the driver behind securitization techniques. Notwithstanding, in light of this book's findings and constructed arguments, it seems prudent to take this analogy further and, again, paraphrase Giulianotti and Robertson (2004) who famously argued that sport, and especially football, represents one of the most sociologically illuminating domains of globalization processes.

158 Conclusions

Inspired by this proposition, this book argues that sport and football also have proven and manifested themselves as extremely illuminating domains of global, national and local securitization processes. Relatedly, empirical records, theorizations and analyses of security discourses, practices and perceptions in sport possess the potential to significantly improve how security is understood or problematized in modern societies. In a nutshell, analyses of sport can illuminate how 'security' is resisted, contested, recirculated or constructed. Fundamentally, this book underscores *exactly this*. Sport must therefore consistently be critically approached – and treated seriously – by social researchers seeking to understand security, surveillance, social control and health security and the potential legacies when applied to sport. Such call leans upon this book's conceptual foundations, empirical findings and future avenues and remains extremely important.

If Goldblatt's (2016) predictions prove rightful, then it remains crucial that the side effects and the legacies of the exceptional security efforts are explored by academics. Indeed, from a scholarly point of view, the forthcoming years present interesting case studies. However, more crucially and beyond academic spheres, they will all be revealing and likely to bring about different unpredicted outcomes (see Roche, 2017). First out is the controversial 2022 FIFA World Cup in Qatar. Then, in 2024, the 'Euros' return to Germany and the Summer Olympics to Paris, before the 2026 FIFA World Cup will be held in Canada, Mexico and the United States. The Los Angeles 2028 Olympics too has been actively resisted by anti-Olympic activists (Boykoff, 2020). To be sure, throughout the 2020s and beyond, every mega-event is likely to be surrounded by intense debates concerning their financial, environmental and social costs.

So, although the respective geographical, political, cultural and social characteristics of the above-mentioned mega-events differ greatly and enable a set of very different risk and security contexts, one thing these SMEs *do* have in common is that even in times of emergency, uncertainty, unknowns or insecurity, the show *must* and *will* go on. And, in the event of a global pandemic, postponements can ensure that the show *eventually* goes on in the modern-day (football) world.

Notes

1 These journals include the *International Review for the Sociology of Sport, Journal of Sport and Social Issues* and *Sociology of Sport Journal*.
2 See, for example, Boykoff's (2020) powerful and critical account of the forthcoming 2028 Summer Olympics in Los Angeles.

Bibliography

Armstrong, G, Giulianotti, R & Hobbs, D (2017) *Policing the 2012 London Olympics: Legacy and Social Exclusion*. London. Routledge.

Bauman, Z (2000) Social Issues of Law and Order. *British Journal of Criminology* 40(2), 205–221.

Beck, U (1992) *Risk Society: Towards a New Modernity*. London. Sage.

Bigo, D (2000) When Two Become One: Internal and External Securitisation in Europe. In M. Kelstrup & M.C. Williams (eds) *International Relations Theory and the Politics of European Integration. Power, Security and Community*. London. Routledge, 171–204.

Bigo, D, Guild, E & Kuskonmaz, EM (2021) Obedience in Times of COVID-19 Pandemics: A Renewed Governmentality of Unease? *Global Discourse* 11(1–2), 1–2.

Boykoff, J (2016) *Power Games: A Political History of the Olympics*. London. Verso.

Boykoff, J (2020) *Nolympians: Inside the Fight against Capitalist Mega-Sports in Los Angeles, Tokyo and Beyond*. Nova Scotia. Fernwood.

Boyle, P & Haggerty, KD (2009) Spectacular Security: Mega-Events and the Security Complex. *International Political Sociology* 3(3), 57–74.

Boyle, P, Clement, D & Haggerty, KD (2015) Iterations of Olympic Security: Montreal and Vancouver. *Security Dialogue* 46(2), 109–125.

Cleland, J (2019) Sports Fandom in the Risk Society: Analyzing Perceptions and Experiences of Risk, Security and Terrorism at Elite Sports Events. *Sociology of Sport Journal* 36(2), 144–151.

Cleland, J & Cashmore, E (2018) Nothing Will Be the Same Again after the Stade de France Attack: Reflections of Association Football Fans on Terrorism, Security and Surveillance. *Journal of Sport and Social Issues* 42(6), 454–469.

Doidge, M, Claus, R, Gabler, J, Irving, R & Millward, P (2019) The Impact of International Football Events on Local, National and Transnational Fan Cultures: A Critical Overview. *Soccer & Society* 20(5), 711–720.

Giulianotti, R & Klauser, F (2010) Security Governance and Sport Mega-Events: Toward an Interdisciplinary Research Agenda. *Journal of Sport and Social Issues* 34(1), 48–60.

Giulianotti, R & Robertson, R (2004) The Globalization of Football: A Study in the Glocalization of the 'Serious Life'. *The British Journal of Sociology* 55(4), 545–568.

Giulianotti, R & Robertson, R (eds) (2007) *Globalization & Sport*. Oxford. Blackwell.

Goldblatt, D (2016) Can Euro 2016 Unite European Culture Where Politics Has Failed? *The Guardian*. Available from: https://www.theguardian.com/books/2016/jun/10/can-euro-2016-unite-european-culture-where-politics-has-failed (Accessed 31 October 2019).

Kennelly, J & Watt, P (2011) Sanitizing Public Space in Olympic Host Cities: The Spatial Experiences of Marginalized Youth in 2010 Vancouver and 2012 London. *Sociology* 45(5), 765–781.

Klauser, F (2010) Splintering Spheres of Security: Peter Sloterdijk and the Contemporary Fortress City. *Environment and Planning D: Society and Space* 28, 326–340.

Klauser, F (2011a) The Exemplification of "Fan Zones": Mediating Mechanisms in the Reproduction of Best Practices for Security and Branding at Euro 2008. *Urban Studies* 48(15), 3202–3219.

Klauser, F (2011b) Commonalities and Specificities in Mega-Event Securitisation: The Example of Euro 2008 in Austria and Switzerland. In C.J. Bennett & K.D. Haggerty (eds) *Security Games, Surveillance and Control at Mega-Events*. London. Routledge, 120–136.

Klauser, F (2012) Interpretative Flexibility of the Event-City: Security, Branding and Urban Entrepreneurialism at the European Football Championships 2008. *International Journal of Urban and Regional Research* 36(5), 1039–1052.

Klauser, F (2017) *Surveillance & Space*. London. Sage.

Lupton, D (2020) Special Section on Sociology and the Coronavirus (COVID-19) Pandemic. *Health Sociology Review* 29(2), 111–112.

Matthewman, S & Huppatz, K (2020) A Sociology of Covid-19. *Journal of Sociology* 56(4), 675–683.

Mythen, G & Walklate, S (2008) Terrorism, Risk and International Security: The Perils of Asking "What If?". *Security Dialogue* 39, 221–241.

Numerato, D (2018) *Football Fans, Activism and Social Change*. London. Routledge.

Parnell, D, Widdop, P, Bond, A & Wilson, R (2020) COVID-19, Networks and Sport. *Managing Sport and Leisure*, 1–7.

Roche, M (2000) *Mega-Events and Modernity: Olympics and Expos in the Growth of Global Culture*. London. Routledge.

Roche, M (2017) *Mega-Events and Social Change: Spectacle, Legacy and Public Culture*. Manchester. Manchester University Press.

Tian, E & Wise, N (2020) An Atlantic Divide? Mapping the Knowledge Domain of European and North American-Based Sociology of Sport, 2008–2018. *International Review for the Sociology of Sport* 55(8), 1029–1055.

Tsoukala, A (2009) *Football Hooliganism in Europe: Security and Civil Liberties in the Balance*. Basingstoke. Palgrave.

Zedner, L (2009) *Security*. London/New York. Routledge.

Index

Note: **Bold** page numbers refer to tables. Page numbers followed by "n" refer to notes.

activism 138–142
Adey, P. 48
Adhanom, T. 4, 103
affective atmospheres 48
Agnelli, A. 106–107
Allianz Arena 140, 141
Andrejevcic, M. 133
anti-social behaviour 50, 83
Armstrong, G. 31n3
Atkinson, M. 25
Augé, M. 47

Bauman, Z. 25, 42, 48
Beck, U. 16, 18–19, 23, 30, 50, 59, 107; pathbreaking (world) risk society thesis 18–19
Bennett, C.J. 20
best practice (or good practice) 41, 42, 69, 77, 131
Betts, R.K. 72n2
Bigo, D. 27, 43, 98, 132, 154
Black September 18
Bono and the Edge 3
Booth, K. 37, 52n2
Bourdieu, P. 25, 52n1
Boykoff, J. 18, 29, 158n2
Boyle, P. 21, 23, 28, 60, 138
Brexit 136
Britishness 139
Brothers Grimsby, The 21n1
Bullingham, M. 112–113, 142
Buzan, B. 22

Case Collective (2006) 39
Cashmore, E. 157
Čeferin, A. 2, 106, 111, 112

Centennial Park bombing 18
Champions League 123, 125
Cheng, V.C. 4
Chomsky, N. 114, 117n5
Christellin, E. 104
Cleland, J. 19, 27, 71, 75, 89, 91n2, 157
Coaffee, J. 135
Cole, C.L. 133
complex security issues 21–27
Copa América 116
Copenhagen School 38
corporate kettling 46
Cottey, A. 37
Council of Europe 41, 42, 66, 76, 77, 79, 85, 130, 131; Recommendation of the Standing Committee (2015) 60–61; Standing Committee of the Convention on Spectator Violence 7, 60, 65; Working Group EURO 2020 84
counter-hooliganism 50, 76, 77
Counter Terrorism Policing 138
COVID-19, 62, 94–117, 123, 137–138; coordinated responses 97–99; and Euro 2020 1, 3, 6, 123–144; invisible enemy, unpacking 108–111; postponement and great collapse 102–105, **103**; security and safety 105–115; as security threats 95–99; and sport mega-events 3–6, 10, 94, 95, 108, 110, 116
crime 26, 49, 50, 101
criminal activity 49
critical security studies: in universe of sport, situating 37–40
Critical Theory 38, 39
cultural capital 52n1

162 Index

Dark Knight Rises, The 31n1
Davies, S. 98
De Bolle, C. 135
Debord, G.: *Society of Spectacle* 23
Dickmann, P. 100
Divišová, V. 68–69
Doidge, M. 69
Domingues, J.M. 98–99
Dunning, E. 89

Eco, U. 114, 117n5
Eick, V. 45
Elbe, S. 97–98
endemic threats 108, 116–117
England 2; group fixture against
    Scotland 5
Englishness 139
English Premier League 125
epidemics 50, 95
epidemic threats 108, 116–117
Estadio La Cartuja 127
EU *see* European Union (EU)
Euro 2004 42
Euro 2008 9
Euro 2020 1–3, 5, 23, 30, 41, 47, 51, 52,
    57, 75, 151, 152; COVID-19 and 1, 3,
    6, 123–144; security pre-planning 60;
    Tournament Requirements 7
Europe: counter-hooliganism 77; COVID-
    19, 4, 94, 103, 106–107, 123, 125, 140,
    151; fan cultures 87; fan cultures,
    problematic implications and impacts
    on 69; fan networks 65; policing 11, 75,
    78, 80, 82, 90, 134, 137
European Club Association 113
European Community 76
European Convention on Spectator
    Violence and Misbehaviour at Sports
    Events (1985) 76
European Union (EU) 41, 77
Europol 136, 137, 138
Euros Policing Team 134
Euro Stadium Operator Workshop (2019)
    61

failure-inspired learning 59
fan(s) 124–128; cultures 87–88; groups
    88; guaranteed presence 126–128, **127**;
    networks *see* fan networks
fan networks: as agents of knowledge
    transfer 83–88; consultation 83–85;
    involvement 83–85; presence of 65–67;
    in security field 76–79

Fans' Embassies 85–87
Fans' Embassies: A Handbook (FSE) 86
fantasy documents 138
*Fédération Internationale de Football
    Association* (FIFA) World Cup 1
field 39; security 27–29, 88
FIFA *see Fédération Internationale de
    Football Association* (FIFA) World Cup
FIFPRO Europe 113
Floyd, R. 38
Folkers, A. 59–60
football 1–12, 156–158; fun networks 27,
    65–67, 85, 87; governance of 61; impacts
    on fan cultures 67–70; pandemic threats
    94–117, 123–126, 130–132, 134–143;
    policing for 41, 63, 75–83; precautionary
    logics 64, 65; security for 18, 23, 25–27,
    29, 36, 42, 47, 49, 61, 88–90; *see also*
    Euro 2020; World Cup
Football Association (FA) Cup 130
Football Supporters Europe (FSE) 7, 11,
    61, 65, 66, 69, 77, 78, 83–87, 89, 90,
    91n2, 91n3, 130–132; *Fans' Embassies: A
    Handbook* 86
Foucault, M. 108–109
Frankfurt School 39
freedom 48
FSE *see* Football Supporters Europe (FSE)
Fussey, P. 42–43, 135

Galily, Y 25
Garcia, B. 88
Garrix, M. 3
German Bundesliga 125
Giulianotti, R. 4, 20, 22, 24, 27, 29, 31n3,
    36, 38, 44, 77, 78, 101, 104, 139, 155, 157
Glasgow Rangers 142
Global North 2
Global Terrorism Database 31n4
Goldblatt, D. 94, 157, 158
Gravina, G. 107
Greenpeace 141
Grix, J. 37
guaranteed fan presence 126–128, **127**
Güney, E. 87

habitus 39
Hagemann, A. 45
Haggerty, K.D. 20, 21, 23, 28, 60, 138
Hancock, M. 126
Hardt, H. 62
Hassan, I. 98
health issues 50

Index   163

Herrmann, J. 141
historical events 18–20
hooliganism 4, 25, 31n3, 41, 49, 64, 68, 77, 83, 90, 99, 101, 116, 135, 137, 138, 143; counter-hooliganism 50, 76, 77
Horne, J. 16
Hutchins, B. 133

Infantino, G. 112
infectious diseases 99–102, 105–107
institutional memory 62–63, 88
International Police Cooperation Centre (IPCC) of the National Football Contact Points 135
international political sociology 38, 39
INTERPOL 136, 137
IPCC *see* International Police Cooperation Centre (IPCC) of the National Football Contact Points
Italy 2

Johan Cruiff Arena 132
Johnson, B. 5

Kallen, M. 136
Kennelly, J. 45, 46
Khan, S. 139
Klauser, F. 4, 20, 22, 24, 27–29, 38, 40, 44, 47, 48, 77, 101, 155
Koch, D. 132

lagacies 4, 16, 17, 26–29, 42, 68, 70, 109, 137, 144, 156, 158
Lauss, G. 22
League Cup 131
lesson-drawing 41, 42, 59–62, 131
Lines, A. 139
liquid security 42–43
London's Olympic Games 2012 9
Ludvigsen, L. 12n2, 71

Manhunt: Deadly Games 21n1
Manzenreiter, W. 16
Marivoet, S. 86
McCann, E. 28, 42
McKee, I. 140
media and policing, link between 82–83
mediation 138–142
medical expertise 128–133
mega-events *see* sport mega-events (SMEs)
Metropolitan Police 138
Millward, P. 8, 142

Molnar, A. 59, 60
Mythen, G. 23, 58–59, 67

National Football Information Points (NFIP) 76
neoliberalism 44, 45
new normal 142–144
NFIP *see* National Football Information Points (NFIP)
nichtwissen 59
Numerato, D. 77–78, 81, 82
Nunes, J. 96–97, 101

O'Grady, N. 63
Olsson, L.-S. 110
Olympic Games: 1896 18; 1972 18, 20; 1984 29; 1996 18; 2010 45; 2012 62; 2016 22; 2020 100
O'Neill, M. 76
Owens, G. 112

pandemics 94–117; coordinated responses 97–99; infectious diseases 99–102; invisible enemy, unpacking 108–111; postponement and great collapse 102–105, **104**; security and safety 105–115; security's 'comeback' 97–99; as security threats 95–99
pan-European turn 1–3
Parent, M.M. 129
Paris School 38, 39
Parnell, D. 155–156
participation 76–79
Pearson, G. 31n3
Peoples, C. 38
pilot events 128–133
Platini, M. 2
Poland 2
policing 3, 8, 10, 11, 21, 27, 29, 31n3, 41, 49, 59, 62, 63, 65, 67–71, 75–90, 124, 131, 139, 140, 142, 151, 153, 155, 156; current issues in 79–82; local and transnational modes of 133–138; and media, link between 82–83; national variations in 79–82; over-aggressive 82; in security field 76–79; style 82
policy 76–79; transfer 28
postponement 102–105, **104**
Poulton, E. 25
power relations and fans, situating 88–89
precautionary logics 63–65
precautionary security governance 21–27
Pyongyang Winter Olympics (2018) 22

recognition 76–79
Reddy, M. 141
Reicher, S. 80
(re)productions of security 36–52; paradigms 40–44; people, spaces and festivity, securing 46–49; securitized commodification 44–46; spatial implications 44–46; specific and general security threats 49–51
research agenda 155–156
risk governance 58+
risk society 16, 30; security in 18–20; sport mega-events in 18–20
Roberts, A. 136
Roberts, K. 94, 106
Robertson, R. 157
Roche, M. 1, 9, 17, 143
Ronaldo, C.: *Ballon d'Or* 47
Rose, R. 28
Rosenberg, C. 104
Rowe, D. 6
Ruetsch, A. 129
Rushton, S. 101

Saint-Denis Convention 60
SARS-CoV-2 *see* severe acute respiratory syndrome coronavirus 2 (SARS-CoV-2)
SD Europe 7, 11, 61, 65–67, 69, 77, 78, 83–85, 89, 90, 91n3, 113
securitization theory 38, 96–97
securitized commodification 36, 44–46
security 2; comeback 97–99; complex issues 21–27; fields 27–29, 88; knowledge networks 27–28; legacies 4, 16, 17, 26–29, 27–29, 42, 68, 70, 109, 137, 144, 156, 158; liquid 42–43; local and transnational modes of 133–138; networks 27–29; (re)productions of 36–52; in risk society 18–20; spectacle 8; spectacular 21; for sport mega-events 3–6, 16–31, 36–38, 40–42, 44–46, 48–52, 69, 88, 134–138; total 20, 21; troika of 9, 57–72, 75
security governance 6, 8, 10, 29, 30, 40, 57, 59, 70, 71, 86, 87, 95, 136, 144, 152; drivers for 153–154; precautionary 21–27, 68
security threats 43, 152; general 49–51; pandemics as 95–99; specific 49–51
Seifert, C. 62
7/7 bombings 20
severe acute respiratory syndrome coronavirus 2 (SARS-CoV-2) 4, 106

Sheptycki, J. 135
Shipway, R. 101
Silk, M. 45
SLO *see* Supporter Liaison Officer (SLO)
SMEs *see* sport mega-events (SMEs)
social change 18–20
social identity 65
Society of Spectacle (Debord) 23
Spaaij, R. 25–26, 31n3, 31n4, 76, 77, 137
spectacular security 21
sport mega-events (SMEs) 1–3, 8–11, 62, 65, 140–144, 151–154, 156–158; COVID-19 and 3–6, 10, 94, 95, 108, 110, 116; fan networks 83, 84, 86; fan presence 127, 128; hosting rights 2; infectious diseases and 99–102; legacies 17–18; modern 68; planning stages for 84; policing 77, 78, 82, 134–138; politics 17–18; preparations 2; in risk society 18–20; security for 3–6, 16–31, 36–38, 40–42, 44–46, 48–52, 69, 88, 134–138; sociology of 17–18; spectacles 17–18; testing grounds 129, 131–133; time-specific 67
Stade de France 64, 69, 155
Stadio Olimpico, Rome 5
Stead, D. 41
St George's Park 136
Stone, D. 61
Stott, C. 31n3
Summer Olympics (2012) 20
Supporter Liaison Officer (SLO) 7, 66–67, 87
surveillance 4, 16, 22, 23, 26, 29, 41, 64, 68, 71, 77, 98, 109, 133, 143, 155–158
Szigetvari, A. 22

Tartan Army 64, 83, 138–142
Taylor, T. 19, 24, 25
terrorism 25, 26, 49, 50, 101, 116; threats 138
Thacker, E. 109, 115
Tian, E. 155
Toohey, K. 19, 24, 25
total security 20, 21
Tour de France 62
Tovar, J. 94–95
transgression 108–109
transnationalization 39, 152
troika of security 9, 57–72, 75; fan networks, presence of 65–67; fans and power relations, situating 88–89; impacts on fan cultures 67–70;

institutional memory 62–63; lesson-drawing 60–62; precautionary logics 63–65; problematic implications 67–70

Tsoukala, A. 23, 76, 77, 137, 138

Turner, M. 27

UEFA Minimum Health & Hygiene Requirements for the Return of Spectators (UEFA) 125

UEFA *see* Union of European Football Associations (UEFA)

UEFA Super Cup Budapest: FSE Review 130

Ukraine 2

Union of European Football Associations (UEFA) 5, 46, 61, 66, 76, 77, 79, 82, 85, 94, 113, 126, 136; EURO 2020 *see* EURO 2020; European Championships 1, 2, 43, 87; *Good practices for safe and secure major sporting events: experiences and lessons from UEFA EURO 2004* 7; postponement of Euro 2020 105; Safety and Security Regulations 41; *UEFA EURO 2020 Tournament Requirements* 40; *UEFA Minimum Health & Hygiene Requirements for the Return of Spectators* 125

UN Security Council 95

Vaughan-Williams, N. 38

violence 26, 83

Walklate, S. 23, 58–59, 67

Walt, S.M. 37

webinars 128–133

Welford, J. 88

Welsh School 38, 39

Wembley security breach 141–142

Whelan, C. 37

WHO *see* World Health Organization (WHO)

Wise, N. 155

Włoch, R. 128

Women's World Cup (2019) 66

World Cup 1, 24, 86; 2002 99; 2006 28, 41, 45; 2010 99; 2018 83; 2022 123, 158; 2026 158; 2030 142

World Health Organization (WHO) 94; Constitution (1946) 96; on COVID-19, 4, 98, 101, 117

Yang, C. 133

Young, K. 25

Yu, Y. 17, 21, 26

Zedner, L. 19, 21–22, 37, 59+

Printed in the United States
by Baker & Taylor Publisher Services